The

Dishonest

Church

JACK GOOD

Rising Star Press
Scotts Valley, CA

IN ASSOCIATION WITH

Rising Star Press
P. O. Box 66378
Scotts Valley, CA 95067-6378
www.RisingStarPress.com

In association with

www.tcpc.org

The scripture quotations contained herein are from the New Revised Standard Version Bible, © 1989 by the Division of Christian Education of the National Council of the Churches of Christ in the U. S. A., and are used by permission. All rights reserved.

Interior design, composition, and copyediting by Joanne Shwed, Backspace Ink (www.backspaceink.com).

Cover design by Chuck Spidell, Illusio Design (www.illusiodesign.com).

Cover photography by Jodie Coston, Lukasz Gumowski, Shun Hong Lee, and Phil Sigin-Lavdanski.

Library of Congress Cataloging-in-Publication Data

Good, Jack, 1935-
   The dishonest church / by Jack Good.
      p. cm.
Includes bibliographical references.
   ISBN 0-933670-09-5 (alk. paper)
   1. Church.   I. Title.
   BV600.3.G66 2003
   262--dc21

                              2003009395

This volume is dedicated to the people of many congregations who allowed me to share their lives, preside at their weddings, officiate at their funerals, and pray with them in their hospital rooms. Especially I recall those who accepted me when I was a student pastor—people willing to teach more than they were taught. For the priceless privilege of sharing the spiritual pilgrimage of these remarkable people I am deeply grateful.

Contents

Introduction

Two interesting and pertinent things happened in the days immediately after I completed this manuscript. First, I read Paul Woodruff's book *Reverence.*[1] Woodruff writes about a significant issue: the loss of a sense of reverence in western societies. He wants this important aspect of life reclaimed. But he wants it reclaimed in a secular form. As one reviewer put it, he wants "to rescue reverence from the clutches of religion."

Woodruff begins his book with an account of a vote concerning gay rights, a political struggle that occurred in the Seattle area. The conservative religious community led a vigorous, hate-filled campaign to defeat an initiative that would have protected gays and lesbians from discrimination. This, for Woodruff, defines religion. An anti-religious bias is evident throughout the remainder of his volume. Who could blame him? In the Seattle event, he saw on display a form of Christianity that thumbs its nose at any scientific knowledge about the origins of sexual orientation. That same form of religion says: "Everyone who is not like me is cursed and hated by God." Woodruff has been taken in by the prominence of this negative style of faith. Thus his volume displays a combination of indifference and antagonism to the entire religious enterprise.

The death of Fred Rogers was the second happening. Fred Rogers designed and produced the Public Television program *Mister Rogers' Neighborhood*. In each of his thousands of broadcasts, Rogers found some new way to invite his young viewers into his imaginary neighborhood, a community where they could feel safe, where they could learn to accept themselves and to cherish all others who shared that appealing place. Mister Rogers did not talk about God; he certainly never pushed any dogmatic concerns. Yet Fred Rogers was a Presbyterian minister, ordained by his church for a special ministry to children. In each of his programs, he was living out his religious vocation. Religious faith, for him, centered in the assurance that at the heart of the universe is a Spiritual Reality who is friendly to the existence of each human being.

Paul Woodruff appears totally unaware that religion can take the form modeled by Fred Rogers. To Woodruff, religion, by definition, is dogmatic, divisive, and anti-intellectual.

Christian churches, and Protestant churches in particular, must bear much of the blame for the misunderstandings of religious faith that are rampant today. Church professionals have been especially remiss in communicating with intellectuals such as Woodruff. Ordained church professionals have been trained in some of the finest academic institutions of our day. The style of faith they develop during their schooling is not, with some important exceptions, dogmatic, divisive, or anti-intellectual. Yet, when they complete their training and begin to lead local churches, these religious leaders hide their newfound breadth and revert to the patterns of their childhood. They do not respect their congregations enough to challenge them. Thus narrow and immature ideas remain in place; religious beliefs are not measured against the insights of secular science. In short, church leaders have utterly failed to present a visible and viable alternative to the style of religion seen in the Seattle initiative.

This failure of religious leaders to share honestly and forthrightly with the laity, a failure with crippling effects, is the subject of this volume.

I have had abundant help in my efforts to identify the problem and suggest possible solutions. Especially I want to thank the members of the two congregations with which I have had extended relationships: The United Church of Christ of Sherburne, New York; and Community United Church of Christ of Champaign, Illinois. The people of these two quite different congregations consistently justified my faith in lay people. They encouraged me to encourage them to think new thoughts and envision their faith in creative ways. When they disagreed with me, they did so with gentleness. Community UCC celebrated the publication of my first book, a volume designed to help those who do not take the Bible literally to see and embrace its spiritual depth. Then they encouraged me to continue writing, even presenting me with the latest in word processing equipment. Many of these church members have read preliminary editions of this volume and have made numerous helpful suggestions. Other early readers included a sampling of the religious professionals that are roundly criticized in this book. They said, in essence, "Preach on!"

Two persons have been especially helpful in dealing with the technicalities of writing. I have been unusually fortunate to have worked with Thomas Devine, an editor at Rising Star Press. Tom's knowledge of the rules of English usage is matched by his skill at persuading me that these rules should be followed. Working with Tom has been one of the most rewarding aspects of the development of this book. Donald Kurtz, a novelist and friend, has read several previous editions of this work. He, in his kind and persistent manner, has encouraged me to sharpen my language and to keep the reader focused on the subjects at hand. Tom and Don should receive credit for any clarity found in the pages ahead, but not be blamed for those places where, despite their best efforts, I engaged in erroneous usage or left ideas murky.

My wife, Diana, deserves the final word of thanks. Her insights and editing skills have been invaluable. She has shared her husband with a demanding vocation for many decades. Now that I have left the pastorate, she shares her husband with a computer screen. Her good humor in the face of my distraction is due largely to the fact that she too has a passion for strengthening a healthy and progressive style of religious faith.

Jack Good
Roanoke, Virginia
April, 2003

NOTE

1.   Paul Woodruff, *Reverence* (New York: Oxford University Press, 2001).

1

A Tragic Divide

*O*ne of my clergy friends boasts of a comment he made in an interview with a pastoral search committee. A somewhat hostile member of the committee demanded to know if this prospective pastor believed in a literal virgin birth. My friend replied that his views on the virgin birth were the same as those of St. Paul. The committee member nodded approvingly, and the discussion went on to other matters.

Paul, as all trained church leaders know, did not mention a virgin birth. So my friend had his private moment of triumph. Clergy tend to see such moments as victories over the benighted folk who occupy church pews. But these are not victories. They indicate, instead, a tragic defeat for Christianity, a potentially fatal division that threatens the very mission and existence of the church.

This was but a single incident. Yet it contains intimations of several sad universal realities.

The first broad reality that emerges from this episode is the fear and distrust with which these two men approached one another. This is amazing, in light of the fact that the interview was held under the assumption that the two might share

1

leadership of a Christian congregation. That possibility had been poisoned from the beginning.

The layman wanted to hold to a tightly defined faith structure that he had learned to protect, with great effort, against the onslaught of modern forces. He feared that his faith would crumble if it were not constantly reinforced by his local pastor. The prospective pastor, on the other hand, feared the power the lay person had over his employment. Thus they held one another at arm's length.

Fear manifested itself in distrust. The committee member knew that prospective pastors must be questioned carefully, or else they might be found to embrace a style of faith quite different from that of the congregation. Apparently he had learned in earlier contacts with clerics that they could be slippery, saying words that sounded right at first hearing but did not stand up under careful examination.

This fear and distrust meant that an opportunity for constructive exchange passed unused. The pastor might have shared his belief in, and deep commitment to, the truths contained in the New Testament stories of Jesus' birth while acknowledging that the historic facts were unimportant to him. This could have led to a discussion of whether the pastor-parishioner relationship implies complete agreement on all topics, or whether that relationship might include occasional disagreement and challenge.

Another broad reality enfolded in the pastoral interview is a fact already implied: The professional church leader and the lay church member approached scripture from decidedly different perspectives. The professional knew that the scripture says little about a miraculous birth for Jesus and that, on the two occasions when it does so, its details are contradictory. He also knew that Paul once implied that Jesus' birth had been by normal means (Galatians 4:4). These apparent contradictions in the biblical record bothered my friend not at all. He had learned to seek biblical truth at another level. The layman, by contrast, was sure that all scripture had to be accepted as true in every sense, or else the authority of the Bible would be completely undercut. Contradictions in the biblical record were unthinkable to him, as was the idea that he could have as pastor a person who did not share his entrenched beliefs.

Yet another clue to a universal condition was my friend's assumption (correct, as it turned out) that the layman before him, even a layman active enough in the church to be appointed to its pastoral search committee, had never been told that Paul was silent on the subject of the virgin birth. The two men shared a denomination in which all religious professionals are trained in the historical-critical method of Bible study. Yet my friend could engage in his strategy of answering/not answering the question with little fear that any of this committee member's former pastors had respected him enough to inform him of the things the New Testament says and does not say about the circumstances of Jesus' birth. His duplicity was built on the safe assumption of inadequate adult religious education.

A very important clue to the condition of the modern church that arose in the interview vignette was my friend's skill in evasion. He had learned how to use words that meant one thing in his own mind ("I do not believe in a literal virgin birth") and a quite opposite thing to the person to whom he was speaking ("If he agrees with Paul, he must hold a traditional set of beliefs").

Actually, my friend is a caring person, and the committee, which did not extend a call, missed an opportunity for effective pastoral leadership. In most situations he is thoroughly honest. He rationalized his behavior on this occasion on the basis that anyone who defines the Christian faith by literal views of biblical narratives deserved to be out-maneuvered.

I understand my friend's position, but I am offended by the way he handled this incident. No matter how one tries, the fraudulence of this scene, and all the deception it implies for the total church, cannot be rationalized. The basic dishonesty to which this episode points has led me to write this volume.

◆

A Distressing Division

The brief exchange between this pastor and this lay member exposes a wide gap between the faith of religious professionals and the faith of those who look to those professionals for leadership. The gap exists primarily because church leaders have failed to share their knowledge with the laity, or to engage the laity in any true ventures of faith. Another reason for the gap is the reluctance of many lay people to surrender belief systems that they sense, at a deep level of consciousness, are inadequate to the present day, but for which they see no substitutes.

In writing, I am motivated in part by concern. I care deeply about the fate of the Christian church, and the mainline Protestant denominations[1] in particular. I have served as a pastor of Christian congregations for more than four decades. The church has formed and defined my life. Despite their many faults, I see local congregations as an indispensable ingredient of a meaningful, intellectually sound religious faith for the modern era. Individualistic faith, spirituality without structured faith, will not carry the day.

I am motivated also by anger. I am angry because so many Christian churches are stale and boring places. Energy goes exclusively into reinforcing old dogmas. The distrust that so often characterizes the relationship between clergy and laity limits creative options. Seldom is anyone challenged to think a new thought, or encouraged to see religion as a stimulating search for truths that will never be entirely known.

The major portion of my anger is directed toward my fellow professionals—those who are trained in theology and who make their living from the church. They, like tradition-bound laity, are motivated by fear. But clergy fear has different roots. Members of the laity fear the loss of their faith; clergy fear the loss of their jobs. The faith of most professionals has expanded far beyond the images of God and Jesus they

acquired as children. Yet they do not challenge the laity to follow them along this broader path. Instead, they have allowed
a small, vocal portion of each mainline denomination to stand
in the way of growth for everyone. This small group threatens
to dismiss local pastors if their fixed belief system is not properly reinforced. If they fail to rid congregations of the offending clerics, they themselves will leave. In the face of such
threats, every idea that might trouble the waters has either
been ignored or diluted in pulpits and denominational publishing houses all across the land. These professionals, almost
all of whom share my deep concern for the church, are killing
the church they love by their lack of courage.

Part of my anger is directed to certain members of the laity,
those who sit passively each Sunday in church pews—passively,
that is, until some of them sense that the pastor is about to stray
from the truisms the lay members were taught as children. Then
they seek out like-minded congregational members. They organize. They send a committee to express their concerns to their
minister. In more serious cases, they ask the congregation to dismiss the offending pastor. I write to say to these people that
their rigid position will not save the Christian tradition; rigidity
violates that tradition and will, over time, destroy what it is
designed to save.

In those same congregations, members exist who are
equally offended by pastoral timidity. They are eager to move
beyond childhood concepts. When their needs are not met,
they say nothing. They do not organize into committees. They
do not visit the pastor with a request for a more stimulating
environment. They either swallow their concerns or else fade
slowly from church participation.

Perhaps these silent people have concluded that asking for
change in Christian churches is a hopeless project. Perhaps
they think they are alone, that no one else shares their concern.
I write with these people in mind. I want to assure them that
they are far from alone.

And I write out of sorrow. My sorrow came to the surface recently when I attended a lecture on the subject of religion and science. The class was made up mostly of retirees. They live in a region noted for its strong, Protestant commitment to Christianity and Christian churches.

The presenter at the session divided the large class into groups, with each group asked to record, on one side of a sheet of paper, the first ten words that came to mind when they heard the word "religion." On the other side of the same sheet, each group was asked to write the first ten words that came to mind when they heard the word "science." The results were both fascinating and discouraging.

Most of the words class members wrote under religion were predictable: "God," "Jesus," "church," "faith," "prayer," "hope," "charity." Other words revealed a darker stance: "hell," "sinner," "dogma," "death." Even in this churchgoing generation, a few negative concepts about religion slipped in: "crutch," "hoax," "conflict."

On the science side, most of the words were equally unsurprising: "evolution," "computers," "inventions," "technology." Not all who participated were science buffs. Among their words were "Greek" (as in "it's all Greek to me") and "required courses."

Alongside the expected words describing science were a few I found startling. Several terms that I want to associate with religion were placed by members of the class on the science side of their sheets. "Mystery" appeared once under religion, but three times under science. Other religious words listed under science included "dedication," "hope," "future," "curiosity," "morality," "beauty," and "endless." Almost everyone viewed science as the field that gets things right: "logic," "exactitude," "proof." "Truth" appeared once under religion, four times under science.

The word that grabbed my attention was "excitement." Excitement was described as an attribute of science, not of religion.

Thus my sorrow. The class session was a reminder that religious faith has come to be known, even among its advocates, as a past-oriented, calcified group of stale ideas. No wonder the majority of our best young people flock to professions in the sciences, professions in which they can pursue truth, and where their explorations are future-oriented and exciting!

It does not have to be so. That must be said more strongly: *It should not be so.* Those who are acquainted with what is happening in the theological world know that *religion is a field where genuine excitement abounds.* New information about the life and teachings of Jesus is emerging. Ways of thinking about the divine—some ancient, some new—are being discussed by people of great intellectual breadth.

Here is the rub: Religious professionals know about the ferment in their field, but they often treat these emerging movements not as sources of excitement but as threats. They refuse to share with those who occupy church pews anything other than the same tired dogma they themselves learned as children. Thus the laity are left with a lifeless excuse for the vital faith they could be pursuing.

The broad purpose of this volume can be stated simply: I write because I am convinced that an honest approach to faith, far from being an attack on religious tradition, is the only way to preserve that tradition. Our faith at its strongest has been known for its sense of adventure. At its best, faith invites its adherents to be seekers. It calls us, as it called Abraham, father of the Jewish people, to set out on a journey even though its precise destination is unknown. Faith is at its weakest when it treats dogma as if it were an ancient fortress that must be defended at all costs.

◆

A Compromised Mission

Religion has often been the truth department of human society. Time after time this foundational fact is illustrated: The Judeo-

Christian tradition has been, and is, committed to honesty. Religious spokespersons frequently call on public servants to be trustworthy in their tasks. Individuals are reminded that truthfulness is basic to human relationships. Honesty is elementary; it is central to the religious mission.

Religion, however, has a problem within its own household. Even while religious leaders have been insisting on trustworthiness from others, they have been reluctant to speak the truth to their own people. Professionals within the church have stubbornly withheld from the laity what they know about the historical Jesus or what they do not know about the Mystery called God. They have been silent on many other important topics that might cause people to reexamine old beliefs or expand spiritual horizons.

Exceptions appear from time to time. When they do, the church marshals its resources and pushes the challenging ideas out of public view. In 1963, Anglican Bishop John A. T. Robinson sent mild shock waves through the church with his book *Honest to God*.[2] Robinson challenged his readers to rise above views that described God as a separate being who lives just outside earth and visits the planet on rare and unpredictable occasions. In 1996, Robert W. Funk caused further consternation with his volume, *Honest to Jesus*.[3] Funk detailed the conflicting pictures of Jesus given in the biblical accounts and insisted that his readers confront the impact of the first century social setting on Jesus' life and teaching. He insisted that the human context of Jesus' life could clarify his relevance to the present day.

Reactions to these writings were remarkable. Articles in both religious and secular publications appeared, assuring the public that nothing had changed, that these writers were aberrations. Soon, everyone was assured, the storm would pass and all would again be comfortable with "the faith once given."

Neither Robinson nor Funk wrote as radicals attempting to undermine Christianity. Their book titles point to a common passion: *honesty*. They challenged the professionals in the

Christian Church to speak clearly to church members about what they know of the divine and the divine role in the world. They encouraged forthright statements about the life and times of Jesus of Nazareth, and about the way the Bible and creeds came into existence. A critic might disagree with Robinson or Funk on the specifics of their arguments, but their basic plea for honesty should be non-negotiable.

Here is the central issue: Pastors and other trained professionals of the church often have developed a system of beliefs that is qualitatively different from the faith they communicate to local congregations. Their individual faith has developed, in most cases, after an intense and sometimes painful time of questioning, dismantling, and reconstruction. For reasons that are not clear, these leaders assume that local church members are either unwilling or unable to survive a similar process. So, in an act of dishonesty that threatens to erode the core of the church's mission, they hold one kind of faith for themselves while the literature they produce for the laity and the sermons they deliver assume another, basically different, style of faith for the non-professional.

◆

Damage

Honesty should be its own excuse for being. When the church practices duplicity with its membership, however, more than a basic commandment is broken. As lies and half-lies inevitably will, dishonesty ultimately undermines the very institutions and concepts it is designed to protect.

Areas of Damage

Here are some particular areas of serious damage, each of which will be explored in more depth in later chapters.

■ *The pastor-parishioner relationship is damaged.*

The modern church, Catholic and Protestant, depends on a healthy pastor-parishioner relationship, one that is constructed on trust. In the present climate, however, trust is in short supply. Clergy assume (mostly incorrectly) that church members are incapable of dealing with naked truth. On their side, parishioners have begun to suspect (mostly correctly) that their religious leaders are not playing straight.

Michael Hout and Claude Fischer, sociologists from the University of Chicago, published an article analyzing the attitudes of the large number of people who have dropped out of religious life over the past decade.[4] Among former churchgoers who continued to express religious convictions, the researchers discovered not just apathy, but active antipathy toward churches and church leaders.

The study revealed that even those who claimed a specific religious affiliation expressed dissatisfaction with churches and church leaders. Fewer than half of all those surveyed expressed a great deal of confidence in church leaders, and that figure dropped to about 10 percent among those with no religious preference.

Of course, when studies are conducted among persons who remain active in the church, a more positive picture is given. But when the opinions of the many who have dropped out of church life are included, the confidence gap between laity and their leaders is shown to be growing wider, and the cost of that gap becoming dearer.

■ *The individual church member is damaged.*

The individual is damaged in a variety of deep and far-reaching ways.

The church member is hurt in faith development. Most church schools teach concepts of God that are, at best, appropriate for children. Adults are seldom challenged to move beyond those ideas. Their vision of God seldom matures beyond what one enlightened church member called a "cosmic bell-hop," a super-strong being who exists primarily to keep me safe and run errands on my behalf. Jesus, whom the Bible presents as a model for sacrificial living, takes on the role of the adult's invisible friend, present to comfort and protect but never to challenge.

The individual is hurt intellectually. Curiosity is stifled. A church that emphasizes established creeds and dogma leaves no opening for the exploration of new vistas. More tragically, these churches reinforce people's tendency to keep their religious thinking at a very low level of cognitive development. At this level, people are expected to believe what they are told simply because religious experts claim to possess a truth that is beyond challenge.

Women and minorities are kept in inferior roles. A few passages of the Bible instruct women to be silent and submissive; several biblical writers condoned slavery. Until the church teaches its people to be discerning in their reading of scripture, these biblical passages will be barriers and embarrassments, with those on the edges of society bearing the brunt of the damage.

Youth feel betrayed. Youth are especially vulnerable to damage by a dishonest church. While their parents and grandparents may have made peace with nagging religious doubts, young people are likely to want to work through those doubts. More than half of those who grow up in mainline Protestant churches will attend college. There they will encounter scientific information incompatible with the faith of their childhood. If they try to reclaim their faith by taking courses in The Bible as Literature, they will discover jarring facts about the origin and development of scripture. Worst of all, they may go home on vacation and confront their pastor with their new knowledge, only to hear the pastor respond, "Yes, I knew all this all along." Their sense of betrayal may require a long time to heal, if it heals at all.

■   *The church as an institution is damaged.*

Damage to the institutional church also takes a variety of forms.

Mainline Protestant denominations, those that are a special concern of this volume, are losing members at an alarming rate. One reason for this loss, I am convinced, is the failure of the church to invite mature and intellectually curious persons into a religious quest.

The Christian church, in both its Protestant and Catholic forms, is losing leaders. Seminaries are mostly filled, but few of their desks are occupied by students who can offer the capable long-term leadership the church needs in its present crisis. Seminaries today find themselves accepting students whose academic records would not win them admittance into other professions. They also gladly accept older, second-career persons whose time of service will be limited. Further, the percentage of seminary graduates who go into parish work is decreasing. Of those who become pastors, a significant number either drop out of parish work or become depressed because they want to drop out and cannot. My conversations with other clergy make me confident that one of the reasons for a high drop-out rate is the conflict between what they have come to believe and what they feel they can safely say in pulpits or church school classrooms. I suspect that those who drop out early are among the most promising young leaders. They have too much integrity to play duplicitous games with their congregations.

A Pact of Silence

Dishonesty damages the modern church because many important issues are simply ignored. A silent pact often exists between pastor and congregation, a pact in which certain difficult issues are to be left unmentioned.

The nature of scripture and the origins of scripture are examples of crucial issues that are generally avoided. And yet understanding particular passages of the Bible is difficult until a philosophy of the Bible as a whole is developed that addresses those issues. Is the Bible the word of God spoken directly to humankind? Is the Bible a divine message recorded by fallible scribes? Or is the Bible a particular community's record of its uneven efforts to understand its role in a God-permeated universe? Only after developing a philosophy of the Bible can the church deal with issues such as the Bible's conflicting advice on divorce, its often demeaning comments about women, and its masculine, monarchial concepts of God.

A basic understanding of the role of the Bible is, sadly, among the last things the leadership of the church wants to encourage. Sermons and educational literature simply refer to the Bible as the Word of God, a classic example of a phrase that means one thing to the professionals who write it and a very different thing to the people who are expected to read it.

Because the human origins of the Bible are not discussed, church members are left in an ambiguous and often hostile relationship with science. How, in an age of science, does the church deal with the many miracle stories in scripture, and where does the church stand on the evolution/creationism controversy? When these subjects are ignored, religious professionals appear to have no knowledge of science, or they seem actually to think the world was created in six days.

Failure to discuss such sensitive issues is itself a half-lie. Half-lies are often more devastating than bold lies.

❖

Two Conflicting Styles of Faith

The most serious damage that can, and probably will, come from the churches' dishonesty is a division between two styles of Christianity. On the one hand, an arid, intellectual faith is emerging, a faith that is taught in academic circles and is held as the private property of the culture's intelligentsia. On the other hand, an egocentric, superstition-filled, miracle-based religion is developing as the faith of the masses.

Optimistically, I state this in the future tense: This division *is emerging*. In reality, I see overwhelming evidence that it already exists. Academics write books for other academics, and they write in a language and style that are almost totally inaccessible to untrained minds. Lay people, in contrast, are more apt to read Christian novels and paperback advice books on how to tap into religion's power to make one healthy, happy, and rich. The gap widens, and as it does, it builds upon itself. Lay people lose touch with the increasingly obtuse thought world of the academic, and academics more forcefully dismiss the "Sunday school faith" of the laity.

Huston Smith, widely read interpreter of world religions, shows deep respect for the Taoist faith. Yet he has this sad commentary on what has actually happened to this once rich religious tradition:

> One way to approach the basic power of the universe is through magic. From this approach to the power of *Tao* comes Popular Taoism, the Taoism of the masses. Popular Taoism is not a pretty sight. We have already said enough about the original doctrine of *Tao* to indicate that it was a concept too subtle to be grasped by the average mind or spirit. It was perhaps inevitable that when the concept was translated to make contact with the average villager and institutionalized around this translation it would be rendered in cruder and eventually perverted terms. To pass from the lofty heights of the *Tao Te Ching* to the priestcraft of Popular Taoism is like passing from a crystal mountain spring to the thick, fetid waters of the stagnant canal. Mysticism becomes mystification and religion is perverted into necromancy and sorcery. There have been long epochs in China's history when Taoism in its popular form could be characterized as little more than a funeral racket.[5]

Smith's description of a bifurcated Taoism should be a warning sign. Evidence abounds that Christianity is moving in a similar direction. A Gallup poll, taken after the beginning of the 21st century, discovered that essentially half of the American public rejects, on religious grounds, the overwhelming scientific arguments for evolution. More than twice as many Americans, according to this poll, believe in a separate being called the devil (68 percent) as believe in evolution (28 percent). Two recent American presidents have questioned evolution, or at least have raised that issue to strengthen their support among those who do.

The walls between professional Christianity and popular Christianity are being built with frightening efficiency, and some of the architects of those walls reside within the Protestant mainline. Recently, in a major city, a congregation invited two professors of religion to give a series of lectures on what is known (and not known) about the historical Jesus. A regional ecclesiastical official sent them notice that he would not allow the event to proceed. In explaining his action, the official wrote, in effect: I cancelled these lectures in order to avoid confusing the laity. Such matters are better kept within the confines of the academic community and among theologians and clergy.

The denominational official had no quarrel with the truthfulness of what was to be presented in the planned lecture series. He simply did not want the faith of an academic made accessible to people in the pews. It would be difficult to deny that this is a major reason why people who want a broader faith are abandoning the church by the thousands.

◆

Summary

Thus a brief episode in a pastoral search interview provides a lens through which a major sickness of the Christian church can be seen and diagnosed. In the following chapter, the pastor-parishioner division will be examined in more detail.

Beyond that, the doctrines and people that contribute to and are impacted by this illness will be identified. The latter half of the book will explore some of the ingredients that can make an exciting religious quest. The quest begins in a tradition whose major strength is its unfinished nature.

NOTES

1. By this term I mean the United Methodist Church; the Presbyterian Church (U.S.A.); the Evangelical Lutheran Church in America; the Disciples of Christ; the American Baptist Churches, USA; the United Church of Christ; the Episcopal Church, USA (which does not consistently identify itself as Protestant); the Church of the Brethren; and other groups that were once influential in the life of the United States and that have, without exception, suffered significant membership losses over the past several decades.

2. John A. T. Robinson, *Honest to God* (Philadelphia: Westminster Press, 1963).

3. Robert W. Funk, *Honest to Jesus* (San Francisco: HarperSanFrancisco, 1996).

4. Reported by *The Los Angeles Times,* May 19, 2002.

5. Huston Smith, *The Religions of Man,* revised edition (San Francisco: Harper and Row, Perennial Library, 1986).

2

The Nature of the Divide

In the first chapter I identified a divide between two styles of faith, an ugly fissure across an already fragmented Christian landscape. Before moving on to explore the people and doctrines that divide the church, it is important to explore the nature of the problem in greater detail.

Being in the Christian church today is much like living in a house infested with termites. On the surface few things seem amiss. We can go about the business of living, paying no attention to the small sawdust piles in the basement and the squeaky floor that signals structural weakness. But we are only postponing the day when the devastating reality will reveal itself: The structure is being eaten away.

Christianity is being eroded. In the United States, the Roman Catholic branch of the faith is growing, but only through immigration. All Protestant branches of the faith are either in decline absolutely, or in decline as a percentage of the population. Signs of restlessness continue to be seen even among those who remain faithful to these slowly vanishing institutions.

Ignoring the problem is not working. Defining the problem is the first step toward a change in direction.

◆

An Evolving Division

Religion, by its nature, tends to divide itself into two styles of believing. Psychological and commercial factors create an inevitable push toward a popularized religion, while intrinsic qualities of the faith resist this process. In general, we could say that a popularized faith emphasizes the rewards of the religion for the individual while saying little about its challenges. This inevitably spawns a counter-movement that seeks to preserve a more intellectually muscular form of faith, one that stresses the needs of the community over those of the individual, and calls for spiritual growth even when growth is painful. The illustration from Taoism, given earlier, shows how this division has expressed itself in that tradition.

In Christianity, the current popularized form of religion often labels itself "conservative" and calls its opposition "liberal," and many commentators have assumed that the major division within present-day Protestant Christianity can be discussed in those terms. But I believe that framing this as a liberal-conservative debate confuses the issues, both because the more basic underlying dynamic is that between popularization and its opposing force, and because the terms "liberal" and "conservative" have lost much of their meaning through misuse.

"Liberal" is a once proud but now battered term that needs to be retired for a generation or two. Its root means freedom. In religious terms, it once meant a style of faith that appreciated tradition but was primarily oriented toward the future. Rigid positions passed on by ancestors were rejected when they blocked the way toward a more just and peaceful world.

The term "liberal" has suffered the worst fate that can fall upon a word: It has been redefined by its detractors. In common usage, it has become a pejorative term implying a form of softheaded, deliberate detachment from the wisdom of the past. I avoid the use of this word whenever possible, not because I disown its original meaning, but because it no longer communicates effectively.

The word "conservative" also has been wounded in modern usage, though to a lesser degree than has "liberal." "Conservative" continues to have positive religious overtones, especially when it refers to cherishing and celebrating the many strengths of the Hebrew-Christian tradition. Since I see myself as a conservator of this tradition, I could call myself a conservative. Yet most of those who call themselves conservatives today would not grant me that label. So, bowing to current usage, in this volume I primarily use the word to describe those who perceive tradition as a fixed reality that can and should be transmitted to new generations in an unchanged form. I disagree with this position, but I recognize that it is held by many persons whose minds and commitments I otherwise admire.

Given these problems with the definitions of "liberal" and "conservative," I believe the once-lively debate using these terms has become pointless. The modern-day divide between Christians cries out to be framed in a different way. Even more importantly, I have described it as a division between *popular* and *academic* Christianity because I believe this pair of terms gives us a more powerful way to understand the current crisis in the church—and to imagine a way out of it. While the fault lines between liberal and conservative and those between academic and popular often run close to one another, they diverge in important ways.

Popular Christianity sees itself as a conservative movement, and, even though I consider this a misuse of language, I will refer to it by that term from time to time. Yet ironically, many spokespersons for popular Christianity have expressed their commitment to the past in such a radical manner that they have removed themselves from the tradition they claim to cherish. Popular Christianity's adoration of the scripture, for example, would be seen as idolatry by most of the thinkers who have been instrumental in forming Christianity. Luther would never have embraced popular Christianity's views of the Bible as inerrant; indeed, Luther wanted to dismiss the entire book of James as a "book of straw." Popular religion's rejection of advanced scientific knowledge also stands outside the tradition it claims to preserve. And popular Christianity's rank individualism is in direct contrast to a religious tradition that has emphasized the role of the community. Ironically too, the bright optimism of popular preachers (God will make everything turn out well for God's special people) seems almost to be borrowed from liberalism (although liberalism and popular Christianity build their optimism on different foundations).

Academic Christianity preserves many of the themes and characteristics of liberalism, but again with differences. For example, liberalism's commitment to justice and peace continues to flourish in the scholarly setting, though in a less optimistic form. Like liberalism, academic faith refuses to reject modern society and secular knowledge, though it keeps itself in tension with these realities. And like liberalism, academic Christianity is unafraid of new ideas; it is constantly exploring fresh concepts and original ways to formulate old belief systems. Yet individual academics vary widely concerning matters of dogma. Some gladly embrace the label of liberal; others strongly reject it.

What academics have most in common, however, is a tendency to speak primarily to one another, using language that is seldom understood by those untrained in the field. Given the weakening of liberalism, and the limited visibility of academic Christianity, the popularizers have been left with almost no opposition in the public forum.

◆

Differences in Style

If I am right in my description of this split, present-day Christians would seem to be faced with an unenviable choice between two limited options: a distant and inaccessible academic style on the one hand, and an insipid, individualistic, popular style on the other.

Note the use of the word "style." The present conflict within Christianity has to do with more than particular beliefs. It has to do with *styles* of faith, too. Both academics and popularists disagree among themselves over details of dogma. But while academics carry on their often esoteric arguments using inaccessible language, popularists have been so committed to accessibility that they refrain from any challenging ideas or from any suggestion that people of faith ever need to grow. This is the first difference in their styles.

Another division between academic and popular styles of faith concerns an approach to religious tradition and the role that tradition should play in the modern day. Followers of popular Christianity embrace their spiritual ancestors as models of faithful living; since they look backward for their examples, the tradition becomes a restraint on social change. Academics, on the other hand, tend to find in tradition a dynamic energy that propels them into the future.

In addition, academics and popularists distinguish themselves from one another by their basic stance toward life itself. To this important subject I will return later.

Damaging as it has been to Christianity in general, this division between academic and popular styles has set the stage for yet another style of Christian believing. This new style has been developed by persons whose spiritual hungers are strong, who have little interest in learning the language of the academics, and who cannot tolerate the narrow views and anti-cultural bias of popular Christianity. This emerging style of faith holds the promise of being a much stronger alternative to popularized Christianity than either the liberal or academic style; yet it is not a total rejection of what is popular. This new style offers the possibility of mediating across the otherwise widening and tragic schism in modern Christianity.

◆

From Academic to Progressive

In a growing but still small number of locations, local churches are trying to overcome the division between academic and popular styles of faith. They sponsor lectures from academics, despite the occasional frowns of their ecclesiastical superiors. They encourage their pastors to share pertinent aspects of their seminary training. They develop adult and older youth discussion sessions in which questions are welcome and absolutes discouraged.

In these settings, a style of faith based on the insights of academics is both transmitted and transformed. What had been an arid, left-brain activity takes on amazing vitality. The result is *progressive* Christianity. Progressive Christianity is the religion of the scholars energized and refreshed until it becomes a lively faith for the masses. Progressive Christianity then stands as a viable alternative to the anti-intellectualism of popular Christianity. In addition, progressive Christianity offers the possibility of narrowing the divide between the two styles of believing.

I speak of narrowing the gap between styles of faith with full awareness of how difficult this task can be. Progressive Christianity is, to a large degree, academic faith released from its scholastic prison. Part of the baggage the progressives carry, then, includes the conflicts that have already been discussed between academic and popular faith. Progressive Christianity distinguishes itself from popular Christianity in several additional ways.

The two styles of faith have quite different ways of identifying authentic adherents of Christianity. Popular Christianity puts great emphasis on dogma and personal confessions of faith. It draws clear, small circles around those who meet its standards, creating an exclusive faith. In contrast, progressive Christianity puts much less stress on dogma. It attempts to draw imprecise and wide circles to include as many people as possible.

The two styles of faith differ even in the harm they may cause. Popular Christianity at its extreme becomes judgmental and rigid. Witch burnings, inquisitions, and religious wars are too frequently the bloody, tragic results. Progressive Christianity carries another set of dangers: Unless care is taken to see that it is deeply and strongly rooted in an ongoing tradition, it becomes a watery system with few defining commitments, a wide but thin blanket placed over ideas that are often distressingly shallow. These, of course, are the familiar charges leveled by "conservatives" against "liberals," and unfortunately, they are not always groundless.

Thus, the division between styles of Christianity continues, but the issues that separate us have taken on new forms. The struggle is now between a progressive style of faith and a popular style of faith. At least one new hope emerges from this change: Dialogue might now be possible. Progressives tend to be less dogmatic than those who earlier claimed the role of liberal, and they, unlike the academics, are not hidden.

Progressives and popularizers can, if they choose, talk to one another. They can engage in dialogues based on the fact that they use similar terms—"God," "Spirit," "Jesus," etc.— and read a common Bible. On occasion the two might even recite the same creeds. Agreement on basic issues is unlikely, but constructive conversations can prevent a wide schism from becoming even wider. Dialogue would help fulfill the mission of progressive Christianity, which, by its very nature, is a mediating force.

◆

The Pastor as Bridge

Progressive Christianity results when the depth of academic faith is added to the energy of popular faith. This merging can be facilitated best by individuals who have experienced both worlds: those who were reared in local churches where popular faith was practiced, and who have also studied in the classrooms of the academics. As you may have guessed, I am describing local pastors.

Local pastors may react to this assignment with understandable horror. Their schedules are already full. Becoming a bridge between two approaches to faith adds another set of burdens. It means clergy must stay in touch with major happenings in the intellectual world. It means they must assist their laity in the sometimes painful transition to new ways of being religious. It means placing their livelihood in danger.

The role of bridge between lay and professional religion may remind many clergy of the story of the cowardly young man who wanted to stay safe during the Civil War. He put on a blue jacket and gray trousers, hoping that the combination of uniforms would confuse anyone wishing to do him harm. The sad ending of this story is that the man was shot in both ends. Most clergy have already been caught in the crossfire of enough other conflicts to have a realistic fear of a similar result.

Actually, the role of bridge between styles of faith need not add to the stress of pastoral life. As this new task is embraced, other tasks can be set aside. Clergy can then emphasize their role as educators, while allowing the laity to take over other duties, such as administration. Even the duties of visitation can be shared across the entire church. Congregations benefit as pastors cease to be lone rangers pretending to be indispensable to every aspect of church life.

Personal Experience

I offer myself as a hopeful example. In an often awkward and almost entirely unplanned way, I have become proof that one can be a bridge between styles of faith and survive professionally to tell the story.

I came into the pastorate near the end of the time when the Protestant mainline was thriving. I had no reason to stop and ask, What is wrong? On the surface, nothing seemed amiss. Yet in my gut I was conscious of something disjointed. My religion classes in both college and seminary were giving me stimulating information about the scriptures and the history of my faith, information I had not heard in the churches of my youth. "This is great material," I found myself thinking. "Why aren't local congregations making more use of it?"

My personal experience is helpful, mostly because it is typical. I come, in fact, from a slightly more conservative than average background. My early faith development took place in the mountainous part of Virginia. We were not technically in the Bible Belt, but close enough to feel its often chilling breezes.

Considering my location, I was fortunate. In the Methodist Church where the seeds of my faith were first planted, I was taught by pastors and church school teachers who welcomed questions as easily as they shared platitudes. The words used by my faith guides, if I could remember them, were probably standard fare. I recall hearing at least the implication that the Bible had been written by the divine, that Jesus was all I needed to know about God, and that the reward for enduring hot Sundays in the sanctuary was eternal life.

Somehow, nonetheless, the blankets of absolutes in which these traditional words were wrapped included holes through which I might breathe. My teachers let me know that the edifice of faith was not so rigid or sacred that it could not be reexamined, and that I would not be condemned if I let my frequent doubts show.

One church school teacher was willing to share with her class a painful episode in her life, an episode that had led her to a faith crisis for which she had found no satisfactory solution. She had suffered a personal loss which nothing in her religious training could explain. A stricken look went across her face when she finished recounting this story. She realized that she had been more self-disclosing than she had intended, spreading, perhaps, contagious doubts. She need not have worried. I have no inkling of what others in the class did with her words, but for me, her sharing was one of the most freeing and growth-inspiring moments in my early religious life. She had demonstrated that one might continue as a person of faith even when basic questions remain unanswered.

From that local church I went to a church-sponsored college located farther back in the hills of Virginia (Emory and Henry College, near Abingdon). My Old Testament professor there was Dr. Loren Dow, a remarkable teacher who carried an aura of profound faith. He taught church school classes at the campus congregation and preached at nearby local churches when asked. He was a person visibly comfortable with himself as a child of God. In the classroom he was demanding, insisting that we master many facts about the scriptures. The Bible, as he taught us, was not a static document but a living one, a volume that he loved and held in high esteem, yet never worshiped.

Dr. Dow forced us to remove our protective blinders and encounter the real words on the biblical page. We came to see—as any objective reader must—that the Book of Genesis contains not one but two creation stories, each with its own take on the nature of God and the manner of creation. Then he helped us to trace these two traditions, which he taught us to call "E" and "J," through the early books of the Bible. He showed us that the first books written in their present form were those concerning the eighth-century prophets,[1] thus establishing the central biblical theme of social justice. Later scripture writers, he pointed out, had much more to say about social ethics than individual salvation.

Some of my classmates, who had matured in more suffocating atmospheres than I, were shaken by Dr. Dow's revelations. One young woman, half in jest but almost in tears, exclaimed once, "Why didn't my mother tell me these things?" She survived the crisis in good style. She has lived out her professional life, despite severe health problems, as an outstanding religious educator. Others have fared equally well. My alumni magazine tells me about many classmates who studied in classes under Dr. Dow. They are contributing to society as lawyers, public school educators, dentists and surgeons. The majority of them are also giving leadership to local churches across the Middle Atlantic States. Acknowledging the human element in the Bible has not hurt the faith of these loyal lay leaders.

Others of my former classmates are now local church pastors. They have scattered, mostly to churches in western Virginia and eastern Tennessee. They are well trained and well informed. They, too, shared in Dr. Dow's classrooms. They know that the Bible is a collection of writings composed by more than seventy very human writers. They know that the question of which writings to include in the Bible has been, and continues to be, a matter of controversy. They know that some of the material in the Bible attributed to Moses includes a description of Moses' death, and therefore could not have been written by him. They know that Paul wrote his letters before the Gospels were composed, and that the Gospels were written, in part at least, to argue with some of Paul's ideas. Yet reports I continue to receive inform me that most of these professionals keep all such matters well hidden from their congregations. With a few important exceptions, they continue to finesse all comments on any subject they consider delicate. Somewhat as a politician might, they tread carefully along the edge of truth and falsehood, using words with which they can live in good conscience but which fail to challenge or engage their listeners. They, along with the vast majority of local pastors, have chosen to reject the role of bridge between styles of faith; they selected, instead, the role of sentinel, guarding the laity from any contamination from the truths they themselves carry.

While learning about the Bible, I was also learning an alternative way of approaching the laity. I attended college at a time when Protestantism was growing so rapidly that it could not fill all its pulpits. I was asked to become student pastor of several country churches near the college. Because no one had told me I shouldn't, I shared with my people the information I was receiving in my college classes. In sermons and adult classes I tried to convey both the spiritual meaning of the scripture and the human context in which it was written. At first this was greeted with mild surprise. The mood quickly shifted to appreciation. The people of these rural communities recognized that they were being respected—that I assumed they were capable of encountering the same knowledge I was absorbing in my college classroom.

My congregations, located far back in the mountains of southwest Virginia, included barely literate laborers; farmers, both tenant and wealthy; schoolteachers and homemakers. Together they made up a wonderful cross-section of rural America. Without exception, they joined happily in the adventure of new knowledge.

Later I continued, through forty additional years of pastoral ministry, to share with congregations the factual information that lies at the foundation of my spiritual life. My methods were honed, but not basically changed. Congregations in a variety of settings responded with appreciation.

A pastor can be a bridge between different styles of faith. Doing so does not require undue sophistication. I was acting as a bridge before I made my first footprint on a seminary campus.

A Changing Population

My personal experience is typical in yet another way. I received education beyond high school. I was only the second person in the Goods' extended family network to do so (my older brother was the first). My father was reared in a religious sect that strongly encouraged him to drop out of school after eighth grade. His help was needed on the family farm. My mother finished high school, but felt no pressure to continue her education. The same pattern held for their siblings. In contrast to my parents' generation, almost all my cousins completed college, and many have earned graduate degrees. Those in the next younger generation of our family attend institutions of higher education routinely.

Yet the Christian church continues to present the same message in the same way, as if their congregations had remained static. This effort at continuity runs squarely into a major problem: Keeping laity in a state of religious ignorance is an increasingly difficult task. As we shall see in a later chapter, the school experience of my family is typical. Educational levels are rising rapidly. As educational levels rise, the entire society is drawn into the information age. All adult church members, those who have college degrees and those who are high school dropouts, read news reports about Dead Sea Scrolls and other discoveries that reveal much about the earthy origins of the Bible. Nonetheless, these well-educated church members find themselves sharing in liturgies and listening to sermons built on the prescientific worldviews of biblical writers. These views create serious discord when placed against the modern knowledge of astronomers who predict lunar eclipses with precision and use telescopes that collect light twelve billion years after it left its point of origin.

The secular world, however, is not the only challenge to the religious *status quo*. The more educated lay persons of the modern age often have the self-confidence needed to set out on religious quests of their own. They may find, without any help from professionals, that they are not receiving the full picture. Some of them will do what the Protestant Reformation encouraged them to do four hundred years ago: read the scripture without supervision.

As they read the Bible, the laity will find evidence that they have been treated with less than full respect. A modern searcher might ask, for example, how the doctrine of the divinity of Jesus came to be.

The church literature I read, and the sermons I heard as a youth, left the impression that Jesus, from the moment of his birth, was recognizable as divine. (After all, do not the most popular paintings of the baby Jesus show a quite visible halo over his head?) This assumption does not survive even a cursory scriptural examination.

One does not have to be specially trained in biblical studies to find evidence that the doctrine of the unique divinity of Jesus developed over several decades. Once a person is emotionally ready to explore the issue, the evidence leaps off the biblical page. Paul, who wrote before the Gospels were composed, seemed to believe that Jesus became the Messiah at the moment of his resurrection (Romans 1:4). The writer of Mark assumed that the divine had selected Jesus for his special mission at his baptism. The birth stories of Matthew and Luke, stories that most scholars assume came later, indicated that Jesus had been the Messiah from the moment of conception. The writer of John, generally accepted as the last of the Gospel writers, extended the role of the Christ back to the world's creation. An unmistakable process of glorification is afoot. The full glorification was not a finished fact even when the New Testament was completed. Yet these *facts* are seldom acknowledged in either pulpit or adult church school classroom.[2]

Perceptive church people will recognize other examples of fudging the truth. Instead of becoming bridges across the divide, pastors often find creative ways to widen the gap between what they know and what they preach.

An example I recall with special vividness concerned a denominational official who, because of her background and office, was a person I wanted to trust without reservation. In a worship service I attended, this ordained conference officer read the scripture. At the end of the lesson she intoned, "I believe it is true. This is the word of God."

Having received no signal to do otherwise, the normal worshiper would take the worship leader's words at face value. "I believe it is true" seemed to mean she accepted the total Bible as literal fact. "This is the word of God" implied that the divine was speaking directly to members of this congregation. But is this what this well-trained, responsible person intended to convey?

In her defense, the scripture reader was sharing in a liturgical practice that has a long history. In congregations of many denominations a worshiper can hear the reader say at the end of a Bible lesson: "The word of God" (a phrase that introduces, even in its simplicity, many ambiguities). Yet it is difficult to defend the unique twist my conference official gave to that tradition. By expanding on the historic formula, the church official was, I fear, playing to a particular audience. The denomination that she and I share includes a conservative element, an element that threatens to divorce the remainder of us if we do not shape up by accepting their package of established beliefs. Especially, we are told by these more rigid folk, we must evidence a stronger respect for the authority of the Bible. The denominational official's desire to placate the biblical literalists apparently overcame her desire for personal integrity.

Also, partially in the worship leader's defense, I am sure she is able to rationalize to herself that her public statement reflects her true beliefs. She does believe that the Bible is a *container* of truth, that at its best it opens and pierces the human condition.

Yet her words carried an entirely different meaning to most of those who sat in the pews. To those who do not have the luxury of spending time each day thinking theologically, the words "I believe it is true" mean that she believes each word and phrase of the Bible to be, both historically and morally, accurate. This includes not only the passage she read in worship that day, but also an account of creation that took place in six days. It also includes movements of armies and nations that cannot be documented by any other historical source. "I believe it [the Bible] is true" also puts this woman in the awkward position of seeming to affirm the biblical admonition that women are not to speak in churches.

Why must the church change its mode of relating to its members? Because church leaders are dealing with a different kind of lay person. Laity in the past have been assumed to be easily fooled. Sadly, this assumption is built in the shape of a boomerang. Once modern lay people recognize that they are being patronized, the lack of respect becomes reciprocal. Those who hear the double meanings offered by religious professionals will either admire their agility or will be angered by their duplicity. The gap within Christianity grows wider.

A few lay people are beginning to plead for leadership that heals rather than aggravates the professional-laity divide. One such person wrote to an ecumenical magazine in appreciation of a recent article that encouraged more serious adult education. He described the difficulty of finding satisfactory literature for a local discussion group: "The vast majority of publications are written either for an uncritical lay audience or for the scholarly community. The former merely espouse what we call 'the party line,' while the latter are usually written in a style that is unapproachable (if not unreadable) by those of us who are not seminary-educated. Even adult educational materials are frequently shallow and simplistic." The same writer continued:

> When arriving at the Right Answers is the desired end of adult education in the church, encouraging lay theology is a great risk. There is always the possibility that lay thinkers will arrive at the Wrong Conclusions, a situation that answerizers cannot tolerate. I know of local pastors who refuse to allow the use of certain adult educational materials in their churches because the class participants might get "the wrong idea." . . . [This] might help explain why lay theology is not more widely encouraged in local congregations.[3]

Such lay feedback should be celebrated, not because it is pleasant to encounter, but because it clarifies the nature of one of the church's major problems.

◆

Pleasure in Power

The need for change should be clear. Change, however, is not taking place. Why? I fear that denominational officials and professional theologians perpetuate the present state of affairs because they have come to enjoy too much their role as sole owners and manipulators of the sacred symbols. Consciously or unconsciously, they leave their church members in a state of semi-darkness because otherwise they would have to share prestige and authority. I do not mean to imply deliberate malfeasance. I do mean to suggest an unconscious pleasure in power. Church professionals assume that lay people who are illiterate in scriptural matters will continue (as long as they remain in the church at all) to be placid, and that they will be satisfied with the often shallow interpretations of preselected scriptures they hear each Sunday. They will not stray in their private readings into unassigned portions of scripture where they might encounter ethical levels that are embarrassingly low, or miraculous acts that mock modern knowledge.

I sense that somewhere, hidden perhaps in the subconscious of church officials, is a fear that lay persons who are truly knowledgeable about the scripture and the history of their tradition will be less dependent upon the ordained leadership of the church. A laity that is well-informed might challenge entrenched bureaucratic priorities and denominational dogma.

Russian novelist Fyodor Dostoyevsky set a scene in one of his novels in the Spanish Inquisition. According to Dostoyevsky's story, Jesus had returned to try to correct the injustices being done in the name of faith. The Grand Inquisitor then confronted Jesus, defending the cruelty being carried out in the name of faith. The Inquisitor's tack was to chide Jesus for the way Jesus had handled his original temptations.[4] Those temptations, according to the Inquisitor, had offered Jesus the opportunity to manipulate people through *miracle, mystery,* and *authority.* Jesus was foolish, according to his antagonist, to have refused these possibilities. People, the Inquisitor insisted, do not want the responsibility of dealing with such matters on their own. Freedom in faith is too heavy a burden for normal folk to carry. The priests and bishops of the Middle Ages were far wiser.

> We have corrected Thy work and have founded it upon
> *miracle, mystery,* and *authority.* And men rejoiced that they
> were again led like sheep, and that the terrible gift that
> had brought them such suffering was, at last, lifted from
> their hearts. Were we right teaching them this? Speak! Did
> we not love mankind, so meekly acknowledging their fee-
> bleness, lovingly lightening their burden, and permitting
> their weak nature even sin with our sanction?[5]

When one looks at the woeful Biblical and theological illiteracy of the laity, an illiteracy in which the church leadership is
complicit, one cannot help suspecting that church leaders continue to enjoy their role in relation to the "weak nature" of those
who sit in our pews. This is a harsh judgment. It is one to which
I have come with reluctance after more than forty years of work
within the structure of the Christian church. But if I am correct
about this, the situation cries out to be exposed and corrected.

◆

The Problem: Unique to the Mainline Churches?

This volume is concerned primarily with the division between
professional and lay religion within mainline Protestant denominations, where I have observed its vicious impact. Other
branches of the faith might experience a similar dishonesty. I
suspect they do.

Many pastors of evangelical, sect-like churches, have earned
degrees from Bible institutes where the subject of study is the
scripture itself. Never would those institutes dream of having
their students study *about* the Bible—the difficulties of its lan-
guages and the social settings from which it arose—as do Protestant and Catholic seminary students. Bible institutes are not
trying to alter their students' faith, only to reinforce what has
been taught in local churches. Theoretically, then, the religious
beliefs of the church professional should be quite similar to the
religious positions of the membership. But not necessarily.

When, in the latter half of the 19th century, Sinclair Lewis was doing research for his novel *Elmer Gantry*, he gathered a group of evangelical pastors for conversations about their beliefs and work. The meetings took place over a period of months. As these pastors came to trust Lewis, they admitted that few of them believed the doctrines they attempted to force on their congregations each Sunday. Lewis found this duplicity abominable, a view he effectively wove into his novel. I have no evidence that a similar situation exists among evangelical pastors today. If it does, however, it is an issue that begs to be addressed.

I strongly suspect that Roman Catholicism has its own issues with clergy/laity dishonesty. Some of the finest biblical scholarship of the past several decades has come from Catholic scholars. Young men studying for the priesthood have been exposed to those insights. They, like their Protestant counterparts, must then go out into congregations where views of the Bible are quite different from the views presented in scholastic settings. Although a Catholic priest carries an authority different from that of a Protestant pastor, he might be reluctant to spend that authority confronting the outdated theological or biblical ideas of his congregations. It would be reasonable to assume that the difficulty of preaching and acting on a faith he does not fully embrace could be part of the reason for the high drop-out rate among young priests, and for the sexual acting-out that has stigmatized the priesthood. I do not have the expertise to explore the impact of pastor/parish dishonesty on Catholicism, although I am confident it is an issue well worth the attention of some of the skilled Catholic sociologists at work today.

Lacking the firsthand knowledge to fairly address the issue of dishonesty in these other branches of Christianity, I will concentrate my attention on mainline Protestantism, aware that the problem being addressed could be much broader.

Mainline Protestantism—Reversing the Trends

The fact that mainline Protestantism has a problem is undeniable. Membership figures are declining. Yet the pool of thinking-oriented people from which mainline churches should be drawing is rapidly expanding. What is causing this disconnect? The question has no easy answers. Sociologists find it easier to eliminate possible explanations for shrinking membership roles than to identify precisely why people persons are leaving church pews. Careful studies have established that mainliners are not leaving in order to become charismatics or fundamentalists.[6] They are not leaving over anger at stands on social issues. They are simply disappearing, vanishing, as it were, in the night.

I have a strong distrust of all critics of the church who think they have *the* answer to the decline of the mainline church. I make no such claim. But I strongly suspect that what is being discussed in this volume is one major factor contributing to membership loss. People who have become accustomed to independent thinking are no longer comfortable sitting in pews where they are told to accept faith structures that were put together in ancient times and in very different societies. An unacceptable conflict has been set up in the minds of persons who have no reason to doubt the insights of astronomy, archeology, and biology.

Modern Protestantism includes people who are referred to by retired Bishop John Spong as "Christians in exile." These are individuals who object to Christian worship that is still dominated by a vocabulary and images that fly in the face of their secular knowledge. They often are spiritual searchers who have struggled without success to read the Bible. Such people continue to tell poll takers that they believe in God and prayer. Yet they no longer experience any loyalty to the church that is the institutional carrier of the sacred traditions.

Some apologists for the faith insist that the church is declining because it has failed to convince these Christians in exile to turn off their minds and accept the "faith once given." To this argument we will return later. At this point it is sufficient to point out that this reasoning does not fit the known facts about decreasing memberships.

Here is an assumption that does fit what we know of those leaving the church: One of the factors that prod them to leave is that they can no longer tolerate the lack of honesty between pulpit and pew. Mature people have despaired of hearing God described exclusively as an ancient combination of Superman and Santa Claus. They have been offended by the lack of a clear statement from the pulpit about the differing worldviews of science and Bible. They have seen too many sly smiles and heard too much innuendo and satire implying that Darwin had it all wrong. This evasion and sleight of hand may have worked once with an illiterate pew. It may continue to work for brief periods with persons whose spiritual and social hungers are intense enough to keep them attached to the church despite the intellectual contradictions. But the effort to impose this approach on everyone in the modern age can only cause further decline of a once proud religious tradition.

The message must go out to all congregations that try to muddy their message to ensure that no one is offended: *The effort to offend no one ends by offending everyone.*

If the assumption described has any validity, then an answer is easy to describe (though not nearly so easy to enact). The lying must stop in all Christian congregations. Even pastors who are committed to a dogmatic approach to faith should play straight with their congregations. How did the dogma come into being? Why were opposing views labeled as heresy? What were the sociopolitical conditions that influenced the form of the dogma?

Here is another, equally important, part of the answer: Another religious option *should* be available for all Christians who are uncomfortable with the dishonesty that tends to collect around congregations with inflexible views. Within driving distance of any person in Western society should be at least one congregation that specializes in challenging people in new directions. This congregation should be one whose roots are clearly in the Christian tradition even while it emphasizes the living, evolving nature of that tradition. That congregation should be one that prods its people to grow in faith and offers resources to help persons harmonize faith and secular knowledge.

When all else fails, try honesty! This is, indeed, the last thing many church leaders want. They fear that even more people will abandon the pews if too much truth begins to flow. Perhaps they are right. Having been fed infant formula for so long, spiritual stomachs may not be prepared for solid food. But here is a hopeful idea: The church has nothing more to lose. Mainline denominations are dying. At worst, a program of honesty will speed up the demise, sparing the patient a painful and lengthy death. More hopefully, the decline can be arrested or reversed. At best, the church could return to its role as the defender of truth—a truth that is applied as fearlessly to the church's internal concerns as to any outside issue. Instead of dying, the mainline churches might reclaim their disaffected members even as they reclaim their mission.

NOTES

1. Amos, Micah, Hosea, and the early chapters of Isaiah.

2. The precise dating of New Testament writings, like so many other aspects of the theological world, continues to be discussed. The point made above, however, regarding the recognition of the special nature of Jesus, would achieve widespread agreement among biblical scholars.

3. Lynn M. Labs, Letters to the Editor, *The Christian Century*, January 20, 1999.

4. The story of Jesus' temptation in the wilderness is told in Mark 1, Matthew 4, and Luke 4.

5. Fyodor Dostoyevsky, *The Brothers Karamazov* (New York: Random House, 1950).

6. See, in particular, the following studies by religious sociologists: Wade Clark Roof, *A Generation of Seekers* (San Francisco: HarperSanFrancisco, 1993); Dean Hoge, Donald A. Luidens, and Benton Johnson, *Vanishing Boundaries: The Religion of Mainline Protestant Baby Boomers* (Louisville: Westminster/John Knox Press, 1994).

3

Honest to Whom?

Jim grew up in a midwest community, surrounded by family members who combined caring relationships with strict adherence to moral standards. The church to which he and his family went each Sunday was an additional source of strength. Strong personal ties made the congregation a place of emotional warmth. People embraced Jim. They expressed an interest in him, inspiring Jim to study hard and to develop his keen mind.

At school, Jim found himself fascinated by science. He did his assigned lessons in his favorite courses, then spent time in the local library seeking more information.

As he grew, discomfort began to set in when Sunday mornings came. He detected that the pastor of his fundamentalist congregation was not happy with the findings of science. Jim heard his pastor state that the concept of evolution was wrong. It was more than wrong, according to this spiritual guide: It was the work of the devil. Astronomers were also engaged in evil work, according to what Jim heard at church. Charting the stars and discovering that the universe was several billion years old violated scripture and thus was to be rejected. When Jim tried to present another point of view in church school settings, his ideas were condemned, not just by the pastor, but by the congregation as a whole. A similar pattern repeated itself at home. Soon Jim began to feel estranged from both his biological family and his spiritual family.

His intellectual curiosity was stronger than his emotional pain. He pressed on in his interest in science. An undergraduate degree was followed by study for a master's degree and then a Doctor of Philosophy degree, all in science.

More than the differences between the worldviews of science and his home church was at stake. His experience taught him that the authorities he had embraced when he had been small were not right about everything. He discovered that his own insights, while not always correct, were accurate enough to be trusted. His time in church became painful, even when subjects other than science were being discussed. He was no longer willing to hear either his pastor or his parents tell him to accept dogma simply because it had been handed down from one authority figure to another. His sense of estrangement deepened.

Marriage and the birth of a son gave him a new source of personal support yet never entirely healed the hurt of his earlier rejections. Neither did new religious communities satisfy his spiritual hungers. He and his wife attempted to be active in a Protestant congregation near a university in which he was enrolled. Here the conflict between faith and knowledge was less severe than in the church of his childhood. Yet, in both adult education and sermons, Jim thought he heard waffling— a failure to clarify how the church related to the scripture's pre-scientific worldview. When he asked questions in educational settings, he sensed he was making other class members uncomfortable. He and his family dropped out of church. He continued to have the feeling that he was being asked to accept propositions simply because of their antiquity. In secular classrooms, he was a participant in the search for truth. In the church building, he was only the recipient of what others had discovered.

Late in his academic career, Jim and his family made one more effort to renew their spiritual quest. They began attending another Protestant church, one known for an honesty that bordered, according to one friend, on the heretical. They found an adult education class taught by a lay person whose knowledge of and love for the scripture was obvious. This instructor felt no need to defend the factual accuracy of any portion of the Bible. His teaching style was to explain the human setting from which a passage of scripture had arisen, and then invite the students to share in exploring the meaning of that passage.

A similar friendliness to science and a high respect for the laity was discovered in the pastor's sermons. This church, Jim found, was a place of faith, one that embraced secular knowledge as an aid in exploring the Mystery at the core of all that is. For the first time in his life, Jim was in a spiritual environment where his questions, his commitments, and his spiritual quest were welcome. He and his family became enthusiastic participants in the life of the congregation.

◆

Typical/Non-typical

Jim is not a typical citizen of the modern age. While more than half of American youth now expect to receive some education beyond high school, less than one in a thousand will achieve the academic level Jim has reached. Yet, by standing out from the crowd, Jim's story amplifies a mental disharmony which increasing numbers of people are experiencing at a somewhat lower decibel level.

Jim is a clear example of what Dietrich Bonhoeffer, nearly a century ago, meant by "humanity come of age." Jim had matured beyond any need for the security of fixed beliefs. He hungered for a faith that was open to adventure.

Not everyone in today's world has "come of age." But a rapidly increasing number of people fit that definition. One does not need an advanced degree in science to be caught up in

the scientific worldview. Indeed, one need be only barely literate to know some quite sophisticated facts. Television news
reports tell of the Hubbell telescope and its stunning discoveries. Archaeological discoveries are announced in weekly news
magazines, linking humankind with distant, evolutionary
ancestors. All media outlets share information that gives alert
persons a basic knowledge of how disease and health interact.
Armed with these facts, people come to worship. In that worship the modern person likely will participate in a liturgy
wrapped in language that is lovely but quaint. The weekly
reading of scripture invites the hearer into a worldview based
on a three-layered universe (heaven on top, hell underneath,
and earth sandwiched in between); worshippers may hear a
biblical story of a time the sun "stood still" (Joshua 10:13). More
likely, they will hear accounts of physical cures that violate the
way they know the human body works.

Many religious people deal with these contradictions by
mastering the art of bifurcated thinking. They allow a pre-
scientific worldview to rule on the Sabbath, while on Monday
they return to an existence that science has made more efficient
and comfortable. But even those who are most successful at
this split thinking must be aware of a gnawing discomfort. This
discomfort is sufficiently widespread to have acquired a name:
cognitive dissonance. When the discomfort grows, a choice must
be made. Either a person must work harder at dividing religious thought from secular realities, or that person will drop
out of the church altogether—an option that has come to be
entirely acceptable in larger society.

This chapter explores the question: "Honest to whom?" I
have traced the journey of one individual from a conflicted
existence to a faith that could be integrated with his scientific
interests. Jim suggests a kernel of an answer to the question. The
honest church will address those persons who suffer from cognitive dissonance; it will attempt to reach those who no longer
look to professionals for fixed answers to every spiritual question. The honest church will embrace those who are determined

to be partners in the exciting search for tentative but satisfying answers to the most pressing questions of existence; it will become a home for those who want to remain attached to the tradition of their forebears, yet who know that tradition to be a flexible guide into, not a static barrier to, the future.

◆

Identifying the Audience

Among the diverse humanity that makes up modern society, there exists a natural and growing clientele for churches that offers an honest and open-ended faith. People for whom the mind is a critical instrument for coping with daily life are hungry for a spiritual home. These people are offended when they are told they must passively accept a basic body of dogma simply because it was handed down from ancient authorities. These people are not willing to be passive recipients of belief systems, especially when the beliefs contradict their understanding of the way the world works.

Formal education is often the catalyst that makes people approach life with more attention to logic. I want to stress, however, that a formal classroom is not the only path that leads toward a thinking orientation. Many highly intelligent people have arrived at that point via other avenues. To this issue I will return later. For now, the emphasis will be on the impact of education on those the church wants to reach. The process of acquiring knowledge alters people in many, sometimes surprising, ways.

Identifying the Audience:
Chaos-Tolerant vs. Chaos-Intolerant

People differ greatly in the amount of disorder they can tolerate. Thus humankind can be separated along lines that suggest the once-popular television series *The Odd Couple*. In part because of the winsomeness of the characters in that program, I have been tempted to call the two groups I am referring to the "cosmic neatness freaks" (like Felix Unger, described by promotional material of the program as "a neurotic neat freak," played by Tony Randall) and the "cosmic messiness folk" (like Oscar Madison, described as "a total slob," played by Jack Klugman). These descriptions, however, are decidedly inelegant and, ultimately, misleading. So I will refer to the two groups as the *chaos-intolerant* (those who, like Felix, insist on imposing order on their world) and the *chaos-tolerant* (those who, like Oscar, have learned to live with disorder, even if they find it disagreeable).

Still, I abandon the phrases "cosmic messiness folk" and "cosmic neatness freaks" with reluctance, for my real concern is one's attitude toward the cosmos. In this sense, what I am attempting to describe is different from the examples of *The Odd Couple*. Neither Felix's pristine desktop nor Oscar's disheveled room is the issue. The real issue is how one deals with chaos in the cosmos—the world at large.

My wife is a fierce enemy of dirt and clutter. Our home, under her direction, has been unfailingly neat and clean. And she confesses to beginning her adult life wanting to carry her war against clutter to universal proportions. She wanted to believe that the cosmos is a morally neat place in which good and evil are distributed in some sensible pattern. Her conversion experience came when she read Rabbi Harold Kushner's book *When Bad Things Happen to Good People.*[1] She continued to attack physical clutter. But Kushner had convinced her to be accepting of the moral clutter that is an inescapable part of living.

Fortunately, both she and I had given up belief in an omnipotent God who oversees a neat system of just rewards and punishments when our eight-year-old grandson died mysteriously and suddenly. If we had tried to cling to a chaos-intolerant position in the face of that event, we would have lost either our faith or our minds. Or both.

My wife's transformation illustrates one additional fact. Inevitably, the number of chaos-tolerant people will increase, and the number of chaos-intolerant people will decrease. Belief in a world of moral order requires constant reinforcement. A single significant event illustrating the random nature of evil has the power to convert a person from chaos-intolerant to chaos-tolerant. Such an event might be a personal encounter with a senseless tragedy. Or it might take the form of reading a convincing book. But once a person has seen the world as a place of moral disorder, it is extremely difficult to turn in the opposite direction. Thus any movement will be overwhelmingly from chaos intolerance to chaos tolerance.

Human longing, however, will tug in the opposite direction. Something there is about humanity that wants to press experience into shapes that make sense. To that end, a significant number of people will begin the journey of faith by embracing a belief in a world presided over by a divine power that micromanages every detail. That belief assures them that, ultimately, good things will happen only to good people, and evil people will be swept away by floods and epidemics. Those who live by this organizing urge want to hold a Bible that is the literal word of the divine. They want a theology that was given by God in correct form to ancient church councils and thus is right for all times and all places.

A friend, a writer, tells of examining the wares in bookstores that cater to Christians of a strongly conservative bent. All the fiction he examined, he reported, had happy endings. The most complicated plots were unknotted in the final sentences. The good guys always won and the good girls always preserved their virtue. This is a description of the kind of world sought by those who are chaos-intolerant. Through literature, movies, and Christian music, they seek to reinforce their view that they live in an orderly universe.

Those who are chaos-tolerant recognize that the world seldom offers storybook endings—final acts in which all problems are solved. As several Psalmists grudgingly acknowledged,

many bad things happen to good people.[2] Those engaged in
the commercial world know how frequently unscrupulous
people are offered coveted promotions, allowing them to
occupy the office where large windows look out across the sky-
line. The baseball manager Leo Durocher may have overstated
his case, but he spoke for all who acknowledge the moral disorder of daily life: "Nice guys finish last."

Barbara Brown Taylor, an Episcopal priest and former local
pastor who now teaches at Piedmont College in Demorest,
Georgia, reported in *The Christian Century* about the difference
in her life now that she has moved from local church priest to
college professor.[3] "In answer to people's faith questions, I hear
myself saying things such as, 'What does it all mean? I don't
have a clue. Do you?' "

Taylor, by these words, places herself in the chaos-tolerant
camp. She is a committed Christian who has no need for fiction
with contrived endings. Instead, she would be deeply
offended, I suspect, by efforts to pretty up a world that she
knows to be in disarray.

Sadly, however, Barbara Taylor implies that while she was
pastor of a local church she would have found it difficult to be
so forthright. She could not, apparently, let herself say, "I don't
have a clue. Do you?" while standing in a pulpit. Honesty is a
luxury she feels she can allow herself now, but she could not
when she led a congregation. But this is premature: it carries us
from the point at hand.

■ *Chaos-Tolerance/Intolerance in Religious Tradition*

The distinction between those who yearn for cosmic neatness
and those who acknowledge cosmic messiness has long
divided people of faith. The biblical account of the ancient history of Israel (1 and 2 Samuel, 1 and 2 Kings) was written by
authors who were chaos-intolerant; they saw their task as not
only to report the past, but, more importantly, to tidy up
human events. A set formula was used in the telling: When the

king (who represented the entire nation before God) was faithful, the nation prospered; when the king strayed from the paths of God, the nation suffered. "The theory of retribution," this is called. History was not so much reported as it was adjusted to the spiritual needs of those who wanted the world to be a sensible place presided over by a Power who hands out just rewards and appropriate punishments.

Many biblical writers rejected the theory of retribution. The writer of the monumental Book of Job, as we will see later, traced the transformation of its main character from chaos intolerance to chaos tolerance. The writer of the later chapters of the Book of Isaiah acknowledged the lack of relationship between the sins of Judah and the punishment they experienced at the hands of the Babylonians. Jesus described a morally messy world in which soothing rains fall on the just and the unjust (Matthew 5:45).

Here, biblically, is the description of a chasm that has existed, and will continue to exist, within the faith community. On one side of the divide is a world of happy endings, a neat interpretation of past events. On the other is the pain of Job, wrestling with a perplexing world he can reluctantly embrace but never understand. On one side of this chasm is a God who controls every detail, the one in charge of ensuring that justice prevails. On the other side is a divine being who labors, not always successfully, against some basic, inextinguishable disorder.

The four Gospel writers continue this division in worldviews. The basic divide is apparent in interpretations of the cross. The first three Gospels (also known as the Synoptics) describe the death of Jesus as a horrid injustice, but one that awakened the disciples to continue Jesus' work. This interpretation sees the cross as an elaboration of the Job story. A thoroughly good person suffers a thoroughly evil fate. It is an earthy story, with earthy implications. The writer of the Gospel of John related this event as if it were the plan of a loving God, an event located on earth but planned in heaven to ensure a redemptive ending. The writers of the Synoptics were attempting to reach the chaos-tolerant. The writer of John aimed his message at the chaos-intolerant.

Identifying the Audience: Stages of Development

Another way of identifying those who seek an honest faith arises from the insights of the developmental school of educational psychology. These students of human growth and behavior trace the way people tend to move through identifiable stages from immaturity to maturity. Several such researchers have identified stages of increasingly complex and effective mental functioning. This process is called "cognitive development." While the researchers who will be quoted here do not explicitly explore the implications of their work for religious faith, those implications are there—and they are enormous.

In 1970, William Perry published his findings about a group of male Harvard students whom he traced as they moved through stages (what Perry called *passages*) of mental development.[4] In his broad scheme, Perry posited nine passages, which he grouped into three major categories. The first category deals with dualism (good vs. evil); the second deals with relativism (all ideas have essentially the same validity); the third brings the student to a level of maturity in which he is able to make commitments in a world of relativity.

The first level of cognitive development, according to Perry, is *basic duality*, a tendency to see the world in polarities of black and white, we and they, good and bad. Young men at this stage tend to identify themselves with authority figures. These authority figures are assumed to be correct in all matters. The young men assume that anyone who takes a position opposite from that taken by their authorities is incorrect and unworthy. They live, then, in a world characterized by two completely unconnected spheres: One is described with the words "authority-we-right"; the other is dismissed as "illegitimate-they-wrong."

Immersion in a challenging educational environment tends to move the learner into a second broad category of cognitive development: *relativism*, or *multiplicity*. In this second level, every person is acknowledged as having a right to one's own opinion. Each opinion carries essentially the same weight as the next. All truth is seen as relative, and the meaning of events depends on their context. The authority figures with whom the student once identified are downgraded but not dismissed. The opinion of the teacher is no better (or worse) than the opinion of the student.

At the highest stages of development, students gradually move toward *commitment*. Relativity still reigns. The world is seen as ambiguous. The student at this stage knows that many questions have no answers at all, and many other questions must be answered imperfectly. Yet, within this murky, muddled world, commitments can be made. In a phrase loaded with implications for religion, Perry describes these students as ready for "commitment within relativism."

A few years later a group of female researchers did a similar study of the mental development of women.[5] They discovered that for women, the earliest stage of cognitive development is *silence*. A significant number of women begin their mental growth by experiencing themselves as inadequate in mind and voice, and thus dependent on external authorities (usually male) for their basic thought patterns.[6] A second stage of development for women is called *received knowledge,* and is similar to the *basic dualism* of men. At this level women are capable of receiving knowledge from all-knowing authorities (again, usually male) but incapable of creating knowledge on their own. After additional growth, women may come to a level of *constructed knowledge,* a stage in which they view all facts in their context, and experience themselves as capable of creating new information.

The stage of constructed knowledge means pulling together many sources of truth. One of the participants in the women's study summarized this well.

> Adele recognized that, although she could still get trapped by her own subjective world and still relied excessively at times on the judgment and evaluation of others, she tended to listen to what she called a voice of integration within herself that prompted her to find a place for reason *and* intuition *and* the expertise of others.[7]

Adele's voice of integration brings to mind similar research done more recently by James W. Fowler. Fowler has studied the way people move through phases of faith development, and his stages correlate well with the two research projects quoted above.

Fowler's final stage of development is called the "Conjunctive stage." As the term implies, this is the point at which integration takes place between previously warring elements. Narrow judgments are discarded. The circle is drawn wide, bringing in wisdom from many previous stages.

> In the transition to the Conjunctive stage one begins to make peace with the tension arising from the realization that truth must be approached from a number of different directions and angles of vision. Faith must learn to maintain the tensions between these multiple perspectives, refusing to collapse them in one direction or another. In this sense, faith must begin to come to terms with indissoluble paradoxes: the strength found in apparent weakness; the leadership that is possible from the margins of societies . . . the immanence *and* the transcendence of God. . . . In what Paul Ricoeur has called a second or willed naiveté, persons of the Conjunctive stage manifest a readiness to enter into the rich dwellings of meaning that true symbols, ritual, and myth offer. As a correlate of these qualities, this stage exhibits a principled openness to the truths of other religious and faith traditions.[8]

We note that the willed naiveté to which Fowler refers is a willingness to embrace myths (for which I will later offer another term) *as myths*. This is quite different from treating myths as literal stories, which would be counter to this advanced stage of development. Fowler's Conjunctive stage correlates well with Perry's "commitment within relativism."

This research into cognitive and faith development lays open the problem faced by tradition-bound churches. These religious institutions see their primary role as custodians of a revealed truth, a truth that must be accepted on faith. Yet this definition of "faith" means receiving crucial information from all-knowing authority figures. Religious recipients of this authority-based knowledge are discouraged from bringing their own experience into play. No room is left for comparing the revealed truths of one's own tradition to knowledge gained by other people in other religions. Conflicting information from other areas, such as science, is dismissed as incorrect or irrelevant. Traditional (revealed) religion thereby asks its adherents to regress to the lowest stages of cognitive development. This sad reality will continue to characterize religious institutions *until churches determine to emphasize the open-ended aspects of faith, its questions more than its answers, its mystery rather than its dogma.*

The mainline Protestant churches have a natural clientele in those who have moved to more mature developmental stages. These persons want to be able to question and possibly renew the faith that has been offered them. They want to be accepted as equal partners in the investigation of spiritual mystery.

Churches tend to boast that they possess a finished faith, revealed by God at an ancient time and no longer subject to modification. They do not seem to recognize that, in this claim, they erect barriers both to the faith development and to the cognitive development of their members. Their anti-growth stance is especially damaging to women. Whenever religious institutions insist on deference to authority figures, their female members are pushed back to *silence,* the lowest and most degrading level of cognitive life.

This anti-growth stance carries a different danger for men. Men are reenforced at the dualistic stage. They are not challenged to move beyond the *we-right, they-wrong* point of development.

The concept "We, the proper possessors of truth" is posited against its opposite, "They, the illegitimate carriers of falsehood." This deadly dichotomy has led to inquisitions and witch burnings; it has contributed to religious wars that continue to the present. More than a simple church squabble over the definition of faith is involved here. Lives are at stake. Entire communities have been destroyed by this *we-right, they-wrong* mindset.

As this chapter was being written, I found a news item concerning a Moslem place of worship in Pennsylvania that had been defaced by fundamentalist (their own label) Christians. When confronted with their crime, the pastor of the Christians responded, "We were simply bearing witness to the truth. Someone has to be right, and someone has to be wrong." No better illustration could be given of the damage done when rigid Christianity reinforces people in the "we-authority-right" vs. "they-illegitimate-wrong" stage of cognitive development.

Education tends to be the catalyst that moves individuals from the lower levels of cognitive development to the higher levels at which people insist on making their own religious judgments. The study of women referred to earlier speaks of the way college students move quickly from the lower to higher levels of mental processing:

> Most of the women we interviewed who still held this [received knowledge] perspective came into our study through the social service agencies or were very young students just beginning their college careers. In the highly selective colleges, where we were able to talk with the same students several times over a span of one to four years, it was exceedingly rare for a student to continue looking outside the self for the source of knowledge. In pluralistic and intellectually challenging environments, this way of thinking quickly disappears. If it is not rapidly dislodged, the student is likely either to drop out or to be pushed out early in the game.[9]

The same researchers indicate the degree to which education has become the enemy of passive belief systems.

> Many colleges, as well as some high schools, are becoming increasingly dedicated to dislodging this perspective [received knowledge] and stimulating the development of more adequate conceptions of knowing. ... Reliance on authority for a single view of the truth is clearly maladaptive for meeting the requirements of a complex, rapidly changing, pluralistic, egalitarian society and for meeting the requirements of educational institutions, which prepare students for such a world.[10]

No wonder formerly strong Protestant denominations are declining! These religious bodies have traditionally been homes to persons of higher than average educational levels. But they are the very people who are now deciding that "reliance on authority for a single view of the truth is clearly maladaptive ...".

If education is changing the way people approach truth, then churches have a limited time for adjustment. The speed with which the United States has become an educated nation is breathtaking. In 1870, a few years following the Civil War, slightly more than 9,300 people received undergraduate degrees. No one received a master's degree, and only one individual in the United States received a doctoral degree. From then until the World War I, the number of degrees went up nearly five times as fast as the increase in population. By the middle of the 20th century, the figures had gone to 432,058 for bachelor's degrees; 58,183 for master's degrees; and 6,420 for doctorates. By 1980, just under one million people received undergraduate degrees each year, nearly 300,000 received master's degrees, and more than 32,000 received doctorates. Today, the growth in education continues apace.

After formal education is complete, other pressures continue to encourage us toward chaos tolerance. Even people with few formal credentials live in an information society that forces them to expand their minds. Thus, it is likely that the number of persons moving into the higher levels of cognitive development is growing even faster than the number receiving formal degrees.

◆

Destructive Impact

If the research cited here is correct, more than cognitive dissonance is at stake. Those who try to sustain a traditional faith in today's world encounter far more than a conflict between facts, such as one's knowledge of the size of the universe bumping against the biblical view of an earth-centered creation. A conflict has been set up at the foundation of a person's being. To *cognitive dissonance* has been added what might be called an *existential dissonance*. The conflict has gone to the root of one's being. Participation in most churches not only presents the member with a conflict in ideas; it pushes that member toward what for many will be a painful regression to infancy, as it were, in their thought processes. When this occurs, basic church loyalty and spiritual hungers may keep church members active for a while. Sustaining that internal tension over a lifetime, however, will require an enormous investment in mental and emotional partitions. Such partitions are highly unstable, and when they dissolve, so does loyalty to the church.

When all these bits and pieces are placed together, the sad situation of mainline Christianity is seen from yet another angle. Denominational officers, presiding over declining memberships, look longingly at the growth rate of conservative groups. They assume a relationship between their own losses and evangelical gains. The process is nudged along by highly vocal conservatives within each national body who insist that their denomination's declines are due to "liberal" tendencies and who threaten to leave if their own chaos intolerance is further aggravated. In response, thinking that they are acting to preserve the institution, mainline leaders tone down any potentially honest utterances. They chide local pastors who cause controversy by calling attention to anything other than approved concepts. They discourage their denominational publishing houses from producing material that acknowledges the problems of a fixed faith in a changing world. The result is that both conservative and progressive people slowly vanish from mainline rolls. The needs of neither are addressed.

Identifying one's audience is more than a marketing technique. Failure to focus has compromised the church's mission. Protestantism needs to recognize who is most likely to be receptive to the message it is uniquely equipped to offer. Instead, church leaders dilute that message. They try to reach everyone, both chaos-tolerant and chaos-intolerant. Mainline churches resemble two economists who went deer hunting. The pair came across a large buck standing in a clearing. Excited, they brought their guns up and fired simultaneously. One missed a foot to the right. The other missed a foot to the left. The economists then embraced and exclaimed, "On average, we both hit the mark!"[11]

The mainline Protestant denominations continue to spray their shots around, missing their target on one side and then the other, all the while hoping that some law of average will redeem their efforts.

Thinking-oriented, chaos-tolerant people need a church home—a fellowship willing to aim a message directly at them. They need a place where their minds will not be affronted by a worldview they and the majority of literate humanity have long since abandoned. They long to find a fellowship in which the ambiguity of their daily experience will be acknowledged. They need to hear a pastor who has the courage, on occasion, to say, "I haven't a clue. Do you?" In short, they seek a church in which honesty is part of the mission.

Denominational officials need to study more carefully the work of sociologists of religion. Research has shown that the decline of mainline churches and the growth of fundamentalist churches are unrelated. The two groups appeal to different constituencies. The fundamentalist churches, with their adoration of the Bible, their charismatic leaders, and services that allow emotions to flow, have aimed their message precisely toward chaos-intolerant persons. A significant minority of the total population responds to their message and their techniques. These churches meet genuine needs of persons who are at a particular stage of religious growth. Thus, such congregations grow.

Mainline churches try to avoid authoritarian personalities. They make the institution the authority. The church is treated as if it is the carrier of a revealed truth no longer subject to question. Authoritarianism remains; it has simply shifted focus. But for many of those who might be attracted to Protestantism, this approach no longer works. Mainline churches tend to deal with people who are not easily cowed by external authorities of any stripe.

Some authority must remain. It is a given in any social grouping. For religious institutions the answer is to shift a significant amount of authority to the pews. But such a shift is strongly opposed by those currently in charge. Because they resist listening to lay persons, lay insights, lay questions, and lay religious experiences, their congregations shrink.

Religion's Divorce from a Thinking Orientation

It is easy to observe the results of the abandonment of persons of thinking orientation. Divorce has taken place between religious faith and the intellectual disciplines. In too many sanctuaries, it is all right to love God with heart and soul but not with mind. A few such churches might survive, even grow in the short run. For Christianity over the long haul, however, the implications are grave. The mainline denominations may endure for a few decades in a truncated, know-nothing form. Soon, however, the term Christianity will apply almost exclusively to those who embrace the emotion-filled, anti-science form of religion, with its mixture of shallow theology and positive thinking.

John Cobb has defined what he sees as wrong with a declining Christianity. He stated his conclusion strongly:

> . . . [T]he church has lost the ability to think. Unless it recognizes that its healthy survival depends on the recovery and exercise of that ability and acts on that recognition, talk of renewal or transformation is idle.[12]

As I pointed out in a previous chapter, youth become especially tragic victims of this separation of thought from belief. They grow up hearing the traditional dogma and its assurance that a God "out there" is concerned about their every act. They also hear the messages, stated or implied, about the sacred nature of every word of scripture. Then comes college—a next step in the life cycle of the majority of youth who are reared in mainline Protestant congregations.

Young people who have spent time in church school classes of typical local churches will have great difficulty holding their old religious ideas through four years of higher education. A few will survive the trauma of rearranging their beliefs in light of new knowledge. Most, however, will simply wander away from a church they can no longer respect.

Churches have found an additional way to abandon their youth. Some college students struggle to be both scientifically aware and religiously devout. Those who seek out a campus pastor who might aid in this faith crisis will look, on most secular campuses, in vain. Protestantism, which was once committed to bringing the mind into the struggle for faith, today has largely left the academic scene. Early in the 20th century, churches began to lose control of the universities they had founded. They then established campus ministries (often known as foundations) to ensure that intellectual growth and growth in faith were not separated. Today, sadly, even the foundations are being cut from denominational budgets.

United Ministries in Higher Education (UMHE) is an ecumenical body that coordinates the campus efforts of ten mainline Protestant denominations. In 1970, UMHE employed thirty-five national staff, many deployed regionally. Excluding staff salaries, its budget was $300,000. By the year 2002, UMHE was down to a national staff of three people, none of whom were regional. The budget had shrunk to $15,800.[13]

Mainline Protestantism is departing from the university setting altogether, leaving the campus to those whose religious views are anti-intellectual, who rage against all forms of modernity, especially against evolutionary concepts. Students (and faculty) of thinking orientation are left with no spiritual home.

◆

Movement from Conservative to Progressive

Here is another sad aspect of the mainline's failure to embrace full honesty. A significant number of people stand ready to move beyond the limits of fundamentalism. Jim, whom we met at the beginning of this chapter, is far from alone. One church sociologist reports that 7 percent of the persons who grew up in conservative churches have, as adults, changed and are now members of mainline Protestant churches.[14] Jim, however, had to launch an extensive search to find a congregation that would provide companionship on his faith journey. No data can be found identifying the number of such people who look in vain.

Alan Wolfe, writing in *The Atlantic Monthly*, explored the efforts of contemporary, conservative Christians to break out of their anti-intellectual box. He found evidence of a strong commitment to honest scholarship in such conservative schools as Wheaton, Baylor, and Pepperdine. The students impressed him. He came to believe that, if the undergraduates of these colleges are any indication, young people brought up in evangelical homes are desperate to engage in serious intellectual inquiry.[15] But despite good intentions from both students and some faculty, Wolfe found, the baggage of a fixed theology made it difficult for students to find the intellectual openness they sought in conservative college settings. At some point, Wolfe seems to imply, these students will break free from their confined backgrounds and spread their intellectual wings. One hopes they will find congregations to support them.

◆

Summary

At the beginning of the 20th century, many students dropped out of high school, and only 10 percent of the population received education beyond the high school level. Strong muscles and an understanding of simple machinery were all that were needed to produce a living. An emotive approach to life was easy to maintain. A desire for a square-cornered world could be indulged.

Today, by contrast, failure to complete high school is rare, and approximately 60 percent of high school graduates pursue higher education. A thinking orientation is encouraged by this expanded formal education; increased learning also nudges persons toward higher levels of both cognitive and faith development. Everyone, regardless of the number of formal degrees earned, lives in an information age in which precise knowledge is essential to survival. The human brain has become a crucial part of coping with life. The proliferation of new technologies challenges every modern person, keeping their minds open to new information and new habits.

Education does more than increase raw data within the brain. It changes the ways people approach life. Engaged minds are more likely to remove emotional blinders and acknowledge the messiness of the moral order. Those minds are apt both to move from chaos-intolerant to chaos-tolerant and to resist dogma that has little to commend it except its antiquity.

Mature thinkers must be invited into the process of making a rich religious tradition relevant to the present day. Honesty is an essential element of this invitation.

True religion is this: to love the divine with all one's heart, soul, strength *and mind*. Yet local churches have divorced themselves from the disciplines of significant thought. The wages of dishonesty are paid in diminished numbers.

NOTES

1. Harold S. Kushner, *When Bad Things Happen to Good People* (New York: Schocken Books, 1981).

2. See especially Psalms 44, 52, and 88. On the other hand, Psalm 1 was written by a neatness freak who insisted that righteous people will prosper in all that they do, while evil people are like chaff which the wind sweeps away. This is a biblical debate to which I will return.

3. *The Christian Century,* June 16-23, 1999.

4. William Perry, Jr., *Forms of Intellectual and Ethical Development in the College Years: A Scheme* (New York: Holt, Rinehart and Winston, 1968).

5. Mary Field Belenky, Blythe McVicker Clinchy, Nancy Rule Goldberger, Jill Mattuck Tarule, *Women's Ways of Knowing* (New York: Basic Books, 1986).

6. One thinks immediately of the advice given by both Paul in First Corinthians and the writer of the book of First Timothy: Women are to remain silent in church and to ask their husbands to explain what has transpired in church meetings.

7. Belenky *et al.,* p. 133.

8. James W. Fowler, *Faithful Change: The Personal and Public Challenges of Postmodern Life* (Nashville: Abingdon Press, 1996).

9. Belenky *et al.,* p. 43.

10. *Ibid.*

11. My apologies to all economists who suffer, unjustly I am confident, from stories like this. This unkind tale was, I fear, too appropriate to omit.

12. John B. Cobb, *Reclaiming the Church* (Louisville: Westminster/John Knox Press, 1997).

13. Data provided by Bruce Larson, Minister for Campus Ministries and Students of the United Church of Christ.

14. Wade Clark Roof, *A Generation of Seekers* (San Francisco: HarperSanFrancisco, 1993).

15. Alan Wolfe, "The Opening of the Evangelical Mind," *The Atlantic Monthly,* October 2000.

4

Honest About What?

N. T. Wright, Canon of Westminster Cathedral in London, is a strong defender of a traditional faith. He also models an openness to new realities and a willingness to enter into dialogue with persons of differing views. In a book co-authored with Marcus Borg, he gives this intriguing insight into himself:

> For seven years I was college chaplain at Worcester College, Oxford. Each year I used to see the first-year undergraduates individually for a few minutes, to welcome them to the college and make a first acquaintance. Most were happy to meet me, but many commented, often with slight embarrassment, "You won't be seeing much of me; you see, I don't believe in God."
>
> I developed a stock response: "Oh, that's interesting. Which god is it you don't believe in?" This used to surprise them; they mostly regarded the word *God* as univocal, always meaning the same thing. So they would stumble out a few phrases about the god they didn't believe in: a being who lived up in the sky, looking down disapprovingly at the world, occasionally intervening to do miracles, sending bad people to hell while allowing good people to share his heaven. Again, I had a stock

response for this very common spy in the sky theology: "Well, I'm not surprised you don't believe in that god. I don't believe in that god either."

At this point the undergraduate would look startled. Then, perhaps, a faint look of recognition; it was sometimes rumored that half the college chaplains at Oxford were atheists. No, I would say, I believe in the God I see revealed in Jesus of Nazareth. What most people mean by *god* in late-modern Western culture simply isn't the mainstream Christian meaning.[1]

Wright's almost offhand remark to incoming students is an indictment of modern church life and a possible explanation for many of the current maladies of the institutional church. His brief conversation with a student suggests an important question. How might such a situation have evolved—one in which two individuals of the same so-called Christian culture have envisioned two different gods? And how could one of them, after living in that culture for nearly two decades, be so surprised by this news?

A lack of honesty is the issue. Something is broken, and the fault lines lie between religious professionals and the laity. The students who came to Wright's office were simply parroting back to him what they had been taught in their local parishes. Canon Wright was the first to inform them that what they heard in their local churches might not be what the pastors who spoke those words really believed.

Most church leaders, those who wear the title "theologian," have stubbornly refused to share with the remainder of the church what lies at the depth of their private faith. Few local church pastors continue to believe in the anthropomorphic god they visualized in their childhood. They take the Bible seriously but not literally. The vast majority of the professional leaders of mainline Protestant churches accept the insights of Charles Darwin, just as they do the insights of modern astronomy. They respect the authenticity of other world religions. Yet, too few church leaders, Catholic or Protestant, have Wright's courage to state openly, in response to immature belief systems, "I no longer accept these traditional and inadequate views."

Lay people must shoulder some of the blame. Many of them are unhappy with the faith they learned at a Sunday school teacher's knee. They want to grow. Yet, since their pastors seem to continue to believe in the old platitudes, lay people fear they cannot share their doubts without being judged harshly by their spiritual leaders. They either continue in the church for the other spiritual and social gifts the church offers, or else they quietly disappear.

◆

The Rejection of Religion

The late 20th and early 21st centuries have become a time of rejection of formal religion. Polls that measure religious preferences consistently report that the fastest growing group in the United States is the non-affiliated.

Rejection of organized religion, however, does not necessarily mean the end of a search for answers to religious-oriented questions. Spiritual hungers abound. Thus, it is common to find people identifying themselves as *spiritual* but not *religious*. This is especially true on college and university campuses.

Recently, a trio of professors of religion made a study of religious practices at four institutions of higher education. The four were widely scattered and varied in nature. In their summary chapter, the researchers included this informative paragraph:

> The undergraduates we interviewed, as well as many of the campus professionals who helped us interpret the religion of undergraduates, preferred to use the words "spirituality" and "spiritual" instead of "religion" and "religious" when describing undergraduate attitudes and practices. James Brand, student government president at South University, summed up a typical student attitude

when he replied in answer to a question concerning whether students on his campus were very religious: "No, but most of them are very spiritual." Like numerous other students we encountered, Brand understood religion to mean institutions or organizations, whereas he took spirituality to mean a personal experience of God or ultimate values. Furthermore, more often than not, "spiritual" and "spirituality" connoted a quest, a journey, something not yet completed, whereas "religion" and "religious" signified something completed, fixed, handed down.[2]

What is it that adults are rejecting when they identify themselves as unaffiliated, and what are students rejecting when they call themselves spiritual rather than religious?

First, all these people are rejecting an institution that claims for itself a godly character that it seldom embodies. Petty squabbles among the membership, conflicts between clergy and laity, and clergy sexual scandals conspire to broadcast a clear and sad message: This institution is not qualitatively different from other human institutions. Add to this the scent of dishonesty between clergy and laity, and we have an institution that is ripe for either reform or rejection.

More than the institution is being cast aside. A theology is also under fire. If asked to summarize the theology (what is often referred to as "the plan of salvation") in which they no longer believe, students who call themselves spiritual would state something like this:

The original man and woman, a long time ago, tried to learn more than God wanted them to know. God punished them by casting a spell on them, a spell they passed on to all their offspring through the act of procreation. This caused all humankind to come under the control of the devil. God then devised a scheme to break this spell. He (the masculine is necessary at this point in the story) impregnated a woman who gave birth to a god-man. This only son of God was sacrificed to cover the price of human rebellion, allowing all those who embrace this story to be restored to proper relationship to the divine. They, after death, will spend eternity with God and Jesus.

Those explaining the "plan of salvation" are likely to continue by describing the plan's ethnic overtones.

Originally, God intended for the Jews to be His chosen people, the channel through which God's message would reach all humankind. But the Jews were not faithful to their part of this agreement and finally rejected the god-man that had been sent. So the Jews were dumped as the chosen people, a role taken over now by the Christians who do accept Jesus as the savior of the world. All the remainder of humankind is still under the old curse and will spend eternity being punished for not accepting Jesus.

How do we know about the "plan of salvation?" Because it is recorded in the Bible, a book that may have been written by people, but those people were so much under the control of God that God is the real author of everything in it.

I have stated the beliefs of a major portion of Christians in a deliberately crude manner. The catechisms used in more formal churches lay out this basic theology with much more sophistication. ("More sophistication" sometimes equals "more *double entendre*.") Yet all of us who have worked with church laity, and especially with college students, know that my description of what people think they are supposed to believe is, in almost every case, accurate.

Despite my obvious dissatisfaction with this "plan of salvation," I recognize its power. When described with more elegance, it becomes a penetrating, mythological statement of human rebellion and redemption—the archetypal truth-story (to use a phrase I will define later). I also acknowledge the depth of its insight concerning the destructiveness of sin and the high price of reconciliation. The concept that God is so thoroughly loving as to pay the entire cost of human rebellion has enormous appeal to all those whose guilt is a burden too heavy to carry. Yet people are rejecting this "plan of salvation" in large numbers, for many valid reasons.

Chief among the reasons for rejection is that the plan is intellectually unacceptable. It makes God sound like an error-prone CEO, constantly trying to correct what had gone wrong with yesterday's decisions. The stories of the gods who frolicked on Mt. Olympus had as much intellectual credibility as this story, when it is laid down in its raw, anthropomorphic essentials.

Another reason for rejecting the plan of salvation is its particularity. First only Jews and then only Christians are assumed to stand in proper relationship to the divine. Other pathways to the divine are dismissed. The seeds of human division and warfare are sown here.

Finally, the "plan of salvation" is rejected because it is not at all in the Bible, except for those who are skilled at a cut-and-paste process of interlacing verses taken from scattered places in scripture. The story of the fall, recorded in Genesis, describes the loss of paradise, but not a curse that will banish humankind from an intimate relationship to God.[3] The mark put on Cain at the end of the Cain and Abel story (Genesis 4:15) is not to demonize him but to protect him. The Jewish people have been reading the story of human rebellion for at least six hundred years longer than the Christians, and they have found no ongoing stigma or need for a human sacrifice to put things right.

This "plan of salvation" is the theology taught in the majority of Christian churches. It is the theology that students enrolling in seminaries are likely to bring with them.

◆

The Religion of the Professional

In seminary, students preparing for a religious profession will likely undergo a culture shock of major proportions. In their classrooms they encounter a faith that is different in much more than particular dogma. They will learn about a different *quality* of religion, one that is aware of the historic doctrines concerning God, but that also acknowledges that an understanding of God is never a finished product. The students will learn that the stories and traditions that introduce them to the divine do not simply drop out of heaven, like milk that flows from a modern dairy, never touched by human hands. The issues are much more complex than that.

As they confront complexity, seminary students find themselves undergoing change. Typically, students enter as chaos-intolerant individuals who treat religious stories and traditions as if they had been transmitted directly from the mind of God. They are likely to leave seminary chaos-tolerant, willing to acknowledge that few religious ideas are thoroughly nailed down and that all information about the realm of the spirit comes to us through the filters of other seekers.

Human Context

Human context is the concept that best defines the difference between the ambiguity-filled theologies that professional training tends to produce and theologies that describe a square-cornered world, the kind that are ordinarily offered to the laity.

Years of immersion in the study of scripture, creed, and church history have taught church leaders to recognize the human settings out of which all religious insights developed. In their seminary training they studied religious history, identifying the social setting in which creeds and scripture were composed. Courses in topics such as "Women and Theology" show unmistakably that the maleness of biblical writers and early church leaders bent the tradition in particular ways. When they speak to the laity, however, these professionals either state openly or imply cleverly that God produced scripture and creed with no consideration for a particular time and place. This one difference radiates its implications outward, causing two astoundingly different styles of religion to develop.

Across the Rocky Mountains lies a line called the continental divide. Rain that falls on the east side of that line falls away toward the plains. Much of it will eventually reach the Gulf of Mexico. Rain that strikes only a few inches away on the westward side moves down the opposite slope and makes its way toward the western states, and eventually into the Pacific.

Human context is like a continental divide in the theological world. On one side are those who reject any thought that humans were influential in producing the stories and doctrines that are the basis of the Christian faith. They become biblical literalists. They embrace the creeds as unchangeable. On the other side are those who recognize the fingerprints of humankind on all religious documents and symbols. They see the Bible as human writings through which the Holy Spirit can and does communicate; they accept basic creeds as important guides in the development of faith, but as especially relevant to the age in which they were written. Those on the contextual side of this divide see nothing as fixed. Their faith is a work in process, a well-grounded system that is open to additional insights.

Paul Tillich once summarized these issues in a single phrase: "The Protestant Principle." The Protestant Principle states that God is perfect. All other realities are imperfect and therefore subject to protest and revision.[4] This principle, which almost all trained Protestant church leaders (and many Catholics as well) would affirm, means that nothing—including scripture, creeds, and dogma—was dropped from heaven in finished form.

Everything that human hands have touched is subject to review. The Divine Spirit may have had a significant role in guiding the development of sacred documents and symbols. If so, human hands and human thoughts were the instruments by which the Spirit was expressed. These hands and thoughts existed in a unique time and place. For example, a particular person or persons wrote each biblical book, sometimes with help from later editors. That person carried biases, and saw the world through the scientific and cultural assumptions of his/

her time and place. The same is true of the development of creeds and the unfolding of church history. *Context*, therefore, is a key concept in understanding the nature of the church's dishonesty. Human context is what, in many Protestant pulpits and classrooms, is ignored.

Those who argue the other side of this issue fall back on the concept of revelation. Revelation is God's self-disclosure. Many church theologians insist (at least when the laity are listening) that the major creeds and the scriptures are ways that the divine has bypassed the limits of the human setting. Those creeds and scriptures are therefore not subject to critique in the manner of other human efforts.

When ancient revelations are assumed to be the only avenue for approaching the divine, enormous problems emerge. Historians have allowed us all to eat the fruit of contextual knowledge. We know how scripture was written and creeds were developed.[5] There is now no going back. The evidence is clear that theology arises out of political and intellectual turmoil. Concepts of God and the ethics of serving God emerge from the give and take of particular moments and particular places. If scriptures and creeds represent moments of divine disclosure uncontaminated by human input, how do we account for the contradictions in these documents, and why would God allow interpretations of them to be so varied?

Some Christians, lay and professional, find it possible to accept some truth from each side of this major divide. Many of those who recognize human involvement in the creation of religious symbols also embrace those symbols as imperfect but effective instruments through which the Divine Spirit conveys its music to humankind. They make a strong case for their position. The profound nature of many of these documents indicates that the writers were genuinely inspired—challenged to share out of the depths of the human spirit. Scripture and creeds might be received as the products of both human context and divine inspiration. Nothing said in this volume is intended to deny that possibility.

Inspiration, however, is not the same as *coercion*. When church people speak to the laity about the inspiration of scripture, they seem to mean that God controlled the writing. I have never understood how *inspiration* has come to imply *control* in religious settings. It carries that meaning in no other context. Ernest Hemingway did his most creative writing when inspired by the sounds and smell of the ocean. But salt air is not credited with his genius. Being near the water somehow motivated Hemingway to reach far inside himself and utilize strengths he could tap in no other setting.

Just so, certain writers of scripture seem have been, at moments, especially sensitive to an indwelling, divine spirit. This *inspiration* (a word that means, both in English and Greek, *in-spirited*; neither precise guidance nor coercion are implied) can help explain the remarkable depth that characterizes much of the scriptures. Nonetheless, the hand holding the stylus and the mind composing the words of even the finest religious history are entirely human.

This dual authorship—God inspiring, man creating—is in line with one of the central proclamations of our faith tradition: God reveals the divine self through incarnation. That is, God moves in and through genuine human flesh. When dealing with the church's core documents, we ignore either the involvement of an inspiring spirit or the distorting touch of humankind at our peril.

The central fact remains: Revelation never comes in pure form. Whatever we know of a spirit realm has come to us through persons who were partially blinded by the circumstances of their time and place, and is therefore subject to future modification.

◆

Clergy Crisis

For students in seminary, exposure to a contextual style of thinking can be wrenching. Such students usually enter the school of theology with the assumption that their instructors will explain and enforce their childhood faith. Instead, they find themselves in an entirely new atmosphere, one in which every ingredient of their previous faith is held before an intense light of scrutiny. In the face of these new realities, the typical seminary student goes through a crisis of faith, that plays itself out in fairly predictable stages.

In the first stage of this crisis, most students, after a few months of study, discover that the faith of their childhood is no longer adequate. Pressing questions appear, uninvited. Can I believe this new kind of religion to which I am being exposed, a religion still labeled as Christianity? This stage is sometimes accompanied by anger at local church professionals who refused to expose the student to these insights. This first stage is a time of danger. No new faith has taken the place of the old. It is a season when some drop out. Almost everyone who does not drop out nonetheless considers doing so.

The second stage is an embrace of the concepts and values expressed in the seminary classroom. With this embrace comes an awareness that faith has not been destroyed. It has been deepened. The new faith is one that offers personal strength and comfort in unexpected ways. Unlike the faith recently rejected, the new one is capable of meeting the challenges of the modern world.

The third stage comes with the move from seminary student to local pastor. Students now reprogram themselves to preach and teach as if their seminary crisis had never occurred. This third stage begins as graduation approaches. It continues into the first months of pastoral work. This time includes so much hectic activity and so many demands on the young pastor that it is impossible to sort out all the reasons for the depression that often accompanies this transition. One ingredient in this depression surely is the effort to preach and teach people who are assumed to have a different set of faith assumptions.

Aware of the problems of reentering the world of the local church, Roy Oswald of the Alban Institute (a group dedicated to the study and improvement of church groups) interviewed a variety of young pastors, asking about their experience of moving from seminary to pulpit. Here is one of his findings. (Note the use of the word "liberal," used here before it took on some of its current negative connotations.)

> The seminary encouraged a liberal orientation while the parish demanded a conservative one. Seminary students were normally exposed to liberal perspectives on social and political problems. The term "ivory tower" is particularly applicable here, as faculty could afford the luxury of speaking out forthrightly on a wide variety of social issues. Taking similar stands in the parish caused conflicts. Clergy were usually discouraged from political involvement and were usually punished for speaking out on social issues. They were rewarded for staying with orthodox, traditional beliefs, and discouraged from expressing uncertainty regarding issues of faith. Being open about personal struggles was usually met with avoidance and criticism. This confused the recent graduates who had been rewarded and supported for openness to personal struggle or a questioning faith while in the seminary.[6]

This third stage of crisis may last through the first several months, even the first several years, of an initial pastorate. Sermon topics on subjects such as the grace of God and personal ethics may meet the expectations of parishioners without violating the integrity of the new pastor. After a time, however, safe sermon topics can no longer be found. Questions arise that must be answered.

All this brings exhausted new pastors to the fourth stage of their transformation. They realize that they are simply stating what they think their parishioners want to hear. They have abandoned their own hard-won system of beliefs. Anger, disappointment, and depression are likely.

One young pastor in the Alban Institute study articulated the problem. One of the surprises he discovered in the parish was "a shaking of theological foundations—one year into first pastorate—losing every belief I held—[I] began thinking I had to build a functioning faith."

I once knew of a dean of a teachers college who often exclaimed, "We bring students here and expose them to the best of educational techniques. Then we send them back into communities knowing that they are likely to teach in the same way they were taught [before they came here]."

Seminaries encounter the same phenomena. They bring students in from parochial parishes, expose them to a broader, more profound faith, and then watch as they go back into parishes to duplicate the limited religion of their childhood. The cost of this, to the mental health of new clergy as well as to the institution itself, is enormous.

In one important way, seminaries and teachers' colleges are different. While those who instruct secular teachers do everything in their power to change their students' mode of operation, seminaries convey at best a mixed message about how their graduates are to handle their expanded knowledge. Seminary faculty tend to assume, along with other church leaders, that the local church is best served if persons in those congregations are not overly challenged. Perhaps they see this as kindness, sparing tender people in church pews the pain of reworking their faith. Yet, in protecting people from pain, they also deny them an opportunity for growth.

For whatever reason, seminary instructors, in subtle ways of which they may not be aware, often communicate caution about carrying their seminary training beyond the school property. Seminaries are thus complicit in the dishonesty that results.

A colleague with whom I once served reports that during a class on the historical setting of a biblical passage, she was clearly instructed by a seminary professor not to tell people in the local congregation about the concepts the class was studying. Few instructors are so forthright. Most find ways to convey the same message by indirection. "Here is something you should know, but it will not preach," is the implied message.

▲

Here, then, is an often ignored but central fact of modern church life. Pastors of local congregations have spent at least three years of intense study of their faith and its tradition. Their personal faith has been examined, usually dismantled and reassembled. Not only the content but the nature of their belief system has been altered. But they have acquired few skills to help them apply their new faith structure in their pastoral roles. The result is often some combination of mental distress and dishonest utterings. Both cleric and congregation become victims.

◆

Broad Differences

The difference between the literal faith with which a seminary student enters graduate study and the contextual faith that this student holds at the end of that time can be summarized in three inclusive categories, and then in seven more specific topics.

First, as they recognize the human influence on all religious concepts, seminarians trade absolutes for mysteries. Popular religion attempts to transform faith into a kind of science: people claim to *know*—sans doubt—about God, Jesus, and the divine nature of the Bible. But in seminary, students come to realize that faith is about the unknown. God is Ultimate Mystery. Students become aware of how wide are the gaps in our knowledge about the historical Jesus. They recognize that many passages in the Bible assign to God actions that no sober humanist or sane follower of Jesus would want to blame on a loving deity. Because religion is based in mystery, many of the religious stories they once accepted as literal are seen anew as mythological. That is, they are stories that probe the depth of life but are not based on fact. Narratives, not facts, are seen as the best means of communicating the faith.

A second broad difference that seminary training tends to bring about is that the religious faith comes to be seen as a participatory activity. Because humans were involved in shaping the faith tradition, humans can be involved in helping it evolve in response to the present age. Seminarians know they cannot be effective in the pastoral role until they take ownership of their beliefs. Informal, evening discussion sessions become as important in this process as what happens in the classroom. Thus theological students move from being passive receivers of a faith structure to being active searchers.

Seminary students usually come to a third new insight: They recognize their tradition as dynamic rather than fixed. In the views they brought with them from their local church they could envision only one concept of God, a God who did similar things at all times and places. Deeper study of sacred texts will reveal how the most ancient views of the divine (a thoroughly egocentric deity) evolve into a God who has responsibility for the entire world. They will recognize other fluid ideas as well. The understanding of Jesus, for example, moves from Mark's earthy concepts to the spirituality of the writer of John.

Seven Particular Issues

The previous three overarching themes emerge through seven particular topics. These seven become a helpful outline of the issues that separate the faith of the pulpit from the faith of the pew.

First is a movement toward an honest understanding of the nature of God. This is the subject of a later chapter of this volume. Here it is simply noted that the concept of God assumed in most Christian churches, a separate being who lives in a nearby place and visits planet earth at random times to deal with special needs, cannot stand intellectual examination. New ways of understanding the spiritual dimension must be offered.

A second area of change in the seminarians' faith is in their understanding of the nature of the Bible. Seminarians tend to enter their professional training with great respect, even awe, for the Bible. Their depth of respect is seldom matched by breadth of information. Few students entering seminary have extensive knowledge of the careful critical work that has been done on scripture by scholars over the past two centuries.

In the seminary classroom, the future pastor will learn that scripture is a collection of writings from a culture distant in time and different in custom. On close examination, it will often seem, to use some of Annie Dillard's piercing words, "an anachronistic, semibarbaric mass of antique laws and fabulous tales from far away."[7] The student will recognize the degree to which the Bible becomes a stumbling block for anyone immersed in a scientific world. They will struggle with metaphors that worked well two thousand years ago but no longer resonate. "The Lord is my shepherd . . ." has a nostalgic ring, but who tends sheep today? Students will likely become fond of stories such as that of Jonah or Hosea, yet be aware that these arise in such strange settings that almost every verse requires explanation to a modern audience.

It is good news, then, to seminary students when they find that the Bible, ancient though it is, is a work still in process. This process takes many forms.

Not even the question of the content of the Bible is settled. Catholic and Episcopalian traditions include eleven books that most Protestant traditions omit. Martin Luther expressed his displeasure that the Book of James was included in the New Testament. In fact, the content of the Bible as it is usually printed today was determined as much by Johann Gutenberg as by any ecclesiastical council —the books he included in his early printings have become accepted as canonical (official).

Important information about the Bible continues to emerge. This is another way in which scripture is a work in process. New facts about the culture and language that produced the Bible are frequently uncovered. With new information comes fresh interpretation.

Seminary students discover that the Bible is the story of a dynamic, evolving tradition. Very few ideas are established beyond question. Those who read scripture without prior assumptions recognize that it sometimes takes on the character of a debating society. Nehemiah feared the influence of foreign wives and had them sent into exile; the writer of the Book of Ruth celebrated the contribution foreign wives made to the nation. Obadiah delighted in the obliteration of his nation's enemies, in particular those who lived in Nineveh; Jonah was sent to save those enemies from destruction. Writers in the priestly tradition insisted that God could best be served by keeping the proper rituals; those in the prophetic tradition minced no words in contending that building communities of justice was the only way to please God. Amos was particularly pointed in his dismissal of the priestly view: "I [God] hate, I despise your sacred feasts ... but let justice run down like waters and righteousness like a mighty stream" (Amos 5:24).

The Bible then becomes a double-edged sword for new pastors. They are apt to want their people to know of, and to become engaged in, the ferment in biblical studies today. Yet, to invite their people into this exciting enterprise means disabusing them of many of their present concepts about the Bible.

Creeds, both their origin and their place in the life of the church, are a third area of reexamination in the life of a seminary student. Seminary students are likely to enter their studies with the common Christian view that creeds are simply a part of the religious landscape. They contain words that are to be recited each Sunday but that are not to be seriously examined.

Creeds, as almost every Christian knows, serve a significant role in worship and personal faith. A common affirmation of faith in a worshipping congregation can be a high moment, drawing the faithful together in a feeling of, if not the reality of, a shared commitment.

The seminary classroom teaches additional facts about ancient creeds. Creeds are revealed to be a witness issued against the specific destructive forces of a particular time and place. But the form that evil takes varies from time to time and from place to place. Therefore, recognizing the human context of creeds is as important as seeing the human context of the scripture.

The seminary student will learn that the basic creeds (Nicene and Apostles') of the church were developed in the third and fourth centuries in the heart of the Roman Empire. Many strong forces threatened to turn the Empire into warring divisions. The Emperor Constantine (who championed Christianity but never officially joined) was confident that a common faith across his territory could contribute to the unity he sought. So he called together church leaders, being careful to secure a majority for the position he espoused, and strongly encouraged them to develop a statement of faith that would define Christianity for all of his citizens.

The bishops began this process by meeting in Nicea in 325. The baggage the various bishops brought contained more than clothing. It included both theological and political agendas. Western and eastern sides of the empire used the session, and the many that followed it, to exacerbate their already raging conflict. Church councils and military battles fed on each other for at least forty years. Murder, betrayal and royal intrigue were part of the complicated, messy undertaking.

Finally, after extensive bloodshed and maneuvering, a creed was produced. That creed defined the faith and thereby branded the heretics. Those guilty of the newly defined heresies were, of course, immediately banished from the church. (At least the more fortunate were banished. The less fortunate were burned or mutilated.)

To those giving leadership to the church in the fourth century, the greatest evil on the horizon was a misunderstanding of the relationship of Jesus to God. They settled that concern on the side of a high Christology: Jesus and God were of the same essence.

Other issues were left untouched. The Nicene Creed has been called the creed with a hole in the middle. It states how Jesus was born, and describes how and why he died. No mention is given of his teachings or acts of compassion, even though they take up the majority of the pages of the biblical accounts of Jesus. The creed focuses on the relationship between the believer and God; it is devoid of ethical considerations. It was designed to meet the particular issues of the time and place of its birth.

By the time all this was accomplished, Constantine was dead and the Roman Empire had a new set of problems.

The Nicene Creed, despite its unsavory beginnings, has done much to give some definition of the Christian faith for seventeen centuries. Sadly, it has also tended to freeze the faith into a form best suited to the setting in which it was composed.

Seminarians know, even as they study the Nicene Creed, that they will give pastoral leadership in a world troubled by a different set of destructive forces. Some old evils have survived and received new names. A dynamic faith needs new statements. Young pastors know this but wonder if they have the courage to disturb the laity with the challenge of creating contemporary ways of defining their faith.

The relationship between Jesus the Son and God the Father is a fourth area in which basic change is likely to occur in the faith of a seminarian. Chapter 7 will deal at greater length about traditional and nontraditional understandings of Jesus. Here it is sufficient to point out that a seminary student's concepts of Jesus' place in the Trinity will probably undergo change.

As some of the ancient creeds indicate, the relationship between Jesus and the God of Jesus' Jewish ancestors has always been at the heart of Christian tradition. On one extreme of the debate are those who say, with direct simplicity, "Jesus was God." Many seminarians will enter their graduate studies

carrying this unexamined view, a view that makes no distinction between the compassionate Jesus who walked the hills of
Galilee and the exalted Christ who, as one creed tells us, "sits at
the right hand of God the Father."

In the academic setting, students will encounter members
of the faculty (and an occasional other student) who take quite
a different stance on this issue. They are Christians who feel
that the concept "Jesus was God" is troublesome, perhaps even
blasphemous. Instead, they see Jesus as a person through
whom the presence of God was especially visible, a wise and
effective teacher, a living demonstration of what it means to be
fully human.

The seminary years give students an extended opportunity
to discover where their own faith falls along the continuum
between a high (Jesus was God) or low (Jesus was a wise
teacher) Christology. They make this discovery in full awareness that some churches have labeled the extremes, especially
the extreme of Jesus as human teacher, as heretical.

As they study church history, however, seminary students
learn that the Christian tradition has included people at all
points along this spectrum, including the extreme ends. The earliest writings about Jesus focused on him as a moral guide. The
Gospel of Thomas[8] and the Q document,[9] both written soon
after Jesus' crucifixion, report him as a compassionate teacher, a
reformer of his Jewish tradition. He was shown to have amazing
powers over sickness and the world of nature. But no word of a
virgin birth, no hint of a return from the grave are found in these
documents. A developed concept of Jesus as co-eternal with the
Creator had to wait for the Gospel of John, a book usually
assumed to have been composed more than seventy years after
the crucifixion. Many people lived out their adult years as faithful followers of Jesus during those seven decades.

A prospective new pastor learns that many various understandings of Jesus held by early Christians found their way
into the four Gospels by which we know Jesus. Some stories
and teachings lifted from The Gospel of Thomas appear in

Mark, Matthew, and Luke. Q is quoted extensively by Matthew and Luke. The Gospel of John was composed in the context of a church that had been given time to reflect on the meaning of its founding figure. Thus, a person seeking support for almost any opinion about the nature of Jesus, from Jesus as teacher to Jesus as exalted Savior, can find that position inextricably folded into the biblical material.

Even a self-identified conservative interpreter of Jesus such as N. T. Wright acknowledges the breadth of the views included in our source material. In the stimulating debate between himself and Marcus Borg, recorded in *The Meaning of Jesus: Two Visions*, Wright had this to say:

> The available sources do not offer a coherent picture. The Jesus of the canonical material is in certain respects quite different from the Jesus of at least some of the non-canonical documents (for example, the Nag Hammadi codices). The Jesus of both of these is scarcely recognizable in the veiled picture of Jesus in the later rabbinical material.

Arguments, then, about who has the right view of the nature of Jesus are mostly pointless. A pendulum has been swinging for more than two thousand years. At certain times in religious history the divine side of the incarnation—the Christ of faith—has been emphasized. Other times have placed the spotlight on the humanity of a physical person—the historical Jesus. The seminary student is likely to receive this information as good news. It broadens the tradition. I find it difficult to label myself or any other person a heretic when I know that faithful followers of Jesus who came before me can be found all across the theological landscape.

Because of the reexamination of this topic that is taking place today, the beginning pastor will spend a professional career watching and perhaps participating in an exciting ferment. With skill (and a bit of good fortune), young clergy might be able to enlist their congregations in the adventure of discovering more about the role of Jesus, the one who is at the center of their faith.

Seminary students are likely, in a fifth area, to undergo change in their views of the relationship between science and religion. In most mainline local churches, the conflict between science and religion is either ignored or decided in favor of religion. When discussed at all, the biblical stories of creation are treated as if they are literal and correct. Many, perhaps most, of those entering seminaries have been exposed to a view that insists that where science and religion are in conflict, religion has the correct explanation for the origin of the universe.

I grew up in a relatively open religious environment. But even there, any potential conflict between science and religion was handled by mentioning the subject as infrequently as possible. My local pastors apparently assumed that we young people had accepted the idea that God created the world in six days and rested on the seventh. Troublesome questions were answered with evasive remarks.

In most mainline seminary classrooms, any conflict between the worldview of the Bible and the modern, scientific worldview is decided in favor of science. Actually, in my seminary, the relationship between science and religion received almost as little attention as it had in my local church. The subject was ignored, however, in a very different way. My Bible professors assumed that science had the correct information about *how* the worlds were made. They further assumed that we students shared this point of view. They showed no sign of wanting to waste time debating the matter. Thus we were freed to move immediately into the religious meanings of the biblical stories.

But when seminary students accept the findings of science, they set themselves up for future conflicts. At least a few of the members of the congregations these students will soon serve will associate acceptance of science with rejection of the Bible. Yet the more thoughtful of the seminarians also know that ignoring the subject should no longer be an option. Christians pay dearly for dismissing the findings of the scientific community, for faith is inevitably the loser when the two are placed in conflict. How many modern people of faith have abandoned religion after the disaster of the Scopes monkey trial in Tennessee, or the effort of the Kansas Board of Education to limit the teaching of evolution in the schools of their state?

The church does not have to initiate a discussion of the relationship between science and religion. That discussion is already taking place, in ways that many anxious clergy may not comprehend. The laity work each day within a scientifically oriented world. They take medications that were tested first on primates who are close to humans in the evolutionary scheme. They read of stunning discoveries in the depth of the heavens, and they hear rumblings of strange happenings described by those who work in a relatively new field called quantum mechanics. They talk about these matters with their coworkers at the water cooler and with family members across the dinner table. They wonder how to reconcile this knowledge with familiar words of scripture. These people would welcome a clear statement from the pulpit acknowledging that faithful religion and sound science can live together as friends. Many of these people would happily join a study course in a local church in which advocates of science and advocates of religion could discuss the relevance of the disciplines with one another.

Seminary students usually received their earliest training in local churches where supernaturalism is assumed to be synonymous with religion. This is the sixth area of significant change in a student's faith. Supernaturalism is a term that describes the beliefs of many of those who embrace popular religion. Religion dominated by supernaturalism assumes that we live in two kinds of worlds. The first is the natural, predictable world we know through our senses. Permeating and sometimes opposing the natural world is an unpredictable arena inhabited by disembodied spirits.

Miraculous acts characterize this second realm. The smallest details of people's lives are determined (predestined?) by the battles that take place between godly and demonic spiritual forces. God is assumed to be in charge of both worlds, although, in some unexplained way, less in charge of the first than the second.

Seminary students who are accustomed to seeing religion in terms of supernaturalism will be forced by the academic setting to think in more concrete terms. In the classroom, the spirits are tamer. Substance abuse, for an example, is seen not as the result of demonic possession but as the result of poor individual choices—choices that can be influenced by helpful pastoral intervention and effective secular therapy. In the seminary setting, miraculous cures, even those described in scripture, are more likely to be scientifically explained than religiously celebrated.

Religion, by its nature, implies a belief in and commitment to something that is super natural. Note, however, how different this concept appears when its two parts are separated. God is super: that is, God transcends the world of objects. God is super, also, in being more trustworthy, more compassionate, and more enduring than anything else known.

Healthy religion, according to insights likely to be taught in seminaries, points to a divine being who is both super and *natural*. People whose spiritual disciplines have brought them close to the divine report that God is as natural as the air we breathe or the water in which we swim. The images of air and water might have been in the mind of the biblical writer who described God as that "in which we live and move and have our being" (Acts 17:28).

The seminary student is encouraged to shift faith away from supernaturalism toward the recognition of the spiritual within the natural. This shift is more than wordplay. It represents a sea change in emphasis. Students are introduced to spiritual guides such as St. Francis and Brother Lawrence, religious geniuses whose major skill was in seeing the infinite revealed in the finite events of everyday life.

Supernaturalism, in its more extreme forms, is sometimes labeled superstition. "Superstition" is a word I hesitate to use, for it is often a judgmental term, used in poorly defined ways. In my more cynical moments I want to define superstition as what *you* believe; genuine religion is what *I* believe.

Nonetheless, superstition is definable. It is, first of all, based on fear. It grows out of an assumption that we live in a hostile universe, filled with forces bent on our destruction. If I make a single error, such as walking under a ladder or crossing the path of a black cat, the fury of the unfriendly forces will be unleashed.

A second characteristic of superstition is its focus on the self. It is all about *me*. Hostile forces are focused on me, waiting for any mistake that will allow an opening to attack me. I must therefore engage in ritual acts of defense, preemptive strikes to keep the evil powers off guard.

Third, superstition has no human context. Like the Greek gods of Mt. Olympus, the forces of superstition often act like mortals. They negotiate, swap ideas, and relish victories over one another. Yet these outlandish stories arise from no human environment. Superstitions do not acknowledge the time and place of their origin.

Healthy religion reverses all three characteristics of superstition. It is based on trust, not fear. It assumes a Sustaining Force that is friendly to our existence. *Even the dark is not dark to Thee* (Psalm 139:12). True religion lifts us above our egocentric concerns and insists that we see the world through a broader lens. *When I consider the heavens, the stars and moon that you have created, what is humankind . . .?* (Psalm 8:3). Finally, true religion arises out of the give and take of daily existence, the joys and pains that weave their way into every life. The most profound moments of spiritual breakthrough are given a time and place. *In the year that King Uzziah died, I saw the Lord, high and lifted up* (Isaiah 6:1).

Persons whose insecurities are deep, especially those who are chaos-intolerant, may attempt to blend religion and superstition. Thus they turn scripture, creed, and dogma into talismans. Worship, instead of being an effort to focus one's life on ultimate values, becomes a charm to ward off evil. "I will not be struck down by any dread disease because I had perfect attendance at church services last year."

Life, as it unfolds, however, proves that nothing protects us from the wrecking balls of outrageous fortune. Opening the Bible at random, for example, and reading the first verse that captures our eyes, is no more likely to give helpful guidance than skimming the advice found in an astrology column. This must be stated more forcefully: *Any effort to use religious language or religious symbols to guard against the fates is superstition.* The effort will ultimately fail. Repeated failures will cause a person either to grow into a more mature faith or to abandon religion altogether.

Seminary students come to maturity in many kinds of local churches. Some of those churches practice a faith that is generously sprinkled with elements of superstition. Favorite hymns are egotistic, using "I" more often than "we." Sermons are based on (and help generate) fear. The concept of God never matures beyond the image of a strong advocate within the pantheon of more evil forces.

Students in seminary are likely to encounter a basic truth: If Christianity is to have any appeal to the many persons who are repelled by supernaturalism and superstition, a broader, more earthy faith must be taught in the classrooms and preached from the pulpits of local churches.

Christianity's insistence on exclusive access to God is a final area of radical change in the seminary student's faith. Many Christian spokespersons have long claimed that only commitment to Jesus can bring a person into a saving relationship to the divine, and finally into the bliss of eternal life. A few passages from scripture reinforce their position. People of all other religious traditions, according to this view, are excluded. Hindus, Buddhists, Sikhs, Muslims, agnostics, and others are left outside the realm of divine concern—godforsaken—no matter how faithful they have been to their religious tenets, no matter how compassionate their lives.

Many modern church members continue to receive comfort in the idea of Christianity's exclusive access to the divine. Sociologists who specialize in religion tell us that the fastest growing churches are those that declare that only Christians have a correct faith. An officer of the Southern Baptist Church received national attention when he announced publicly that God does not hear the prayers of Jews. The idea that my group is right and all others are wrong will always have strong appeal.

Sustaining the belief that one has a lock on truth is easy when a person is surrounded by those of similar opinion. As long as those who are excluded live a long distance away, Christian spokespersons can describe other faiths in any degrading way they choose. Challenge is impossible.

No longer is it true, however, that the non-Christian "pagans" are strange people who live in distant cultures. For example, followers of Islam, whose faith, especially after the tragic attacks of September 11, 2001, has been stereotyped as hard and militant, may now live on the same block where I live. In the flesh, they are likely to be as gentle with their children and as caring for their neighbors as any Christian in the same neighborhood. Building stereotypes of Islam is more difficult when the faith is represented by a human face rather than a threatening idea.

Diana Eck, Director of the Pluralism Project at Harvard University, has described the new realities of American culture.[10] Three hundred Buddhist temples stand in Los Angeles alone. Muslims now constitute one of the major minority groups in the United States. Every other major world religion is represented here in numbers that most persons would find surprising.

Not only do we now meet persons of other faiths in our neighborhoods, we must also listen to them as they respond to our exclusive claims. Eck quotes a New York Swami whose Hindu faith insists that the Holy can be approached from many paths. "To think you own the Almighty cannot but be counterfeit. No real experience of the infinite presence of God can leave you condemning your neighbor."

Seminary students find themselves in a setting in which sympathetic contact with other religions is mandatory. No self-respecting seminary professor of world religions would try to interpret Islam, for example, without inviting an adherent of Islam, or at least introducing materials written by persons of that faith.

When the ideas of other faiths take on human flesh, the negative views once taught in local church school classes fall away. A more open stance results. If the seminary class in world religions has been well taught, the student is left with an awareness of how unfair has been Christianity's presentation of other faith traditions.

Yet, in this almost forced broadening, the students' experience is simply the ordinary experience of Americans magnified. Because of formal and informal contacts now taking place between people of different faiths, the laity has become a participant in the emerging new openness. Polls among Christians, including those of more conservative groups, indicate that more than 80 percent of those who identify themselves as Christians acknowledge that truth can be found in other religions.

Graduates of today's seminaries know that they will sacrifice their integrity if they enter a pulpit and assure a congregation that Christians know the only path to salvation. They also know that surrendering this belief will be difficult for some members of their congregations. The stage is set for either skilled pastoral intervention or for conflict. The other alternative, one too often chosen, is to pretend to believe in Christian exclusivity while saying as little as possible on the subject. Poisonous dishonesty finds many ways to express itself.

◆

Summary

Several years of intense professional training tend to nudge religious professionals into a more open, more dynamic faith. They come to know how the Bible, the creeds, and church history have unfolded. Once they have eaten the fruit of contextual knowledge, it is extremely difficult to return to the faith of their childhood. But they have also experienced a surprising fact: Expanded horizons do not weaken religious faith. They strengthen it. These emerging professionals have recognized the power that faith can release in human life, especially after it has been stripped of the most troublesome aspects of supernaturalism and superstition.

Next, seminary graduates must leave the sheltered world of the classroom and confront congregations of people with a wonderfully complex set of needs and desires. The issue of honesty accompanies them each time they enter their new pulpits; it impacts many other pastoral contacts. The way honesty is handled in these early months of a new ministry will set a pattern for a lifetime.

Almost a century has passed since Dietrich Bonhoeffer told the church it must learn to deal with people who have "come of age." Not long afterward Rudolf Bultmann listed several traditional doctrines of Christianity that he considered outdated and superstitious. More recently Bishop John Spong published his list of ways Christianity must change in order to reclaim those he called "Christians in exile."

Church professionals must hear these voices—the voices of Bonhoeffer, Bultmann, Spong, and all those in pews who are hungry to be given adult food. Congregations in villages, cities, and rural areas all contain people who want to be challenged, persons who have already moved in their cognitive development beyond the stages at which truth is passively received. These vital people might remain in the church and in the Christian faith if religious professionals can summon the courage to make an honest confession: "The outmoded doctrines that are troubling you, I do not believe in either."

NOTES

1. N. T. Wright and Marcus J. Borg, *The Meaning of Jesus: Two Visions* (New York: HarperSanFrancisco, 1999).

2. Conrad Cherry, Betty DeBerg, and Amanda Porterfield, *Religion on Campus* (Chapel Hill: The University of North Carolina Press, 2001).

3. Naomi H. Rosenblatt, a Jewish psychotherapist, offers an alternative reading of the biblical story of rebellion in a book she co-authored with Joshua Horwitz, *Wrestling with Angels* (New York: Doubleday, 1995). She insists this is a story of human maturation, a coming-of-age with all its attendant growth pains.

4. Paul Tillich, *Systematic Theology,* Volume Three, Part V, Section II (Chicago: The University of Chicago Press, 1963).

5. For a carefully researched description of the development of the Nicene Creed, see Richard Rubenstein's *When Jesus Became God* (New York: Harcourt Brace and Company, 1999).

6. Roy Oswald, *Crossing the Boundary Between Seminary and Parish* (New York: Alban Institute, 1980).

7. Annie Dillard, *Antaeus,* Autumn 1989.

8. An early description of the life and teaching of Jesus, lost for centuries but recently rediscovered.

9. A hypothetical collection of Jesus' teachings. Many, probably most, New Testament scholars assume that the Q document was the source of much of the material in the Gospels of Matthew and Luke.

10. Diana L. Eck, *A New Religious America: How a "Christian Country" Has Become the World's Most Religiously Diverse Nation* (New York: HarperSanFrancisco, 2001).

5

From Fear to Affirmation

Why do church professionals resist an honest relationship with the laity? What could possibly motivate Christians to perpetuate a divide between their own style of faith and that which they attempt to cultivate in their congregations? I have tried to discover answers to these perplexing questions.

Fear often plays a role in creating illogical situations. So it is in the professional/laity split. Four fears, all emanating from the professional side, are at the base of it all. These fears lead to behaviors that cannot otherwise be explained. Tragically, these fears have been handled in ways that are counterproductive, creating the very realities that caused the fear.

Fear number one is that ordinary people who attend worship will react negatively if asked to embrace a mature faith. Many religious people bring a particular style of belief with them to worship each Sabbath. Surely, it is assumed, they will believe in that same manner throughout their lives. If challenged to change, they will become defensive and perhaps even seek out another congregation where their former ways will be reaffirmed.

The second fear lives hidden within the first. Church leaders tend to distrust lay persons in general, and the intellectual power of the laity in particular. If church members are allowed to think for themselves, they might be seduced by their own logic. Perhaps they will embrace ideas that the church, long ago, labeled as heretical. Unguided reason can carry us down blind alleys. Reason makes people think they can be self-sufficient. Our salvation is by faith alone, the major Protestant reformers insisted. Thus, the logic (or illogic, as it may be) continues, congregations must accept on faith what is sometimes unacceptable to the intellect. Because they distrust the mind, those same leaders distrust genuine religious education. Thus what is advertised as learning becomes, in reality, indoctrination.

The third fear is that honestly exposing the human roots of our religious tradition—church history, creed, and dogma—will cause that tradition to lose its spiritual power. Those who suffer from this fear are confident the tradition must be treated as a special kind of history, a record of divine interventions, unlike other human activity. Otherwise, it is argued, the tradition will have little positive influence on people of faith.

A fourth fear, like the second, might be subsumed under the previous heading, but it is such a large concern that it must be lifted out and examined on its own. This fear is that the Bible, if exposed to probing examination, will lose its power as the carrier of a holy tradition.

All four fears are based, in part, on reality. People have been known to leave churches when challenged to embrace new ideas. On some occasions a distorted form of human reasoning has led individuals and groups to hopelessness or violence. Confronting the messy way that creeds were developed and defended can be painful. Changing the way the Bible is viewed can put stress on long-held belief systems.

Nonetheless, I insist that all four fears are, ultimately, unfounded. More than that, I want to show that allowing those fears to dictate our actions will cause the church to create the very results that were feared. *Failing* to encourage people to alter their belief systems will cause a greater membership loss. *Failing* to encourage a proper use of the mind is the most likely way to send people down blind alleys. *Failing* to educate the laity about the human context of tradition, and scripture in particular, will create a loss of respect for those sacred realities.

◆

Personal Experience

Many factors cause me to believe that we must examine and reject our fears. Personal experience is one of them.

An experiment early in my ministry brought me to what might be seen as radical conclusions. I preached a series of sermons on the overall theme of "Things I Do *Not* Believe."

The sermons came from a commitment I made to myself as I finished seminary. I determined that the knowledge I had acquired about the nature of the Bible and the place of doubt in a strong belief system would not be treated as dirty secrets to be kept from the supposedly fragile folk who sat in church pews. I would be honest. I would lay out the basic elements of the Christian faith while acknowledging those points on which I had personal reservations. I would encourage my congregations to examine, and then to take ownership of, their own beliefs. If this caused damage to people and churches, and if honesty proved impossible to sustain, I would seek another line of work.

The title of my sermon series was negative, and, to those in the congregation, potentially frightening. If I had a chance to relive those Sundays, I would change that title. I have come to recognize that it is possible to share honestly even while preaching positively on themes about which my own beliefs are ambiguous. At a profound level, people know this important fact: Doubt authenticates faith. So faith and doubt can be wrapped in the same package. In many cases the two should be wrapped in the same package.

Actually, the messages in my series were not so destructive as their label implied. For example, one message concerned a literal interpretation of the virgin birth. On that Sunday I assured the congregation that the birth stories in Matthew and Luke were placed in the Gospel accounts for an important reason: They are tender ways of pointing to the unique nature of Jesus of Nazareth. I encouraged my parishioners to embrace the truths within these stories.[1] I assured them that I had no quarrel with anyone who believed the accounts to be historically accurate. I simply asked that they be tolerant of those who saw the birth accounts as additions made to the biographies of Jesus by the early church—a position I affirmed as my own. I reminded them that many people of the first century lived out their entire adult lives in the forty or more years between the crucifixion of Jesus and the writing of the Gospel of Matthew (widely accepted as the first New Testament writer to describe a miraculous birth). Many, perhaps most, of these early Christians had no reason to believe that Jesus was born in other than the normal way. They were faithful disciples. Some were martyrs. They laid the foundation for the church.

The point of my sermon was not to prove the birth stories untrue. (How does one prove a negative?) The point was to indicate that a belief in a literal virgin birth has not been, across history, a necessary part of Christian commitment. Other sermons in the series were, likewise, an effort to broaden the tradition rather than deconstruct the faith.

The sermon series was given to a congregation composed of a typical slice of small-town middle America. The church was located on the village green of a community in upstate New York. Each Sunday I looked out at a collection of laborers, small-town merchants, public school teachers, an occasional doctor or dentist, and a few farmers. The educational level was somewhat higher than that of the immediate area, but not significantly higher than a national average. There was no reason to think that this congregation could handle my outburst of honesty any better than the majority of Christian congregations scattered across the nation.

I approached the series with anxiety that stopped just short of panic. At best, I anticipated an encounter with a significant number of angry individuals who felt that their faith had been undermined. At worst, I had fantasies of a visit by church officials asking that I seek another parish. I announced at the beginning of the series that I would not greet the congregation following the service in the normal fashion but would, instead, station myself in a room near the sanctuary where anyone with questions, concerns, or anger could see me in relative privacy. I followed this procedure for three of the six Sundays in the series. No one sought me out. I then returned to my practice of fellowship following the service. Again, I braced myself for anger. Instead, I received smiles, nodding of heads, or occasional comments such as "Thanks for your honesty." Another: "I have thought that way for a long time. It was good to hear from the pulpit that I was not so far off base."

My series of messages on what I did not believe was given in the second year of my pastorate in Sherburne, New York. I remained in that position for fifteen additional years. We were (and are) a part of a denomination that is shrinking at an alarming rate. Much of the loss is from churches in towns and villages like Sherburne. Across nearly two decades, however, we in Sherburne enjoyed slow but steady growth in both membership and financial giving. And honesty remained a hallmark of the relationship between parishioner and pastor.

Perhaps I was lucky. I prefer to think I stumbled onto an important truth: Congregations are not nearly so fragile, nor so unsophisticated in their faith, as many pastors assume. Church people have seldom been given a safe setting in which to express their questions, or to state their reservations about such matters as biblical miracle stories or creeds that no longer speak to current issues. When offered such settings, when assured that they will not be condemned for an opinion different from the orthodoxy they were spoon-fed as children, parishioners are more likely to respond with a sigh of relief than a cry of anger.

Perhaps I got away with this[2] because my sermons were more affirmation than negation. Rather than telling the congregation that the tradition in which they had spent their lives was wrong or inadequate, I stressed that their tradition was inclusive. The tradition continues to be large enough, I insisted, to include those who accept the beliefs that were passed on to them as well as those who feel those beliefs need to be reexamined. As I shared my own spiritual struggles, the people felt trusted and thus affirmed.

Another reason for the positive reaction to this series of messages may have been that people sensed it emerged out of genuine caring. I would like to think this was true. They recognized that I wanted them to have a faith built on solid ground that was not subject to breakage by the impact of new information.

Admittedly, this effort at honesty might not be so well received in every place. Modern Christian communities include a significant number of individuals whose spiritual existence is built on a literal and fragile belief system. Such persons react in anger when the pulpit fails to reinforce a narrow, old-time religion. To their credit, however, such people seldom run away. (In nearly forty years of ministry, I have lost only one family whose exit might be blamed on too much spiritual openness.) Persons who have been challenged will stay and struggle, often engaging in an almost desperate effort to convert me and thereby find additional approval of their carefully crafted faith. In such cases, emotional concerns become intertwined with issues of belief. Gentle pastoral care, and not an argumentative bout, is the appropriate response. These exceptions do not change the basic reality: Honesty from the pulpit is almost never the precipitating factor in breaking a church relationship. People may want a firm foundation for their faith, but they are smart enough to know that dishonesty is not an ingredient of stability.

That early experience in the pulpit taught me to have more trust in the laity and less trust in the fears that have often controlled the behavior of church professionals. Most of the people in pews want clergy to be honest. They might dread the pain of adjusting long-held beliefs. But at a significant level they know that the belief systems that seemed appropriate to their ancestors do not work for them.

Today, most adults have learned to be suspicious of absolutes. They have discovered that truths they once were taught as immutable in other fields—science, for example—have been radically revised. Why should religious dogmas, concepts about the less-defined world of the spirit, not also be subject to reexamination? Occupants of the pulpit can no longer sally forth under the banner of absolutes and expect unquestioning parishioners to follow.

◆

Confronting the Fears: Affirming the Laity

The church, then, must move from fear of the laity to an affirmation of laity. I am convinced that the vast majority of those who occupy church pews will respond positively to teachers and preachers who assume that nonprofessional church members are capable of change and growth. Many parishioners are weary of being passive recipients of ancient wisdom poured down on their heads each Sunday morning with no acknowledgment of its original setting. They will enthusiastically respond to an invitation to become participants in a search for ways to apply enduring truths to an evolving human society.

Respect is a precious gift the pulpit may offer to those who occupy pews. The laity want to know that they are seen as competent people fully capable of facing the world as it is. Respect means recognition by the pastor that people have moved beyond the early stages of cognitive development and are ready to think more broadly. They want guidance, not dictation from so-called experts. Respect means celebrating the fact that people are capable of making the sometimes difficult modifications that are required in the presence of new information. Most of them are willing, when required, to undergo the pain of spiritual surgery rather than live with the constant ache caused by non-sustainable beliefs.

Clergy, nonetheless, tend to be paralyzed by caution. They seem to assume that the removal of any one building block of a parishioner's belief system will cause the entire structure of faith to crumble. This fact reveals the underlying problem. Pastors often assume that the structure of faith that sustains their people is a house of cards. Respect means assuming that the people in church pews have a more solid grounding than their pessimistic clergy seem to believe.

I do not mean to overstate this optimistic view. At many moments in my work in the Christian church I found myself despairing of the church and of church members. Asking people to join in the process of change and growth can be a discouraging business. On the other hand, my moments of greatest optimism have been provided not by church bureaucrats, but by lay persons of modest formal preparation. I recall those who challenged me to greater integrity when, in preaching, I used faulty logic or built, and then attacked, straw men. I cherish the memory of people who, when I asked members of a congregation to write down their questions, took the risk of sharing profound doubts with me. I recall one man of simple educational credentials, a person who had spent his life hearing the Gospel described in purely individualistic terms, who nonetheless took a courageous, lonely stand when faced with an issue of racial justice; he knew in his heart more than he had been taught to formulate in his mind.

The church will not be reformed by whipping its people into shape on doctrinal matters. The church will realize its potential power when its lay members are acknowledged as capable of sharing in the development of a faith that can be sustained in the face of present-day realities. The clergy's fears of those in the church pew must be transformed into affirmation.

Sadly, most persons are unlikely to find themselves affirmed in modern Protestant churches. Instead, they will be told that God has acted in ancient times and far-off settings, establishing a body of beliefs that are no longer subject to question or modification. In other words, they are encouraged to regress to the lowest level of cognitive development, a level in which they accept the wisdom of experts.

Our faith tradition actually affirms, rather than fears, human nature. Scripture writers assumed that their readers were capable of growth. Why else would those writers present their people with new ideas or revisions of old ideas?

Affirming the laity simply means following the example of Jesus. On several occasions, as the Gospel writers tell the stories, Jesus turned questions back on the questioner. "But who do *you* say that I am?" (Matthew 16:15). Or, again, "What is in the law? How do *you* read it?" (Luke 10:26). These were not rhetorical questions but efforts to involve Jesus' followers in the search for elusive truth. Rather than hold his authority for himself alone, Jesus sent his disciples out with the power to heal (Matthew 10:1). Despite their slowness in absorbing the truths he presented, Jesus continued to show great respect for the potential of his disciples.

Affirmation does not imply a shallow optimism. Our tradition affirms humanity in realistic terms. The second chapter of Genesis gives a balanced picture of what we are. This account tells us that we who carry the image and breath of God are "dirt-people," composed of the most elemental ingredients. Any spiritual glories we manifest are matched by a caldron of earthy, defensive, erotic, sometimes violent drives. Our dual nature can, and often does, cause rebellion against our better selves. Any person who has reflected on life will recognize this biblical description of humankind.

Forty years of pastoral ministry have convinced me that people join churches to be affirmed as spiritual beings, as children of God. Painfully aware of their destructive nature, they seek to have their spiritual nature strengthened.

◆

Confronting the Fears: Affirming the Mind

Affirming persons means respecting human intelligence. Church members want to bring their total selves—their souls, their bodies, and their minds—into the religious arena. If their minds are abused, they will vote with their feet and silently disappear.

The Protestant emphasis on sin is one of the ways minds are abused. Many of the church fathers and almost all the Protestant reformers stressed that humankind was in a state of rebellion (sin) over which we have no control. Because of sin, the reformers taught, people are estranged from the divine. At its extreme, the doctrine became the idea of *total depravity*: that is, humankind is so corrupt and unacceptable to God that we are incapable of doing anything to redeem our status. Especially, we cannot reason our way into the good graces of the divine.

William Schweiker of the University of Chicago Divinity School spoke recently about the tragic results caused by the pessimistic view of human nature held by certain strands within Islam, Judaism, and Christianity.

> There are those in each tradition who argue that human reason is so distorted or so feeble or so impotent that we cannot, ever, make valid moral judgments about how to live rightly. Given that, we must utterly submit all thinking to those who can claim rightly to interpret the decisive revelation of God's will . . .
>
> Within ultraconservative Roman Catholicism . . . one must submit to the infallible teaching of the papacy and magisterium. Within fundamentalist Protestantism . . . this means an attack on all human inquiry and the demand for complete submission to a literal reading of the Bible. These kinds of revelationalism . . . are the backbone of fanatical and authoritarian movements around the world and within each of these traditions.[3]

This attempt to discredit the human mind has, unfortunately, put the church at war with part of its own tradition.
Wisdom is an important part of our spiritual ancestors' understanding of God.[4] In the Hebrew Scripture, wisdom is considered a part of the divine nature. The writer of the Book of
Proverbs personified wisdom and gave her a feminine voice.[5]
Wisdom, according to this writer, was with God from the
beginning of time and assisted in the act of creation. Known
sometimes by the Greek name *Sophia,* this aspect of God is ech-
oed in the famous Prologue to the Book of John (John 1:1-14):
"In the beginning was the word (logos) . . . All things came into
being through him, and without him not one thing came into
being." Jesus, in John's Gospel, continues the role assigned to
Sophia, the wisdom of God.

Ultimately, the argument that reason is a hindrance to faith
dies by falling on its own sword. All negative conclusions relating to reason are reached through logical processes. The advocates of this position find themselves in an embarrassing
position. They have used reason to conclude that reason is too
sinful to be helpful. That bird will not fly!

To think, therefore, is to move toward the spiritual center.
The fear of reason, not reason itself, takes one away from our
religious foundation.

Affirming the Mind through Worship

The weekly service of worship offers great opportunities to
affirm people and to affirm the human mind. Lay participation
in the service is important. For the past three decades I have
insisted that at least one lay person share in the leadership of
any service of public worship in which I was involved. Lay people (including youth) can effectively read scripture, lead
prayers, and give children's messages. At least once a year the
laity should take over leadership of a church's entire service.
Lay sermons can be powerful statements of how faith enters into
conversation with the secular world. Young people, especially

while members of confirmation classes, should have the experience of planning and leading services, including presentation of
the message.

During most of my ministry I have set aside one Sunday
each year as "feedback Sunday." On those days, I do not plan a
message. Through the newsletter, I alert the congregation
about what is to happen. On feedback Sunday, members of the
congregation find in their bulletins a blank sheet of paper. Time
is given early in the service for people to write questions, suggestions for future sermons, or simply comments. The ushers
gather the completed sheets. While the lay liturgist conducts
the service, I take these papers into my office and choose five or
six questions to which I can respond on the spot. I return to the
pulpit and give my comments. The remainder of the congregation's questions and sermon suggestions are filed. They
become important resources when I am doing long-range sermon planning. People seem to find this process exciting. They
pay closer attention during the remainder of the year, hoping
that their contribution will stimulate a sermon.

An Episcopal priest who is a friend shared with me that all
his sermons have been planned in response to input by a lay
committee. In addition, at one service each month, the entire
congregation has an opportunity to talk back to the preacher.
On occasion a special group is convened to give more precise
evaluation of a series of sermons. The congregation of which he
is priest has expanded steadily despite a difficult location and
limited parking, both of which would be seen as disadvanta-
geous by "church growth experts."

Creative clergy and creative laity will find additional ways
to affirm the skills and interests of lay persons through the service of worship.

Affirming the Mind through Education

Honest, effective education of the laity is the church's finest
way to show respect for its people and their mental skills.

Congregations that want to grasp this opportunity will plan education that encourages serious study by people of all ages.

Two central goals should govern the educational program of the progressive congregation. The first is to move gradually from an exclusive focus on experiential learning, appropriate to the youngest students, to a balance between experiential and fact-based education. Experiential learning is appropriate for people of all ages; yet, as students grow, they also need certain facts, honestly presented, that will help them be responsible members of the religious community.

A second, and equally important, goal is to challenge students to move forward through the stages of cognitive development; otherwise, they will never be equipped to be participants in the search for ultimate truth.

■ Education of the Very Young

Young parents are eager to find an affirming style of education for their children. They seek church schools that meet their definition of excellence. The attractiveness of the literature, the atmosphere of the classroom, and the skill of the teachers are all important to parents.

But I cannot recall ever having been asked by any parent whether their child would be taught proper doctrine. Those who have come to our doors are asking that their children be allowed to wrestle with truth.

Honest, effective education should begin with the youngest students. Before children are able to think clearly about the nature of God, they can experience what it means to be cared for in a God-like manner. Nurseries must be caring, clean, happy places. Those who staff church nurseries must know that their every act toward an infant or toddler will create a lifelong association with the church and thus with the divine.

As the child matures, age-appropriate education begins to involve the mind. Children can learn that church congregations are groups where divine love is embodied in compassionate people. The Bible can be introduced as an important book that describes the way people have searched for spiritual meaning. The effectiveness of education is doubled when it is both absorbed by the mind and experienced through hands-on projects.

Preserving and passing on the tradition involves teaching certain facts. Students will learn about the lives and ideas of those who have helped shape the history of their faith community. They should know the historic creeds and how those creeds supported the people who developed them.

Experiential education supplements and expands this sharing of facts. Roger Shinn, an excellent religious educator of the 20th century, once defined the goal of Christian education as "introducing the student into the Christian community."[6] N. T. Wright spun out an equally felicitous phrase when he wrote of "living in the story."[7] Educational programs that invite the student into a tradition are affirming. Even young students can participate in important religious activities, such as collecting materials to send to children in mission schools, and visiting and assisting in local mission projects.

Practicing honesty with young children has its own set of challenges. Children tend to ask for literal answers. "Is this story true?" means true in the historical, factual sense. The teacher often gropes for ways to respond. The temptation is either to sidestep the issue, or to knowingly lie by saying, "Yes this is true," in hopes that a later teacher can straighten out the resulting confusion.

Despite its difficulties, honesty must be established as foundational for education. To the question, "Is this story true?" an appropriate answer could be, "We do not know. Perhaps this is a made-up story. But what we learn from this story is very true and very important."

Too much emphasis on doctrine can be especially destructive to children. Children may hunger for concrete answers, yet the church errs when it implies it knows more than it does about God and the will of God. I learned this at an early age.

The church in which I grew up taught me that love was the primary characteristic of the divine; they also wanted me to believe in a deity who was all-powerful, a micromanager of human life. One day I went to high school band practice and learned that a sister of the trombonist who sat beside me had died. How could I reconcile a loving and all-powerful God with this tragedy? My church had not prepared me to handle this question.

Helen Goggin, religious educator from the University of Toronto, says this about efforts to teach the love of God:

> ... [I]n most churches children will sing hymns about an almighty and all-powerful God, often with the use of military imagery. They will hear a teacher say that it is God who determines what happens in the world. How then do children reconcile these images of God with the violence and suffering they see on TV or with what many children today experience in their own homes and neighborhoods?

Goggin continues with suggestions for shifting some of the concept of power from the divine to the child:

> So instead of teaching children that God has all the power and determines everything that happens, what if we taught children that the choices they make as individuals are equally important in the course of history? What if we began at a very early age to help children see that they are creating themselves in this wonderful world where God offers them the best possibility for their current situation? What if we emphasized that we are free individuals whose choices in every moment of our lives can make a difference? Each child could be helped to see that they contribute something to the happiness or despair of the place in which they find themselves. What if we spoke of redemption in terms of their participation in actions that create goodness and reduce harm to others? What if we challenged them to be co-redeemers of their world?[8]

If I had been taught as Goggin suggests, I still would have been distressed by my first intimate contact with death. Yet I would not have been tempted to put the blame on God. Instead, I might have felt the first stirrings of a call to a profession in which I could help people make their way through such disasters—stirrings that would come later and under different circumstances. I might have seen the relationship between my friend's grief and human foolishness, foolishness such as our tendency to put resources into frivolous playthings or military instruments of destruction rather than adequately funding the search for medical cures.

■ Older Youth: Confirmation Training

Confirmation comes at a major transition moment, as a child is evolving into a youth. More than hormones are changing in young lives. Cognitive development is occurring; self-esteem issues are arising. It is crucial that the church seize this opportunity to show respect for the student's rapidly emerging abilities. Here Roger Shinn's point becomes reality: Education makes the student a part of the religious community.

Effective confirmation trainers will find creative ways to ensure that class members experience themselves as participants, not only in the activity of church life, but also in the search for truth. One of the most effective ways to create this experience is to encourage students to write their own creed.

At Community United Church of Christ in Champaign, Illinois, my role in confirmation training has been to meet with the class for an extended Saturday morning session once a month. In my last meeting with each group, I ask them to compose their own creed.

The early part of this important session gives me an opportunity to explain the role and structure of creeds. Creeds are, I inform them, statements made against the demons. (Junior high schools have great fun with the concept of demons. They are able, however, to recognize both the poetic nature of this statement and the truth it carries. Destructive [demonic] forces play on their lives each day.) The trinitarian structure of most Christian creeds is also explained. With that background, the young people are asked to work in small groups composing their creed. This creed becomes their positive statement made against the negative forces that they currently experience. The result is shared by the congregation on the day they are confirmed. Here is the creed written by a recent group.

Creed
Confirmation Class 2000
Community United Church of Christ
Champaign, Illinois

We believe in God, the Creator

Who is constantly revealed to us, who gives us strength to do things we could not do before,

Who has created us to be good, who changes us during our life to be better. Who judges us not by race, tongue, age or gender. Who, when we sin, restores us and shows us better ways.

Who has come to us in Jesus,

Whose example helps us deal with the problems of our day;

Racism, violence, family problems, drug abuse, disrespect for religion;

Who returned from the dead when he was resurrected at Easter;

Who continues to work

In the church, through people who follow their beliefs, people who are sustained by Him, and share their faith with others;

Through those who preach and teach;

Through youth who learn who God is and who help continue God's work;

Through the divinely inspired evolutionary process, working to improve the human race, showing Her creativity in many other ways.

To God we give glory. To God we give ourselves.

Writing this creed accomplished several important goals:

- ◆ It increased both knowledge of and respect for the tradition into which the young people were about to be confirmed.
- ◆ It helped the young people be active participants, not just passive recipients, of this tradition.
- ◆ It helped the young people experience the relevance of the tradition to their own lives. They identified the demons against which their personal faith must contend, some quite explicitly, some with admirable subtlety (such as sexism that limits God to one gender).

■ Education for Older Youth and Adults

Religious teaching has traditionally been an enterprise aimed primarily at children. One of my favorite aphorisms states that Jesus taught adults and played with children. Modern churches tend to turn this example on its head: We teach children and have social events for adults. Fortunately, a growing number of congregations today are searching for more effective ways to educate older youth and adults.

Education of youth and adults must be done honestly, or it should not be done at all. In large numbers of congregations, what are called adult classes are actually social groups (and are usually very effective in this role). They discuss a biblical passage on Sundays to justify the space they use in the educational wing of the building. But serious grappling with issues is systematically avoided. These classes serve an important purpose but would more correctly be labeled as fellowship groups.

Churches that approach their mission honestly must develop strong programs of education that actually draw youth and adults into the search for religious truth. Almost every denominational leader knows this to be true. Yet there is little agreement on how this clear goal should be achieved. The problems are considerable.

Finding good adult education materials is difficult. They are expensive to develop, and, once developed, they must be sold in quantities large enough to justify the cost. As a result, denominational publishing houses are reluctant to publish any materials controversial enough to cause their more conservative congregations to shop elsewhere.

Denominational magazines were once effective educational tools, but in almost every case such magazines have proven too expensive to sustain. So, while religious hunger increases in the general population, the nutrition to sate that hunger becomes increasingly scarce.

Finding qualified and available teachers for adult education, especially education that is challenging and growth inducing, can also be a discouraging task. Smaller congregations, those that make up a large portion of major Protestant churches, have a special problem in this regard. Those churches tend to seek out a curriculum that will not discourage even the least qualified person who might be willing to fill a slot in a church school staff.

William Placher looked at the problem of religious education for older youth and adults and came to this pessimistic conclusion:

> So many of our churches have become boring and depressing places. So many of the brightest children of our church members are going to Buddhist retreats or reading about Celestine prophecies or God knows what. They aren't seeing churches as places where they might go to think seriously about their religious questions.[9]

No easy answers can be found to the pressing problems of adult religious education. But surely one part of the solution is for trained pastors to take a more active role. This may mean actually teaching. It may mean becoming a teacher of the teachers. Such active participation in education is essential if the clergy are to fulfill their role as bridges between academic and popular styles of faith. Another solution, for churches that have the financial wherewithal, is to employ qualified persons to lead classrooms.

The upshot is this: People have a strong hunger for education that is honest and affirming. Too often churches, instead of satisfying those hungers, patronize their members. Thus church members continue to vanish. Churches can do better. They must do better. Otherwise, members *should* continue to vanish.

◆

Confronting the Fears: Affirming a Dynamic Tradition

Christians are the recipients of a dynamic tradition. Our history is full of debates and question marks. Our faith ancestors were not passive containers into which a received truth was poured. They were searchers sharing in the venture of discovery.

Faithfulness to this past means finding ways to sustain its excitement. The effort to pass this tradition, unchallenged and unchanged, to future generations is a sure way to kill it. This rich tradition can be preserved only by allowing it to evolve.

In the Jefferson Lectures in the Humanities, given in 1983, Jaroslav Pelikan remarked, "*Tradition* is the living faith of the dead; *traditionalism* is the dead faith of the living." That pithy sentence offers the possibility of celebrating tradition while seeking to bring that tradition into a living relationship with the present.

Sharing truth with a congregation does not mean waging a campaign against outworn beliefs. Instead, the effort at honesty must distinguish between a tradition that is celebrated, and a traditionalism that freezes faith into forms that are no longer viable.

Traditionalism is so strong in some churches that it provokes radical, sometimes counterproductive, means to dislodge it. A problem emerges when pastors, after years of struggle, finally allow themselves to share vital information about the makeup of the Bible, or about the ways dogma has developed. When their fear-caused inertia is finally overcome, the result is often something close to a pastoral explosion—a sneering attack that translates into "You don't really believe all that old stuff, do you?"

But "that old stuff" will not go away quickly. Nor should it. The tradition, even in its more rigid forms, has shown amazing staying power. Ritual, scripture, music, and other artistic expressions continue to inspire commitment and elicit positive memories. Religious tradition, especially when it is honestly interpreted, can continue to be a rich environment in which people can grow. In that hallowed soil, enriched by the insights and questions of modern followers, individuals will continue to be supported in faith.

Ancient rituals and concepts need fresh interpretations. But they are not to be dismissed. Our religious tradition offers us roots that burrow back more than two thousand years. This vital antiquity is to be celebrated.

Baptism is an illustration of an ancient ritual that continues to serve a dynamic tradition. The roots of this rite go deep. Baptism predates the Christian movement. It was used by our Jewish ancestors in faith as a means of receiving non-Jews into their faith.

In my belief system, nothing magical or supernatural happens in baptism. Along with many other Christians of today, I have long since given up any idea that people are born with a stain of sin that must be washed away in the waters of a baptismal font. Instead, baptism is an affirmation of a person's primary identity as a child of God. The ritual marks the beginning of participation in an ongoing religious tradition.

Instead of release from an inherited state of sin, I prefer to see baptism as a symbol of adoption, as do both Paul and the writer of Ephesians (Galatians 4:5 and Ephesians 1:5). Adoption in the literal sense means embracing, and being embraced by, a new family. Along with the new family come a new family tree and a supportive set of traditions.

One of my favorite cousins was adopted into the Good family. She is an amazing person. My aunt and uncle adopted Carol when she was seven. In her earlier years with us she let us know that she considered some of the ways of the Good clan to be strange. As a teenager she rebelled. When she reached adulthood, she sought out and found her birth parents. She was then forced to choose which family would receive her primary allegiance. Her decision was to give her loyalty not to those who had given her biological life, but to those who had given her acceptance and care. Today, she is one of our clan's most faithful members. She helps plan family reunions. She gives compassionate attention to her aging aunts. She has broadened our religious affiliation by her Baptist membership, yet she moves easily among the remainder of us who are Methodist, Church of the Brethren, United Church of Christ, and Mennonite. She lives her life in her own unique and effective way. Yet her major decisions are made in the framework of the Good family, its traditions, and its network of relationships.

I am confident that Carol continues to view some members of the Good family as strange and a few of our traditions as unworthy. (She is, in this sense, no different from all of us who were born into this group.) Membership in this tradition does not come with a rule book governing her every decision. It is a framework in which she lives. It tells her who she is. Knowing who she is has helped her make the many responsible decisions that have characterized her adult years.

The writer of the Letter to the Hebrews knew the meaning of adoption. In his view, the followers of Jesus have been taken into a community of caring people that knows no boundaries of time or space: "Therefore, since we are surrounded by so great a cloud of witnesses . . ." (Hebrews 12:1). How can one live at less than one's best with this cloud of witnesses symbolically looking on?

Baptism has brought all of us into a particular kind of family, a sacred family defined by its search for ultimate truth. This family began with the call of Abraham, continues through the exciting episodes of the Hebraic Scripture, and reaches a fulfilling moment in the life, death, and new life of Jesus. That tradition endures through centuries of church expansion. It continues today across the globe in its countless, sometimes contradictory, forms. It includes both the tragic and the heroic, the perpetrators of the Salem witch trials as well as the martyrs of the civil rights struggle. We inherit it all in our adoption into the faith family.

The Bible is the family album of this community of faith. Church creeds are statements of what are (or have been) common concerns. Services of worship are family gatherings, renewing commitment to one another and to shared values. The family's sacred rituals are its ties to the past, reminders of the cloud of witnesses whose past sacrifices are a challenge to us to achieve a present faithfulness.

Judaism—at least in its most vibrant branches—has always been more comfortable than Christianity with an open tradition. I am fond of the aphorism that where three Jews are gathered, there are four opinions; this captures Judaism's wonderful and playful delight in issues that continue to be undecided. According to the research discussed in Chapter 2, this dialectic thinking represents one of the higher levels of cognitive development.

A careful study of the Christian tradition shows that it, like its parent Judaism, has embraced a surprisingly broad array of concepts. The huge tent called Christianity has been able to offer shelter to remarkably divergent, sometimes contradictory, ideas. Traditional church fathers stressed the otherness of the divine, while Christian mystics celebrated God's immediacy. Monastics retreated into the wilderness to live lonely lives of prayer, while the majority of the faithful chose to live within the ambiguities of community life. The early church lived nonviolently (as have remnants within the modern church) until the later church developed the doctrine of just war.

I consider myself both a conservative and a progressive. I am a conservative in my love of this broad and nourishing tradition. I am conservative also, in that I want to preserve the dynamism that characterizes Judaism and has been essential to Christianity in its more vital eras. Being a conservative in this regard also makes me a progressive. As a progressive I want to explore new vistas concerning core issues. What is the nature of the Ultimate Reality we have called "God"? How do we best serve God? Is human nature basically sinful, or is humankind a little lower than the angels (Psalm 8:5)? How can we achieve social justice? What is the meaning of the death and resurrection of Jesus? What is the relationship between Jewish law and Christian morality? My desire to keep these issues open is progressive because it seeks and welcomes new light. But this progressive stance is also conservative. It seeks to conserve and continue the style of openness that defined our spiritual ancestors. I have been adopted into this marvelous tradition, and I want to conserve its dynamic nature.

As a progressive, I want my beliefs to be compatible with my understanding of the physical world. But this, too, has a conservative thrust. Not only were the early keepers of the faith comfortable with debate, they were also comfortable with the relationship between their concepts of God and their understanding of the material world. *They brought their finest scientific insights to bear on their faith.* If God formed the world, then the nature of the world should tell them something about its Maker. Thus a Psalmist could exclaim that the heavens are "telling the glory of God, and the firmament proclaims his handiwork" (Psalm 19:1). They were awed by nature, even though their views of nature were, from our vantage point, flawed.

Today, those who ask that our faith be exposed to new scientific information[10] are not attempting to take Christianity in new directions. They are attaching us to the most ancient aspects of our faith. The effort to mediate between science and religion is as old as faith itself. Continuing that effort is both progressive and conservative.

People who espouse ideas similar to those in this volume are often accused of being "troublemakers." Or, to use a common phrase, those who want to think outside the box are seen as being eager to "upset the apple cart." The apple cart, however, cannot be protected by locking its wheels. Apple carts are constructed so their life-giving fruit can be moved from place to place, offered to a variety of people in a variety of settings.

Again we see illustrated the central idea of this chapter. Traditionalists fear losing the power of the tradition, so they circle their wagons of ancient ideas to preserve the tradition in some unchanging forms. Ironically, the major threat to the tradition's preservation is just this refusal to allow it to evolve.

The concept of a Christian faith that is rigidly fixed, dogmatically established for all times and places, is an oxymoron. Christianity is, by definition, open. It continues a tradition that has always welcomed new insights, that has looked unblinkingly toward the future. It is always in process. Those who insist it must be handed forward in an unaltered form violate it in the most basic way.

◆

Confronting the Fears: Affirming the Bible

Honesty acknowledges and celebrates the human element of the scripture. Far from diminishing the Bible's impact, such acknowledgment increases its spiritual power.

The Bible is usually presented in churches as if it were filled with firm rules and eternal truths. Hearing this, people become confident that they can turn to its pages and find answers to the perplexities of their lives. But when they actually open the Bible and read, their assumptions are blown away by the winds of reality.

Honesty concerning the Bible will begin when we clearly identify its nature. The Bible is not an answer book. It is, as mentioned earlier, the family album of a community of faith.

As a family album, it is the arena in which family debates take place. The debates are not shouting matches; they are usually subtle, encased in narratives or folded into poetry. They are present, nonetheless, and the careful reader will not miss them. Any effort to paper over this fact, to pretend in the name of divine authorship that all biblical writers took similar positions on all topics, does violence to the obvious meaning of their words.

The church pays a high price for its efforts to hide the contentious nature of scripture. One example comes from the ethical arena. The Christian church, especially its Protestant branches, has insisted that Jesus came to set aside the Jewish moral law.[11] Unquestionably, Paul argued that slavish obedience to every recorded law was not necessary. Salvation came instead through divine initiative, through faith in the grace of God. But other parts of the New Testament show that Paul's position was only one side of a vigorous debate. Matthew attributed to Jesus words that reflect an internal struggle in the young church:

> Do not think that I have come to abolish the law or the prophets; I have come not to abolish but to fulfill. For truly I tell you, until heaven and earth pass away, not one letter, not one stroke of a letter, will pass from the law until all is accomplished. Therefore, whoever breaks one of the least of these commandments, and teaches others to do the same, will be called least in the kingdom of heaven; but whoever does them and teaches them will be called great in the kingdom of heaven.
>
> (Matthew 5:17-19)

The church has been deeply wounded by presenting only one side of this debate. The loss of allegiance to any basic body of moral law has made it easier for the church to engage in violent crusades, to torture its heretics and hang its witches. Salvation by grace offers no excuse for failing to behave as compassionate citizens of the divine realm. This debate begs to be reopened.

An honest approach to scripture reveals how a knowledge of the time and place of biblical events expands scripture's impact. Many passages of the Bible achieve their full power only when seen in their human contexts.

For example, the 65th chapter of Isaiah is a beautifully constructed vision of a peaceful society. Every reader, even those with no background knowledge, will be moved by the vision. These verses reveal the world in its full potential, free from the rancor and violence that robs us of *shalom*. Yet, the reader who knows the context will find more.

19   I will rejoice in Jerusalem,
            and delight in my people;
        no more shall the sound of weeping be heard in it,
            or the cry of distress.
20   No more shall there be in it an infant that lives
                but a few days,
            or an old person who does not live out a lifetime;
        for one who dies at a hundred years will be considered
                a youth,
            and one who falls short of a hundred will be considered
                accursed.
21   They shall build houses and inhabit them;
            they shall plant vineyards and eat their fruit.
22   They shall not build and another inhabit;
            they shall not plant and another eat;
        for like the days of a tree shall the days of my people be,
            and my chosen shall long enjoy the work of their hands.
23   They shall not labor in vain,
            or bear children for calamity.

                                        (Isaiah 65:19-23)

This text was written in Babylon during the Jewish exile. The memory of the defeat of their nation had been burned into the mind of the writer. After a long siege, Babylonian soldiers had overrun what the Jews had thought to be an impregnable defense. The protection they had anticipated from their God had failed to materialize. Further, the Babylonians had wanted slaves as the spoils of war. So the victors prepared the able-bodied among the Jews for the long trek to the north. Some, however, could not make that arduous trip. Infants were a hindrance; thus babies were taken from their mothers' arms and slaughtered. The elderly would be another problem. They, too, were executed. Homes that Jews had constructed with their own hands were left for others to inhabit. Crops, carefully and laboriously cultivated, would be harvested by outsiders.

Once the passage is properly set into this context, certain phrases leap off the page with new power: "No more shall there be in it an infant that lives but a few days, or an old person who does not live out a lifetime. They shall build houses and inhabit them; they shall plant vineyards and eat their fruit." The passage becomes much more than an attractive vision of an idealized existence: In context, it becomes the tear-soaked testimony of a wounded people. All those who have suffered tragic losses can find in this passage a point of contact with their spiritual heritage.

The Gospels are replete with additional examples of the importance of context. The account of Jesus walking on water is an important one.

To those who assume that the Gospels are historically accurate, the story of Jesus walking on water is a strange story with no apparent purpose other than to show that Jesus had power over nature. But what does this mean for followers of Jesus in the 21st century? A warning sign can almost be seen over this account: "Jesus could walk on water, but do not try this at home." Tragically, the traditional reading of this story reinforces the idea that Jesus was basically different from me, and that I can never expect to model my life after his.

Those who have studied the Bible critically know that the story of Jesus walking on water was written several decades after Jesus' death. By then the church was beginning to structure itself. Issues of leadership were in dispute. Some people wanted the church to be led by those who could claim kinship with Jesus. Others wanted the disciples to be in charge. Of the disciples, Peter was considered the strongest leader.

The writer of the Gospel of Matthew was in Peter's corner. Yet he recognized that Peter had developed a reputation for impetuousness. The arguments in favor of Peter's leadership included the fact that he had been one of Jesus' closest friends and had learned directly from Jesus. But could he be trusted with a major responsibility? Matthew knew that the best way to further Peter's cause was to acknowledge both his strengths and his weaknesses.

Three Gospel writers tell the story of Jesus walking on water, each with different details. All three show Jesus exercising a power greater than those of nature.

Matthew's telling is the longest and reveals his particular agenda. Matthew adds a second scene, one that puts the focus on Peter. When Peter saw Jesus striding across the waves, he shouted, in essence, "I am a man of faith, I can do this too." Jesus, impressed by Peter's courage, invited his friend to leave the safety of the boat. For a few moments Peter, like Jesus, was supported by the sea. Then Peter became distracted by a strong wind. Fear took over. He began to sink. Jesus had to reach out to him to keep him from drowning.

The story of Peter on the waves may have been based on some actual event, but it is highly unlikely the story unfolded in precisely the way it is told. Much more likely, Matthew edited the original event to influence the choice of leadership for the young church. Peter's assertive but sometimes shaky faith gave him the potential to lead. But beware, Matthew seems to be saying. *Peter can give effective leadership only when his faith stays strong and his attention remains focused on the example of Jesus.*

If taken literally, this account seems to do nothing but put Peter in the position of a buffoon. If seen against the background of the early church's sparring for power, it becomes an important statement about church leadership. Effective leadership will come from those who have developed a deep personal faith, and who themselves remain focused on Jesus. This fact has as much relevance today as in the first century.

On a larger stage, the scriptures are the means by which religion's commitment to truth confronts the secular world's love of lies. Secular philosophy often ignores the weakness of humankind while denying evil and death. Christianity, in contrast, acknowledges our brokenness. The cross, our central symbol, brings death before the worshipping community each time that group gathers. Christianity's message of hope is made precisely in the face of this symbol of despair. The Bible is an effective carrier of this astounding message *to the degree to which it participates in the brokenness*. The scriptures emerge out of the pains and triumphs of human life. Because the words of scripture arise out of authentic human settings, its words of hope are all the more powerful.

An honest reading of the Bible not only enriches its high moments. It also releases the church from feeling it must defend the low points of scripture. The instances in which the divine is depicted as ordering ethnic cleansing, and the many passages in which slavery is accepted as a normal part of the social setting, can be accepted without distress. They are simply assumptions of a former time. An evaluation of women as worth only 60 percent as much as men (Leviticus 27:1-4) can be acknowledged as the view of our spiritual ancestors without feeling that such an ethic is laid on us in our time. Such otherwise embarrassing passages become benchmarks against which to measure the distance other scriptural writers traveled. Some writers rose above the ethic of their time to decry war, to celebrate the potential contributions of an escaped slave,[12] or to recognize a woman, Lydia, as a leader of the emerging church.

The church that opens the entire scripture to its people, acknowledging both the ugly and the beautiful in the biblical landscape, has affirmed its people as being able to deal with truth in all its complexities. Equally important, that church has released the full power of the Bible.

The same paradox attaches to the use of scripture that pertains to the remainder of our religious tradition: Those who are perceived as radicals are actually the conservators. Respect for the Bible means acknowledging its human grounding. The greatest danger to the Bible comes from those who want to paint it in supernatural hues that an increasing number of modern people find offensive.

◆

Summary: A Biblical Insight

A final example of how honest interpretation brings the meaning of scripture to light is pertinent to all that has been said in this chapter.

A writer, whose name we do not know, set the event somewhere around the 15th century BC. According to the tale, the Jewish people, freshly released from slavery, complained as loudly about their new nomadic status as they once had about their old confinement. Permanent homes were a luxury they could barely recall. The food found in the desert was repulsive. Other tribes harassed them. According to the biblical writer, God lost patience with all their belly aching. A plague of poisonous serpents was sent as punishment. The danger of death by snakebite was added to all their other troubles.

Moses, their leader, appealed for divine mercy. Then comes this intriguing passage:

> And the LORD said to Moses, "Make a poisonous serpent, and set it on a pole; and everyone who is bitten shall look at it and live." So Moses made a serpent of bronze, and put

it upon a pole; and whenever a serpent bit someone, that
person would look at the serpent of bronze and live.

(Numbers 21:8-9)

The tale seems outlandish. The words clearly are not to be
taken literally. Nonetheless, when the fog of pre-scientific
assumptions is brushed aside, an important truth emerges: *Facing the reality we fear often carries the potential for our healing.*

This ancient narrative can be helpful as we consider the
topic of honesty between pulpit and pew. Pastors are often
deeply threatened—panicked may not be too strong a word—
by the idea of sharing with congregations the insights they have
gained in their own faith development. Any effort to challenge
lay people to a more mature faith is perceived to be as poisonous as a serpent bite, threatening the well-being of the pastor as
well as the very life of the modern church. So the issue of faith
development is pushed to the background, while more manageable concerns, such as repair of the church building's leaky
roof and plans for the summer picnic, are brought to the front.

Ignoring the danger is not working. Too many local
churches have become stale, anti-intellectual places. Members
are drifting away. A new approach is essential. Perhaps Moses
heard God correctly. The most effective means of healing is to
place our fears in a visible place and to gaze squarely at them.

Facing our fears forces us to acknowledge the wrong-
headedness of the church's desperate effort to avoid an honest
wrestling with faith. An increasing number of persons seek to
grow beyond the religious concepts of their childhood. They
hunger to be like the lilies of the field that illustrated Jesus'
vision of a new way of being in the world. They desire roots
deep in the nourishing soil of the past, coupled with the sun
and rain and space needed for growth. They want, in other
words, to stand at the intersection of a dynamic tradition and
an open future.

NOTES

1. In the following chapter I will explain why I have come to call accounts like the descriptions of Jesus' birth "truth-stories" rather than true stories.

2. This is the phrase that came to me as I was first composing this sentence. On reflection, I determined to leave it as it was first written. What an interesting insight into the mind of a pastor! I speak, I am confident, for many pastors who allow themselves to engage in truthfulness from the pulpit and do not suffer adverse effects. The common feeling: We got away with something.

3. Quoted by Carol Zaleski in *The Christian Century,* December 19, 2001.

4. An entire portion of scripture is known as wisdom literature. This includes Psalms, Proverbs, Job, Ecclesiastes, Lamentations, and portions of other books.

5. See, for example, Proverbs 7 and 9.

6. Roger Shinn, *Education in the Christian Community* (New York: The Pilgrim Press, 1960).

7. Wright and Borg, *The Meaning of Jesus.*

8. Helen Goggin, "Children and the Church in the 21st Century," *Creative Transformation,* Volume 7, Number 4, Summer 1998.

9. William C. Placher, "Helping Theology Matter: A Challenge for the Mainline," *The Christian Century,* October 28, 1998.

10. The intersection of science and religion will be explored in Chapter 8.

11. I have argued elsewhere that Paul intended to set aside the law concerning circumcision, not the entire body of moral laws. Jack Good, *The Bible: Faith's Family Album* (St. Louis: Chalice Press, 1998).

12. See the Book of Philemon for the Bible's only suggestion that human slavery is not the will of God. And even there the suggestion is indirect. An anti-slavery message can be found only by reading between the lines.

6

Honesty Brings Endurable Pain

The title of this chapter has gone through a number of trans-formations. "Honesty Can Be Painless" was my first effort. Part of me wants to think that a shift toward honesty could be accomplished easily, and that almost every person in almost every congregation would hold celebrations to welcome any sign of emerging openness.

Then I thought again. I recalled that my own development came with a price. While in seminary, I realized that the old tru-isms no longer worked for me, and that I could not go back to local churches and preach the same message I had heard in my youth. I had arrived at that point in the seminarian's crisis when old beliefs had lost their power but no and no new set of beliefs had been developed. I did not know what I meant when I spoke the word "God." The miraculous elements of scripture had become problematic. I felt empty. "Who could possibly look to me for spiritual sustenance?" I asked myself.

While struggling with my doubts, I cross-registered from Boston University for a course at Harvard Divinity School. Paul Tillich was teaching there. His course saved me as a parish pas-tor. Tillich taught me to seek the divine not in the heavens above, but in the depths of life. God is best described, according to Tillich, as "the Ground of All Being." He also taught me to see the profound truth in biblical stories that may not be historically accurate.

My crisis of faith was, by the standards of many of my classmates, short lived. Those were, nonetheless, tough days. I cannot claim a painless transition to a different style of belief. Why should I expect others to make the journey more easily?

The next edition of the chapter title included an effort to be cute: "Honesty Can Be (Relatively) Painless." This idea, too, quickly died. At some point in this process, a church member who is also a psychiatrist read an early version of the chapter. He caught me up short. "Why use the word 'painless' at all?" he asked. "No genuine growth takes place without pain. Besides," he continued, "who wants to join a group that asks nothing of them?"

Dr. Ken Gilbert was absolutely correct. No pain, no gain. Respect for the laity includes respect for their willingness to choose to move into that zone of discomfort which surrounds every adventure in growth. I dropped the word "painless."

Truthfulness, the subject of this entire volume, finally made its way to the surface. In most congregations, a shift from duplicity to honesty will cause some measure of distress. For a few individuals, the discomfort will be extreme. Of this, however, I am convinced: The vast majority of people will survive the transition to a more open style of faith and remain as committed Christians. They will do more than survive; they will grow spiritually. More than that, an honest presentation of faith might draw back some of those who have drifted away. Finally, the point I wanted to make was clear: Honesty involves *endurable* pain—pain that is the acceptable price of significant growth.

◆

An Experience of Loss: A Barrier to Evangelism

Moving from duplicity to honesty causes pain, but not only to the individual church member. The institution also will pay a price (though, as I will argue later, any short-term losses will become long-term gains).

Progressive churches will probably never experience the rapid growth that has characterized some conservative movements. The reason is simple: The shift to honesty means surrendering the old as well as embracing the new. Sorrow over faith lost, therefore, must precede joy over faith discovered.

The word "evangelical" is a key to understanding some of the different growth patterns within the larger Christian community. The word means "bearer of good news." For many conservatives, religion is an experience of spiritual ecstasy. The more outgoing of them have little hesitation in attempting to share that joy with friends and relatives. They easily slip into the role of evangelists. The joy they find in their faith is multiplied as it is shared.

For a progressive Christian, in contrast, the first step in religious growth involves the surrender of long-held certainties. A neat and predictable world in which a parent-like deity protects the children of faith must give way to a messy universe in which moral living has little or no impact on material success. Biblical stories that once were seen as literal accounts of a God-controlled universe must be reinterpreted as products of human imagination. Giving up these once steadfast beliefs can be agonizing.

Progressive Christians will see parallels between their religious development and their childhood surrender of the Santa Claus myth. Necessary, but wounding.

Progressive Christians naturally are more hesitant to be *evangelical* about their religion. Who wants to invite friends and relatives to share the sorrow that comes from setting aside so much of what once provided comfort?

Even though conservatives move toward happiness by a more direct route, progressive Christians must never cede to them the emotion of joy. People who have watched the certainties of the past disappear might feel for a time that nothing matters, that no religion can address their needs. Then they discover that it is possible to believe in a new way. This new-found joy goes to a depth previously unknown. They come to recognize that they are held by a creative Power that sustains and encourages them even though they cannot fully understand either the Power or the process. The progressive Christian understands the meaning of resurrection in a way that those who have never surrendered their childhood faith may never appreciate.

Progressive Christians can also be evangelists. Their process, however, is more complex. A simple "Are you saved?" might express the invitation of a conservative church member. They assume that they are urging a switch from secularism to religion. The progressive Christian must ask for more. Their witness is often expressed to persons who are already religious but find their belief systems inadequate. In this case, the question becomes: "Are you willing to surrender the comfortable certitudes of your past in order to explore mysteries that will never be solved?" The complications grow.

The point is this: Few people are likely to approach their neighbors and invite them to embrace a faith that begins in grief. Progressive churches, then, will rarely grow in the spectacular manner of some conservative branches of faith.

Skilled leaders, both lay and clergy, can lessen the negative impact of a transition in faith. The pain can be made endurable. Better yet, the pain can be transformed until it becomes, like the pain of many medical interventions, a surgical step in the direction of health.

I am convinced that the vast majority of current church members will survive the needed changes, and that they will come out stronger at the far end of the process. As for the institutional church, new faces, faces of Spong's "Christians in exile," will return and claim the places left by those for whom the pain was overwhelming.

The loss is real, but the loss is endurable. I am confident of this because I have observed religious transformations working themselves out in the lives of many parishioners and many congregations. By embracing honesty, people grow. Congregations grow.

◆

Finding One's Audience

Since growth first involves loss, the question before the mainline churches is this: What portion of the population is most likely to respond to an invitation to a pain/growth combination? The obvious answer is that chaos-tolerant people are more likely to endure in the face of an ambiguous message than those who are chaos-intolerant.

Traditional wisdom once taught that the major Protestant denominations were losing members to evangelical groups largely because of liberal tendencies. This directly contradicts my own experience. It also contradicts the findings of skilled sociologists such as Dean Hoge[1] and his associates. Their careful work indicates that the growth of conservative churches has not been at the expense of any other established congregations.

Dean Hoge acknowledges that neither he nor any other sociologist of religion has uncovered any one simple solution to the puzzle of why conservative churches grow while mainline Protestant congregations shrink. They have simply been able to eliminate the major theories that, up until now, have been suggested.

Honesty, or the lack thereof, between professionals and laity is a subject that has not been studied. Indeed, it would be a difficult issue to put under a microscope. Yet it is surely one important reason for the different growth patterns of conservative and mainline Christians. Conservatives, as has already been pointed out, are better at identifying their potential audience (the chaos-intolerant) and aiming their message toward those people. Their message may stretch mental credulity at many points, but it is stated with clarity. Mainline churches, on the other hand, try to appeal to everyone. They dilute their message in hopes of offending no one. Thus the growing number of seekers to whom honest questions rather than rigid answers might appeal are left without a church home.

Along with Bishop John Spong and others, I believe that our society includes many who have already gone through the experience of grief over the loss of their former faith. These "Christians in exile" continue to believe in a divine realm, an Ultimate Mystery that breaks through in an especially luminous form in Jesus of Nazareth. These discouraged but still vital seekers are ready to embrace a faith in which honesty is a central element. The number of such people is large enough to suggest that growth for progressive congregations is highly likely. Growth of any sort would be a significant change from the steady declines suffered by Protestant denominations over the past several decades.

◆

Reasons for Optimism

Overall, I am optimistic that the transition from the present stance of duplicity between clergy and pew to a state of openness involves *endurable* pain. I find a number of reasons for confidence.

The first reason for optimism is this: I am convinced that more people than most church leaders realize are ready *at this moment* to hear a spiritual message that is compatible with the physical world in which they live.

A friend, a member of the clergy of a denomination more conservative than mine, whose church is in a city noted for its traditional values, tells of an incident that took place after a service one recent Easter. Two faithful members of his congregation were overheard as they approached their cars just after worship. One paused and asked the other, referring to the service from which they had just emerged, "Do you believe all that stuff?" The other took a moment to reflect before replying, "Well, no, I guess I don't." Then the topic was dropped. The next Sunday both were back in worship. I could recite many other incidents of a similar nature.

Belief systems are not nearly so important to the average church member as church professionals tend to assume. A significant number of people join churches for social contacts, for the rituals they provide at transitional moments of life, and to satisfy a desire to wrap their lives in the mantle of the sacred. Mentally, however, they reject much of the dogma and most of the supernaturalism that confronts them each Sabbath. National poll-takers will hear these people affirm the traditional concepts: belief in God, prayer, Bible, Jesus, etc. They say these things because they think they should, or because they are embarrassed to admit, even to themselves, that they believe otherwise. But in unguarded moments, such as occurred in the parking lot of the church described above, the truth spills out. Their mental reservations are enormous.

When church professionals share their own doubts with lay people, the reaction is likely to be not anger, but relief. The guilt the laity had been carrying about having an inadequate faith disappears. They welcome an invitation to join a search—even if the search is for answers to puzzles that can never be fully solved.

Polling methods have not yet been devised that will allow these people to state their doubts without fear of judgment. No one knows, then, how many such persons exist. But evidence accumulates, pointing to a much higher number than most church professionals suspect. The best evidence for this doubt comes from the large crowds that gather in places across the globe to hear speakers such as Marcus Borg, John Spong, Karen Armstrong, and John Dominic Crossan. If these people are an indication of a widespread hunger, then a transition from duplicity to honesty can take place with much less pain than is usually assumed.

Willingness to Reexamine the Scripture

A second reason for optimism might be seen as a subheading of the first. New data indicate that church people are more flexible in their scriptural attitudes than their spiritual leaders suspect.

The Bible has a central role in the life of mainline Protestantism. Recent surveys suggest that the laity of mainline denominations are ready to look at the Bible with new eyes. They are prepared to accept scripture as a carrier of a sacred tradition rather than as an idol to be worshiped.

Not long ago the Presbyterian Church (USA) polled their membership for views on scripture. It is important to note that Presbyterians are a national body, with a presence in all parts of the United States. Presbyterians have attained higher than average educational levels and thus are accustomed to approaching matters with their minds. They also have a reputation for taking seriously the authority of the Bible.

Results of the poll revealed that only 14 percent of those responding felt that the Bible is without error in any matter. A larger number, 23 percent, believed that the Bible is accurate in its teachings about theology and ethics, but not necessarily in matters of science and history. Essentially half of the respondents (48 percent) affirmed that the Bible is both the inspired word of God and a thoroughly human document. Eleven percent of those responding felt that portions of the Bible, including material concerned with theology and ethics, may not be the inspired word of God. The remaining 4 percent accept the Bible as merely the record of the moral and religious experiences of Hebrews and Christians.

Pastors and religious educators, then, in this Bible-centered denomination, can assume that slightly more than one in ten of their congregants consider scripture to be inerrant. The remaining 86 percent are open to an examination of the human element on the biblical page. Yet the materials printed for educational work in this denomination, as in others, are careful to avoid offending even a small portion of the membership. The needs of the vast majority of Presbyterians, people who may want clearer explanations of the troubling elements of scripture, are ignored.

A somewhat similar survey of the membership of the United Church of Christ (UCC) brought comparable results.

The UCC is often labeled a "liberal" denomination, so openness on matters of scripture and dogma might be expected. However, the UCC, like its Presbyterian cousins, has deep roots in the Reformed tradition of Protestantism. Other roots of this denomination reach back to New England evangelism and to such Bible defenders as Jonathan Edwards. The average educational level is similar to that of Presbyterians.

The responses to the UCC survey were made, not surprisingly, by unusually committed persons. Ninety-four percent of the 8,000 people who filled out survey forms feel very close or somewhat close to God. An even more impressive 96 percent see the Bible as either very important or somewhat important in their lives.

Those of us who want to encourage the laity to increase their biblical literacy and develop an overall philosophy of the scripture will find this survey, in an ironic way, encouraging. Nothing in the survey indicated that the participants already possess a body of facts about the Bible, nor that they have a consistent framework for understanding it—nothing, that is, that must be surrendered before more adequate concepts can be absorbed. People cherish the Bible as a concept but have little knowledge of what is in it. Less than 20 percent of the respondents could name all of the Ten Commandments, and only 55 percent could accurately quote even one.

The survey also indicated that churches, at least of this one denomination, have failed to help persons think through their attitudes toward biblical authority. Inconsistencies were rampant. In the survey, 61 percent strongly agreed that people inspired by God wrote the Bible. Yet only 50 percent felt they should trust what the Bible says. Ninety-two percent affirmed that the Bible teaches that Jesus was born of a virgin; less than 70 percent have this doctrine as part of their own faith. All this becomes what an educator would call a "teachable moment." The laity of the United Church of Christ are virgin soil for those who want to encourage genuine wrestling with scripture.

Perhaps what appear to be inconsistencies in the UCC responses might be evidence of an emerging discernment. Respondents seemed ready to distinguish truths that are enduring from truths that were relevant only to an ancient time. With little encouragement from denominational publishing houses or from local clergy, people may have prepared themselves for a more profound understanding of scripture. These survey results reveal the need for intelligent sermons and also for good educational material, written with respect for the maturity and the probing questions that laity bring to religious matters.

Willingness to Surrender Superstitions

Another reason for optimism is that *people are being challenged from several quarters to surrender their superstitions.* In an age of science, progressive Christians are not required to make this case on religious grounds alone.

As indicated in Chapter 3, the word superstition must be used cautiously. It was noted that superstition is egocentric; it is an effort to protect oneself from hostile, demonic forces; it exists without reference to any human context. Superstitions are ineffective efforts to cope with issues over which we have no genuine control. They are attempts to manipulate the fates. Or, in simpler terms, superstitions are our efforts to make our own luck.

Despite all their faults, superstitions can be comforting to even moderately insecure people. Without superstitions, people in crisis must face the fates without protective armor. In the short run, superstitions can be useful; eventually, of course, they prove to be hollow. One of the kindest things a church can do for its people is to encourage them to cope in other ways. Honesty means acknowledging that, in the final analysis, we *are* defenseless against the randomness of life.

Science is, along with progressive religion, a second force pushing modern people away from superstition. The greatest contribution of science is not in medical advances or in space exploration; its greatest accomplishment is in ridding people of the fear of living in a demon-infested world. A scientific age means that people can walk through a cemetery at night without fear of being accosted by the ghost of an angry ancestor. We no longer need blame the gods for lightning that burns down a home, or evil forces for the illnesses that bring us low. No longer must we spend our days fearing that disembodied powers are standing over us, waiting to pounce when we make a misstep. We can expend our energy searching for the real causes of pestilence and disease. In this new atmosphere, our fears remain, but they are more manageable because they are based on reality.

Life experiences are a third set of forces that encourage us to surrender our superstitions. As an early teenager, I owned a worn but comfortable baseball cap. I wore it to at least two consecutive baseball games with friends, games in which my results with a bat far exceeded my ordinary efforts. The cap became my good-luck piece, and for a time I wore it in every game I played. Alas, the law of averages took its toll. The cap was discarded months later, after I finally admitted to myself that no piece of cloth could change the fact that I was not designed for great feats on an athletic field.

Life experiences can discourage us from turning religion into superstition. A few years after I abandoned my not-so-charmed baseball cap, I began carrying a small New Testament/Psalms volume given to me by a local chapter of Gideons. I seldom read its words. I carried it not for its wisdom, but for the warm feeling, the sense of strength and protection it offered. I look back on this with a touch of embarrassment, but no particular guilt, for it was a harmless way of dealing with adolescent anxiety. Had I made this a lifelong practice, however, I would have turned a carrier of the sacred into a good-luck charm.

All efforts to take control of the fates have this in common: They ultimately reveal themselves as powerless. When churches lay this truth openly before their people, they provide more than an act of honesty. They also provide an act of kindness.

▲

Here, then, are major reasons why most congregations will find ways to move with minimal disruption from duplicity to honesty: Those in church pews are ready to reexamine their beliefs. In particular, they are ready to look at the Bible with fresh eyes; they are pushed by many forces to surrender their superstitions. In short, church members are much better prepared for honesty than their leaders assume.

◆

The Pastor's Role as Bridge

As indicated before, local pastors are the key to preventing further broadening of the gap between a popular and shallow faith on the one hand and an academic and arid faith on the other. The pastor is in a position to ease the pain of change by understanding both worlds and interpreting them to one another.

Developing a Bridge Vocabulary

Language is key. One of the essential elements needed to interpret the academy to the pew is a vocabulary that will help connect these two worlds.

Words have power beyond any formal meaning. Words carry emotional as well as intellectual baggage. Vocabulary is a major reason why instructors at institutions of higher learning have difficulty communicating with people who follow other lines of work—a split referred to as "town and gown." Those who spend their working hours immersed in the world of ideas come to speak a unique language. The language of a professor and the language of a neighbor who is an accountant may sound similar, but the meaning of certain words used by these two people can be light years apart.

Bridges can be constructed between the thought world of the seminary and that of the congregation only if a local pastor learns to hold these two in tension. Instead, most pastors avoid this issue by setting aside the knowledge they gained in their professional training. In most cases, they keep a few impressive textbooks on their library shelves as reminders of a past season of their lives. Although they might continue to find pleasure in thinking privately in the vocabulary of the scholar, they preach and lead worship in the vocabulary of their congregations. Two tragic things then happen: The congregation is denied the intellectual nourishment that might be mediated through the pastor's education, and the pastor pays at least an equal price, a price measured in a different coinage. As was pointed out in Chapter 3, pastors suffer a painful dissonance between what goes on in their heads and what they feel they can say in public.

Pastors who try to challenge their congregations with a richer vocabulary usually find that some words carried over from the academic setting are inadequate. Unless the congregation is given extensive preparation for specialized terms, the use of them will spread more alienation than understanding. Who wants, on a pleasant Sunday, to be confronted with a sermon sprinkled with terms such as *exegesis* (precise interpretation of a particular scriptural passage) or *theodicy* (the problem of evil in a world created by a good God)? Such concepts can and should be introduced. The terms themselves are, in most church settings, off-putting.

The word "myth" is a prime example of a term that has different meanings in various settings. For those who understand its original meaning, "myth" deals with a key element of biblical faith. Biblical stories of miraculous events are, in academic circles (including theological seminaries) described as "mythological." Unfortunately, "myth" has one meaning to those schooled in anthropology or theology and an entirely different meaning on Main Street. To those who think academically, "myth" refers to the deepest, most profound form of truth. One theologian remarked to his students, "Do not say a thing is *only* a myth; say, instead, it is nothing *less* than a myth." Sadly, however, this rich word has lost its power for all except those who relish the rarified intellectual atmosphere of a Joseph Campbell or a Paul Tillich. When the biblical creation stories, for example, are referred to from the pulpit as myths, the vast majority of lay persons will assume that those accounts have been dismissed as meaningless stories appropriate only for children.

I want to suggest another alternative. The second possibility is not a perfect solution but it carries us past the difficulties of other options. Pastors and Bible teachers can learn to refer to otherwise troublesome Bible events as *truth-stories*. A truth-story is a narrative told in order to convey meaning rather than fact. Its dramatic details attach its message to the lives of its hearers. Truth-stories often contain elements that their original audience would consider remarkable, even outlandish. The outlandish elements are signals that the message relates to more than a particular event; the message impacts life in its broadest sense. The narrative then acts as a vessel in which a truth deeper than its surface details can be carried.

The concept can be understood by visualizing the message of the truth-story as if it were a liquid held in a container. From that container it flows easily from situation to situation. Audiences in different times and situations can receive this truth because of its fluid form.

Truth-stories appear in many guises. For example, Thornton Wilder's popular drama *Our Town* powerfully confronts its audience with the preciousness of everyday human relationships. The play begins with scenes from a simple New England home. Then tragedy strikes. A mother dies in childbirth. The mother, Emily, not yet ready to surrender her earthly relationships, makes an arrangement with the heavenly authorities to return to her previous home. She is given one day to relive an intimate event she had originally taken for granted. In reliving that day (a birthday), she becomes aware of how much relational warmth had been missed, by all involved, on that important day. The details of planning a birthday celebration had overshadowed the human meanings of the day. "Why don't you ever *look* at one another?" Emily asks in a moment of pathetic frustration.

No one insists that the story line of *Our Town* is historically true, in the pallid and literal meaning of "truth." Instead, the drama *carries* truth—carries a truth that is more profound because it transcends and is separate from its container.

Jesus' parables are truth-stories. He told, for example, of a man who was traveling from Jerusalem to Jericho. Thieves set upon the man, beat him, and left him for dead. Two Jewish religious functionaries passed him by before he was rescued by a Samaritan—a member of an ethnic group most Jews had been taught to despise. Was this story *true*? That is, did it actually occur on a particular day in human history? Interestingly, this question is seldom asked, for it is quite irrelevant to the message the story conveys.

The story of the Good Samaritan is a clear example of the way Jesus constructed his parables. Each parable is carefully attached to the realities of life. The road from Jerusalem to Jericho was, in fact, a dangerous path. That a man might be set upon by robbers, beaten, and left for dead was quite within the realm of possibility; it was even a frequent occurrence. From this point on, the realism of the story diminishes. What a coincidence that the next two people to pass the wounded man on that busy road represented groups known more for righteous words than for compassionate deeds! Then came a Samaritan. Here the reader moves across a boundary from the coincidental to the unbelievable. The distrust, even hatred, between Jew and Samaritan was long-standing and deep. That a Samaritan, especially one riding a healthy animal and carrying coins in his purse, would be moving freely in this Jewish territory was unlikely in the extreme. The Samaritan then acts in idealized terms. His generosity knows no limit. By this point the sensitive reader is aware that the story is not built on surface facts. How droll it would be to ask if this event happened on a Wednesday or a Thursday. The story has to do with more important matters.

The truth that is held in this story is entirely fluid. In Gentile churches, it is assumed that the focus is on the Samaritan. The moral is assumed to be self-evident: We are called to offer aid to those who have experienced some reversal in life. The fact that the helper and the helped are of different ethnic backgrounds may be noted by non-Jewish readers, but it is usually acknowledged only in passing. "Good Samaritan Laws" refer to legal protection for those who give assistance in situations such as auto accidents. No ethnic implications are implied. From a Gentile point of view, this is a proper application of the story.

It is helpful, however, to try looking at this story through a different set of eyes. The original audience was Jewish. Jews would never have identified with the Samaritan; hostilities were too deep. They would have seen themselves in the role of the wounded victim. A new message arises: *People of God are called to set aside their ethnic pride in order to accept aid, regardless of the human channel used to deliver that aid.*

The parable of the Good Samaritan is a truth-story with amazingly broad implications. Its insights are adaptable. The short drama has validity in many settings.

Here, then, are the three characteristics of a truth-story: First, it is realistic enough to establish its relevance to common life; second, it is strange enough to signal that it is not to be taken literally; and third, it is fluid enough that its truth can be applied in a variety of settings.

Truth-stories are encountered on almost every page of scripture. The creation stories of Genesis are containers filled with religious (but not scientific) truths. The many miraculous healing stories of the Bible are most valuable when allowed to convey a message about the compassion of God, or to give added esteem to the individual performing the act of healing. The treasures in the birth and resurrection stories are magnified by seeing them as truth-stories.

One must assume that some truth-stories are based on actual events. The actual events, however, become secondary to the insights carried in the drama. Just as a skilled novelist takes genuine events and molds them into a narrative that immerses the reader in the depths of life, so biblical writers took real human events and adapted them to the larger task of conveying holy truths. Some special circumstances may have marked the beginning of Jesus' life. Certainly something happened at the end of that life to inspire the disciples to believe that he was a personal presence with them as they continued his mission. The precise nature of this something in each case has been lost in the ancient and often garbled records. Yet the *meaning* of these stories continues to guide the Christian church.

▲

The chances of a smooth transition to an honest faith greatly increase when pastors find a vocabulary that bridges the gap between the academic world and the world of the pew. Identifying many of the narratives of the Bible as truth-stories serves this purpose. It lifts the burden of having to believe literally in accounts that are often unbelievable; yet the term affirms the importance of these stories. Rather than attacking the faith of the believer, this new addition to a pastor's vocabulary can broaden and deepen that faith.

"Exegesis," "theodicy," "Biblical criticism," and similar terms should be left in the pastor's study. Honesty in the pulpit does not mean that the *vocabulary* of the academics must be utilized. Creative local pastors will find fresh words to communicate the *concepts* that these important, scholarly terms represent. These new words can then become the building materials with which a bridge is constructed between academia and the local church pew.

◆

Growth Is Possible: Expanding Congregations

My optimism begins with the belief that individuals are ready for growth. I am equally optimistic about the church as an institution. Honesty can help congregations expand. While explosive growth will not be the result of honesty, steady growth for progressive Christianity is highly likely.

To test this idea, I surveyed two groups of churches that have indicated that they practice full honesty with their congregations.

The first group is made up of congregations associated with the Center for Progressive Christianity (TCPC). TCPC is a loosely knit association of congregations that attempt to minister to persons who have not been satisfied with Christianity as it is commonly presented. No group of radicals, this group begins its eight identifying principles with a clear statement about the role of Jesus Christ. These eight principles are worth noting:

> By calling ourselves progressive, we mean that we are Christians who:
>
> 1. Have found an approach to God through the life and teachings of Jesus;
>
> 2. Recognize the faithfulness of other people who have other names for the way to God's realm, and acknowledge that their ways are true for them, as our ways are true for us;
>
> 3. Understand the sharing of bread and wine in Jesus' name to be a representation of an ancient vision of God's feast for all peoples;
>
> 4. Invite all people to participate in our community and worship life without insisting that they become like us in order to be acceptable (including but not limited to): believers and agnostics, conventional Christians and questioning skeptics, women and men, those of all sexual orientations and gender identities, those of all races and cultures, those of all classes and abilities, those who hope for a better world and those who have lost hope;
>
> 5. Know that the way we behave toward one another and toward other people is the fullest expression of what we believe;
>
> 6. Find more grace in the search for understanding than we do in dogmatic certainty—more value in questioning than in absolutes;

7. Form ourselves into communities dedicated to equipping one another for the work we feel called to do: striving for peace and justice among all people, protecting and restoring the integrity of all God's creation, and bringing hope to those Jesus called the least of his sisters and brothers; and

8. Recognize that being followers of Jesus is costly, and entails selfless love, conscientious resistance to evil, and renunciation of privilege.[2]

At the time of my survey, TCPC included sixty-eight congregations in twenty-two states and the District of Columbia. Two of these were non-denominational congregations, and two were ecumenical campus ministries. Mostly, they were small-to moderate-sized congregations.[3]

The majority of TCPC churches identified themselves as either Episcopal or United Church of Christ (with a smaller scattering of United Methodists and Presbyterians). Both these denominations, in the last year in which figures were available, lost 1 percent of their national memberships. Together, the fifteen congregations of the United Church of Christ that are also members of TCPC neither gained nor lost members in the year previous to the survey. More than thirty Episcopal congregations had, at the time of the survey, affiliated themselves with TCPC. In contrast to the denomination's losses on the national level, the Episcopal churches in my survey reported far more gains than losses. One reported a tripling of membership since publicly affiliating with TCPC.

Membership changes for TCPC churches of other denominations were positive, but the number of congregations was not large enough to be statistically significant.

So in these two major denominations whose national bodies are in decline, I found that several congregations—congregations who are willing to announce openly that they are more interested in the journey toward truth than in the embrace of a static, absolute truth—are *not* in decline. As a whole, they evidence significant growth.

The second group I surveyed is made up of congregations that have played host to a series of lectures known as "Jesus Seminars on the Road." The Jesus Seminar itself is a group we will meet again in the final chapter. Here it is sufficient to indicate that it is a highly provocative group of New Testament scholars who meet regularly in an effort to learn more about the historical Jesus. They are committed to making their findings known as widely as possible. They make themselves available to congregations that will host them for a weekend of lectures on the subjects they are currently exploring.

My survey was done early in the life of the Jesus Seminars on the Road program. Only six congregations that had taken part responded to the survey requests. These six congregations are located in four states and the District of Columbia. They are affiliated with four denominations, three of which are national bodies currently suffering membership declines. These six congregations, however, have enjoyed, over the past decade, a combined membership increase of 16 percent.

Much more impressive than these limited membership figures are the testimonials of clergy and laity in churches of the two groups surveyed. One recently retired pastor reported:

> I have been teaching redaction-critical studies for years and use that approach consistently. My classes are very popular and bring in people from other congregations to attend.

Another pastor speaks for a church that is determined not to be caught up in marketing techniques:

> We have only been a member of the Center for Progressive Christianity for six months, however we have been a "progressive" church since our inception over twenty years ago. We are more likely to measure our success in the size of the good works our members do rather than our size in

members. Overall, our membership has been stable over the past year, and five years. We are near the maximum size our building can handle, and have a great reluctance to divert our funds from our charitable good works to facilities. Consequently, we are not aggressively recruiting. For example, our web site does not feature our address. Being a progressive church is our identity. Most of our members left other churches looking for a church that would be more supportive of progressive endeavors.

A pastor of a Pittsburgh congregation of a highly structured denomination wrote this:

Our progressive stance was welcome in a very conservative diocese that continually fought doctrinal battles. We were large enough to be able to ignore all but the worst of it. Frequently my vestry would write open letters to the bishop that would be circulated all over the place. This brought a lot of people out of the woodwork who were sick and tired of the fundamentalism and literalism of many of the other parishes.

Essentially, what we tried to do was to preach the Gospel, not try to inculcate dogma. The Kingdom of God was the theme of the place with all that it includes: forgiveness, reconciliation, healing, peace, inclusion and joy. It made for a lively and active congregation that was intimately involved in alleviating whatever misery that we could see in our community. I think this is the work of the church, not beating people over the head with nuances of doctrine.

Not all responses were so positive. One pastor reported a recent church split, a conflict to which their progressive stance contributed. She added, however: "Now we are confident; the new visitors all embrace this [progressive stance] enthusiastically."

A few respondents reported membership growth of a size that a fervent evangelical might envy. An Episcopal priest from

California reported that his progressive church had tripled in membership over the past five years. He added:

> We have welcomed many previously unchurched people, had a good number of adult baptisms, and also welcomed people who identify themselves as returning and recovering Christians who want to make a new relationship with our tradition, with the church, and (in some instances) with Jesus, but have had to come to terms with hurtful experiences they had in other, more restrictive and judgmental expressions of Christian faith.

The same priest explained the rationale of the former church dropouts who have come to them: .

> Members report that intellectual honesty, willingness to hear and discuss moral ambiguity, a nonjudgmental and welcoming stance toward gay couples and gay and straight single people deepen their experience of the work of God. We have a sizable number of families with children who say that this is the kind of religious and Christian environment they want their children to experience.

Another Episcopalian, this one from Ohio, gives an equally enthusiastic witness:

> St. Mark's Episcopal Church has seen significant growth over the past five years. A decade ago this inner city congregation was recovering from eight years of conflict with the previous rector with only 40-50 elderly faithful in the pews on a Sunday morning. Today we are a beacon in the Toledo area and the Diocese of Ohio. Average Sunday attendance is 150-180 people and growing quickly. . . . [I]n 1998 our pledge base jumped by over 25%.

Persons with a strong sociological bent may be inclined to dismiss the responses to these two small surveys as anecdotal. A larger and more carefully constructed study is needed to establish just how honesty between pulpit and pew affects church membership growth. The data related here, however, are enough to cast doubt on the common assumption that full disclosure of biblical and doctrinal information will cause memberships to drop.

From my surveys I conclude that at least this much can be said: In a variety of situations, representing churches of many sizes and situated in a variety of regions across the United States, honesty has resulted in membership growth. Until someone does a wider study that proves these churches (more than seventy in number) to be an anomaly, I will hold to the conclusion that honesty can contribute positively to the health of the institutional church.

◆

Summary

Here, then are some basic realities: Honesty about the human context of scripture and creeds encourages personal growth that is painful in the short term and freeing in the long term. Dishonesty about these matters tends to block individual growth. Worse yet, dishonesty reinforces people in early stages of cognitive and faith development. In contrast, presentation of a faith freed from superstition can stimulate development in individuals; it can also nourish moderate and sometimes impressive growth in religious institutions, reversing the alarming decline that mainline churches have experienced in the past decades.

As shown in Chapter 3, it is clear that the number of people who are prepared to seek an open faith is increasing. This fact should be a major source of hope for all mainline Protestant congregations. We have come, in other words, to that pleasant point where the pull of the ideal of honesty is joined by the push of sociological trends. It is an opportunity to be seized.

Calling this a painless process is obviously an unrealistic dream. The symbol of the cross confronts us with its wisdom:

Some encounter with pain, some willingness to move through pain, is essential if the journey is to take us toward new life.

NOTES

1. Hoge, Luidens, and Benton, *Vanishing Boundaries.*
2. Quoted from the Center for Progressive Christianity web site, www.tcpc.org.
3. In the relatively short time between my survey and the submission of this manuscript, TCPC expanded to 186 congregations located in eight countries.

7

Jesus: Answer Man or Puzzle Maker?

"Jesus Is the Answer," bumper stickers proclaim, without, sadly, indicating the nature of the question. Precise assumptions lie behind that imprecise slogan: "Whatever the nature of your deepest questions, you will find a clear answer in the way Jesus lived and in what he taught. Your strongest felt needs will find their satisfaction in a relationship with the living Christ." The person who designed that bumper sticker had been listening to what is said in modern churches. That person had not been reading what is said in scripture.

The bumper sticker measures the perfidy of modern Christianity. Religious professionals speak to their congregations as if Jesus had, indeed, offered easy answers to each person's individual questions. The church makes no objection when people want to believe that Jesus was mostly about *me*, *my* wants and *my* fears, especially *my* fears of death. Acquiring a ticket to a life of bliss beyond this life seems, in many liturgies, to be the sole reason for loyalty to Jesus. All this is presented as if it were grounded in scripture.

Contrary to all this, a serious reading of the New Testament reveals that Jesus never intended to be an answer man. Instead of making human problems go away, he seemed intent on creating a new set of concerns. Through both words and example he defined the requirements of discipleship: acts of compassion, especially acts aimed at those the remainder of society had rejected; acts that upset the conventions of unjust societies; sacrificial living, even to the point of joining him in crucifixion. Attempts to meet those requirements greatly complicate life. Questions, not answers, multiply.

◆

A Divided Faith

Jesus, who has acquired the title of "Christ," is the heart of the Christian faith. Calling oneself Christian acknowledges something definitive in the life of an itinerant peasant of Nazareth.

Yet no other part of the faith exposes so clearly the gap between the faith of religious professionals and that of the laity. What is taught in the academy describes a figure that would be hardly recognizable by those who attend weekly worship in the average Protestant sanctuary. Seminary students learn about the Jesus of the academics. They return to preach a Jesus who is familiar to the masses. Dishonesty abounds.

By preaching a popularized Jesus, pastors open themselves and their congregations to a major problem. Doctrines of Jesus seem to offer the greatest temptation to those who want to transform religion into superstition.

Popular religion often depicts Jesus as if he were a good-luck charm. He is the defender of each believer, the one who carries prayers and concerns to God. Jesus is seen as a protector, one who keeps bad things from happening to good people. The Jesus of popular religion was a divine intervention in history, unaffected by the social, economic, or political realities of his time.

On the other hand, those who have studied the biblical records in depth tend to arrive at a very different understanding of Jesus. The contrasts are severe:

- The popularized Jesus protects the person of faith from life's overwhelming problems; the biblical Jesus leads the follower into conflict with the powers and principalities, a conflict that can lead to suffering or even to death.
- The popularized Jesus promises a blissful, eternal existence beyond the grave; the biblical Jesus focuses on the current world, encouraging a quality of present living that is worth preserving into an infinite future.
- The popularized Jesus lifts the burden of our guilt from us, paying with his blood the price for our sins demanded by God (or by Satan, or by both); the biblical Jesus adds to our burdens, insisting that people of faith carry crosses of their own.
- The popularized Jesus insists that people worship him; the biblical Jesus asks that people follow him.[1]
- The popularized Jesus gives simple and inflexible answers to each of life's perplexing problems; the biblical Jesus gives often cryptic teachings that modern followers must struggle to interpret for their own time and place.
- The popularized Jesus is based almost entirely on the resurrected Christ, a spiritual presence that transcends time and place to become a protective, comforting companion for every age; the biblical Jesus was bound by time and place, a historic person who lived amid the complexities of daily life.

Popularized Christianity is, then, egocentric to the core. While it includes enough authentic references to the actual life and teachings of Jesus to make it seem real, it also contains large portions of superstition. Jesus, in this view, is an adult equivalent of the child's invisible friend. One of popular Christianity's most frequently used hymns states:

> What a friend we have in Jesus,
> All our sins and griefs to bear . . .[2]

The alternate view also stresses the presence of an eternal Christ, available to inspire us and put us in touch with our spiritual strengths. The resurrected Jesus promised that he would continue with his disciples, much as a dying mother promises to be a continuing influence in the lives of her children. This promise was given in answer to the problem of how to continue Jesus' mission.

The living Jesus, then, will not hold our hand through life's inevitable and often petty problems. Instead, the spirit of Jesus will inspire us to find the strength necessary to encounter the excruciating pain that accompanies a life of absolute faithfulness. A hymn popular among progressive Christians states:

> Grant us wisdom, grant us courage,
> For the living of these days . . .[3]

The Role of Dogma

Any church that makes Jesus the subject of dogma is skating on the edge of dishonesty. Jesus, as presented in the scripture, was a man of action, not a weaver of dogmatic patterns. He practiced a radical openness, thereby destroying walls that had separated people. He gathered his closest friends from the edges of the social world. He showed respect for prostitutes. He counseled compassionate treatment for occupying soldiers and even accepted at his table the hated tax collectors. Yet the popular church that was formed around Jesus has used its savior figure to build barriers between people. It has done this by stressing doctrine over discipleship.

Centuries after Jesus' time, the church would produce a series of dogmas and creeds that, like modern-day sound bites, would attempt to make Jesus intelligible to those who were poorly equipped for intellectual digging. Popularization of the faith might be justified in that setting. Lacking the recording equipment that makes sound bites possible, the developing church achieved the same effect by visual glimpses. A glance at an icon, a stained glass window, or a statue would teach an easily absorbed lesson, or reinforce a dogma. This approach was excusable, perhaps even helpful, when the majority of Christians were illiterate and accustomed to being told what to think.

Simplification has always been a path to popularity. Chaos-intolerant people exist in large numbers, and they inevitably will have their day. Nonetheless, simplification is a violation of both the essence and spirit of Jesus' remarkable life.

Popularization through dogma has had the tragic result of robbing Jesus of his humanity. Jesus is fully God and fully man, the dogma insists. The human side of that equation sounds mundane. The divine part is startling and thus grabs more attention. It is also the most difficult part of the dogma to believe. Thus liturgies stress, Sunday after Sunday, this part of the doctrine. The result has been to turn the biblical challenge on its head. Instead of following a Jesus who was thoroughly immersed in a human setting, as scripture invites us to do, we find ourselves worshiping a purely divine Christ from whom all evidence of humanity has been extracted. Embracing his style of life becomes a non-option. "I cannot live the way he lived. He was a god!" Such is the sad result of oversimplification in the effort to attract adherents.

In professional circles, the same short dogma has a different impact. The term "simplification" is, in that setting, both untrue and unfair. Though "Jesus was fully God and fully man" makes an effective sound bite, and can be heard at a simple, surface level, a person who listens a second time can no longer label this dogma as simple. Indeed, theologians of every age have written book upon book trying to interpret it. Perhaps the effort to clarify this concept requires great exertion because, at the end of the day, it is impossible to explain. Some aspects of divinity and some aspects of humanity are mutually exclusive. For example, divine foreknowledge would make it impossible for Jesus to experience normal human emotions. If a divine Jesus had known that Lazarus would be resurrected, his tears at the death of this friend were a sham (John 11:17-44).

Church dogma, then, tends to widen the gap between the religion of the masses and the religion of the academy. It becomes an unintended example of a worst possible scenario. For those (usually nonprofessionals) who seek simple answers, dogma can be a quickly memorized nugget that answers surface questions while making no demands on the believer. On the other hand, those (usually professionals) who are the self-appointed keepers of the deeper meanings of such dogma find themselves with ideas that are complicated to a fault. Neither in its simplicity nor its complexity can dogma bring together the religious professional and the religious laity.

It is clear from reading the Gospel stories that Jesus never thought of himself in dogmatic terms. The church moved far from its roots when it argued, at Nicea, over whether Jesus was of a similar essence, or the same essence, as God. (This was the famous debate in which a single Greek letter [an iota] added to a particular word made a difference between orthodoxy and heresy.) Jesus refused to give clear answers when asked about his role. He never requested "Worship me." His challenge was "Follow me."

The first Christian creed was not a dogmatic statement but a political statement. "Jesus is Lord" was affirmed by early followers who were commanded by Roman authorities to perform acts of worship to Caesar. By their simple three-word creed, members of the young church asserted that their lives would be guided by the example of Jesus, not by the dictates of a Roman tyrant. No cosmological implications were intended.

Building Walls

Dogmatic beliefs came into being largely for the purpose of establishing the Christian church as separate from the Jewish community. Indicating that Jesus was God incarnate was a sure way of distinguishing followers of Jesus from those traditional Jews who were scandalized by the idea that God would take on human flesh. From its beginning, Christian dogma was designed to erect walls.

As soon as the separation between Christianity and Judaism was an established fact, Christians began using dogma to build new walls—this time between themselves. Political intrigue and bloodshed followed in the wake of dogmatic debate.

In the modern age, theological debate usually takes place in a more tranquil manner. Yet, the presence of more than 350 separate groups of Christians in the United States alone, each claiming to have the only precisely correct belief system, is evidence that the power of dogma to divide is undiminished.

The divisive power of dogma should be amazing to anyone who carefully reads the Gospel stories. Those stories affirm, time after time, Jesus' reckless inclusiveness. Today, tragically, he has become the excuse for one of the most extensive systems of human division the world has known.

◆

Creator of Puzzles

A dishonest church has distorted Jesus to make him appealing to those who are chaos-intolerant. This first-century Jew has become part of a worldview in which a clear solution awaits the asking of any precise question, and messy problems are dismissed as nothing more than the concerns of people with messy minds. The Gospel stories present Jesus in an opposite way.

Instead of being an answer man, Jesus seemed determined to be a creator of puzzles. When someone asked him a straightforward question about the identity of one's neighbor, Jesus responded not with a clear definition but with a story (Luke 10:29-38). Those who heard and understood that story were given a truth they had not sought: We are socially interconnected, even with those we enjoy despising. Yet, as was explained in the previous chapter, the precise nature of one's neighbor was left a bit vague. At another time, Jesus seemed to indicate that his stories were told to confound rather than clarify (Matthew 13:13).

An honest church will shift its emphasis from Jesus the answer man to Jesus who invites his followers into a journey of discovery. Those who are chaos-intolerant will find this change distressing; the chaos-tolerant will find the invitation appealing.

What Is Unknown: Jesus Himself

The puzzles begin with Jesus himself. Honesty should cause the church to acknowledge the limits of its knowledge about this man who stands at the headwaters of its faith. Four canonical (accepted as biblical) records of his life and teachings exist. A fifth account, the Gospel of Thomas, is assumed by many scholars to be among the oldest records. It tells primarily of Jesus' teachings and contains no account of his birth or resurrection. Other records of a similar sort continue to be found. Most of these early accounts are consistent about many aspects of Jesus' life and teachings. In a number of other ways, the records differ significantly.

In a book referred to earlier, *The Meaning of Jesus*,[4] N. T. Wright, the more conservative of its two writers, makes this simple comment: "The available sources do not offer a coherent picture." Here, from a scholar who is considered a conservator of the faith, is all one needs to move from duplicity to honesty. The sources are inconsistent. Wright has substituted a question mark for the exclamation point that one hears from most pulpits. His comment shows how easily one may be honest without abandoning the beliefs of generations of forebears.

As a youth I was taught one way to deal with the Gospels' inconsistencies. The educational materials of a major denomination told me that the four biblical writers were simply giving different views of the same person. A popular illustration compared the four Gospel writers with four blind persons describing an elephant: One had touched a trunk, one had encountered a leg, another the tail, and yet another felt the enormous torso. They each offered a different description of the same reality.

I found this explanation unsatisfying. I wanted to object that the Gospel writers were not blind, and that Jesus was not an elephant. The differences in the Gospel accounts were more than views from different angles. It was clear to me that some of the facts in one Gospel contradict facts in the other Gospels. Was Jesus a person who made elaborate claims for himself, as recorded in John, or should we accept the more reticent Jesus of the first three Gospels? Did he go to Jerusalem to cleanse the temple at the beginning of his public ministry, as one writer claimed, or did this event take place at the end of his life, as in the other three accounts? Why should two writers tell of a miraculous birth (with quite different details), and two ignore altogether the manner of his birth? Clearly, the records were in conflict.

Later, in college and seminary, I would learn reasons for inconsistencies in the Gospel records. I was shown evidence that each of the four Gospel writers had a particular reason for writing, and that those reasons affected the way the story of Jesus was told. Additionally, I was taught how the young church wove its concerns in and around the actual teachings of Jesus. Or, to put all that another way, the Gospel stories are in part a history of Jesus and in part a mirror held up to the conflicting concerns of those who told that story.

The upshot is this: A reader of the four Gospels sometimes encounters the authentic words of Jesus, while at other times the encounter is with the struggles of the early church, presented as if they were the words of Jesus. This reality, one that will seem radical to many who occupy church pews, is common knowledge among religious professionals. Yet these professionals continue to teach and preach as if every word attributed to Jesus in the New Testament were verifiably his.

How, then, is the lay person to know the difference between the teachings of Jesus and the insertions of the early church?

This is a difficult question, complicated by the fact that even the scholars disagree on an answer.

Perplexing as that issue can be, it has a silver lining. It shifts the religious endeavor from memorization of dogma to exploration of mystery. Pursuing that question can be stimulating. It can be a path to growth.

Searching for the Authentic Jesus

At several points in relatively recent Christian history, scholars have attempted to determine the nature of the *real* historical Jesus. The challenge is daunting. Records are both ancient and contradictory. Gospel writers, as already noted, approached their tasks with their own, often contrasting, agendas. The highly complicated social setting of Jesus' day contributed to the confusion.

As they have pursued an understanding of Jesus, even the best of scholars have found it difficult to rid themselves of their biases. They have searched the ancient texts looking for Jesus and found, to no one's surprise, what they wanted to find. Scholars who took a dim view of human society researched the subject and announced that Jesus was primarily concerned about preparing his followers for a life beyond this life. Other scholars worked with the assumption that it is possible to improve life on this earth. They found that Jesus was primarily a social reformer. As one wise individual put the matter, searching for the historical Jesus was like looking into a deep well; what looked back from the bottom of the well was not the image of Jesus but the reflection of the researcher.

Despite all the problems, the task of understanding the historic Jesus is too important to abandon. Recently, a group known as the Jesus Seminar, mostly instructors of the New Testament on American college campuses, has attacked the subject. Their method was to look at each individual biblical statement attributed to Jesus and to ask which of these comments can safely be defended as coming from Jesus. They aimed to winnow out the statements reflecting the hidden agendas of the Gospel writers. They hoped that out of the list of authentic statements of Jesus would come a clearer, less biased, picture of who he truly was.

The first task for this group was to develop guidelines for determining which of Jesus' biblical sayings could be attributed to him. When, for example, a saying was found in several sources (more than one canonical Gospel, the Gospel of Thomas, or an early writing called the Q document), it was given a higher level of trustworthiness than sayings that appear in only one source. When a saying clearly related to the power realities of the young church, as in the case of Peter being given the keys to the kingdom (Matthew 16:19), it was assigned a lower level of probability. Platitudes common to Jesus' day were likely to be downgraded. But comments that cut across the grain of the conventional wisdom of first century Judea were assumed to be authentic. Why else would they be included? Each scholar, having examined a statement in light of the guidelines, voted on each biblical saying of Jesus, using a scale of authenticity from highly likely to highly unlikely. In this procedure, the negative votes have dominated. More sayings of Jesus have been put under a cloud of suspicion than have been embraced as authentic.

As could have been predicted, the work of the Jesus Seminar has met strong resistance. Church professionals have been loudest in their complaints. When one listens carefully to their objections, it becomes clear that mostly they are not disagreeing with the particular findings of the Jesus Seminar. They are complaining that secrets meant to be shared only among the professional elite are being offered to the general population.

Members of the Jesus Seminar have compounded the hostility by publishing their findings in readily accessible volumes. When invited, they have taken the results of their research into local churches for weekend seminars.

Defenders of the work of the Jesus Seminar have perceived the motivation of the group quite differently from its critics.

They note that these Bible scholars are not the first to raise questions about which teachings of Jesus could be accepted as authentic. The first organized movement to raise such questions was a group of German scholars who, more than two centuries ago, submitted the Bible to the same methods of critique that they applied to other works of literature. They concluded that the Gospel stories were a blending of many voices, and the teachings of these stories reflected a variety of motivations. The most radical of those scholars found themselves wondering if there had been anyone like Jesus at all, or whether any of the sayings in the Bible were genuinely his. In particular, the wide-ranging mind of Albert Schweitzer examined the evidence and the work of scholars who preceded him, and concluded that precise knowledge of the historical Jesus was impossible to acquire. We can confront him, but not fully understand him, Schweitzer concluded, and made that thought memorable in the closing words of his *Quest of the Historical Jesus:* "He comes to us as one unknown . . . ".[5]

Thus the work of the Jesus Seminar, according to its defenders, was an effort to rescue the historical Jesus, not to destroy him. From their studies has emerged a consistent, though hardly complete, picture—a picture of a remarkable man who existed in a particular social setting. He had an identifiable set of concerns and a unique style of teaching. A person named Jesus did exist, they have concluded. His profile can be established. Against this profile, each of his reported statements can be measured. The result is affirmation, not negation.

Few people agree with every detail of the methods or the results of the Jesus Seminar. The members of the Seminar have many disagreements among themselves. That is why they vote. Their purpose is not to achieve final, unassailable answers but to open a dialogue, and to lay out ground rules for a search that has crucial implications. They intend to include as many people as possible in the search, thus overcoming the division between knowledge-levels of lay and clergy. In short, the appeal of the Jesus Seminar is to those whose cognitive development allows them to deal easily with ambiguity and to move comfortably among the many question marks that reside within the Gospel stories.

What Is Unknown:
The Meaning of Jesus' Teachings

The teachings of Jesus are often as much a puzzle as the details of his life. His followers are required to follow a poorly marked path through a thicket of obscurities. Surprisingly, however, this difficult route can be enormously stimulating. The journey can become its own excuse for being.

As was noted earlier, fixed systems of belief are barriers separating people. Questions, by contrast, are inviting. Once a stimulating question has been posed, people from all starting points are welcome to join in the search for answers.

Each year the American President and his staff sponsor an Easter egg hunt on the White House lawn. Children from all over the heterogeneous capital city participate: Rich and poor rub elbows, an amazing number of ethnic groups appear; the bright and the dull are together. When the search for eggs begins, all such potential barriers are set aside. The thrill of the search transcends every human division.

By emphasizing questions rather than answers, puzzles rather than solutions, Jesus demonstrated a unique approach to religion. His was an inclusive style. He offered enticing hints at truths not fully formed, and by that opened the religious search to all. It was not by accident that his followers, after his death, would find ways to set aside the ethnic barriers of Jesus' ancestral faith and invite the entire world into this vital tradition.

Without doubt, the disciples found Jesus' teachings, especially his parables, to be difficult intellectual hills to climb. Both Mark and Matthew attempted to put the blame for this on Jesus, indicating that Jesus had intended to share inside information with the disciples, information that the general population could not grasp. "To you has been given to know the secrets of the kingdom of heaven, but to them it has not been given." This strange statement is then amplified: "The reason I speak to them in parables is that seeing they do not perceive, and hearing they do not listen, nor do they understand" (Mark 4:11-12, and Matthew 13:11-13). The Fellows of the Jesus Seminar quickly concluded that these are unlikely to be authentic words of Jesus, because this effort to distinguish between an inside group and an outside group is entirely foreign to the inclusive mission of Jesus.[6] Nonetheless, the inclusion of this passage in the Gospels shows conclusively that Jesus' teachings were never easy and that his ideas were not quickly grasped, even by his closest friends.

Walter Wink offers a similar explanation for Jesus' refusal to give clear teachings. If he had allowed himself to become the answer man, Jesus would have denied his followers the opportunity to discover the answers that lie in their own God-given wisdom. In other words, had Jesus monopolized the role of Messiah, others could never find the messianic roles to which they might be called.

> Jesus *could not* tell others he was the Messiah. For if he told them, they would not have to discover the Messiah within themselves. And if they did not discover the Messiah within themselves, they would not learn that they had such powers of discovery within themselves. And if Jesus did not enable them to discover such powers within themselves, he was not the Messiah.[6]

If Wink is correct, and I am convinced his insights must be taken with utmost seriousness, then Jesus spun out puzzles rather than set answers because of his profound respect for his followers. The modern church should take note.

Jesus seemed to have shown no hesitation in admitting that his own knowledge was limited. Both Matthew and Mark record an encounter in which Jesus was asked about the events that will precede the fulfillment of time. "But about that day and hour no one knows, neither the angels of heaven, nor the Son, but only the Father" (Matthew 24:36, and Mark 13:32).

Since Jesus' comments have been frequently misunderstood from the beginning, applying his thoughts or duplicating his actions on the modern scene requires both insight and creativity.

Jesus often taught by example. But his actions also left questions in their wake. The accusations made against him have become a measure of the degree to which those who knew him best misunderstood him. "He eats with tax collectors and sinners" (Luke 15:2). In almost every known society, sharing a meal is a sign of equality and social acceptance. Jesus apparently insisted on accepting persons who others considered unacceptable. He used his table as a symbol of a new way of putting communities together. In Jesus' new society, walls that once separated people are symbolically broken in the literal breaking of bread. Jesus' contemporaries were scandalized by his eating habits and clueless about the implications of his actions for their lives.

Another accusation against him recorded by the Gospel writers was that he violated the Sabbath by his healing work. Jesus demonstrated consistent respect for the rules of his tradition. Yet, in a vivid truth-story that reveals how his earliest followers perceived him, he demonstrated that restoring a withered human hand was of an even greater value than ancient rules (Mark 3:1-6, Matthew 12:9-14, Luke 6:6-11). Rules could be bent or broken when compassion made such actions necessary. Thus he left us not with a self-enforcing set of inflexible laws but with a question that must be asked again and again in each new set of circumstances: When is it acceptable to observe the spirit of a law by breaking that law?

The Role of Parables

People looking for easy answers will be especially affronted by Jesus' parables. No simple fables, these. They are, as Bernard

Brandon Scott has insisted,[8] a new way to imagine our world. If their meaning were self-evident, interpreting them would be easy and all interpreters would agree. Yet we know that interpretations vary widely. Parables, then, are much like impressionist paintings. The eye of the viewer is called on to supply a significant amount of detail. Viewer and artist become partners in the creation of a finished work.

Parables make demands on those who hear them. Parables are not allegories (even though Gospel writers, in editing their material, sometimes treated them as if they were). The various actors in the stories are not fixed symbols, but are doors through which a hearer can enter the story. The door one chooses determines what the parable means.

Two of the most popular of Jesus' teaching stories demonstrate the variety of ways these stories can be interpreted. In Chapter 6, I noted how the parable of the Good Samaritan (Luke 10:30-35) may be appropriated differently by Jewish and Gentile audiences.

The parable of the Prodigal Son (Luke 15:11-32) is another tale that allows many applications. The name by which the story is known indicates the degree to which personal guilt influences our efforts at interpretation. People assume the story is focused on the younger son, his misdeeds and ultimate redemption. This is one valid way to see the narrative.

Others might want to rename this "The Story of the Forgiving Father." In that case, we experience the tale as a call to be more forgiving of the tragic mistakes made by those closest to us—even the mistakes that are costly to us.

Yet a third option in this family drama is to enter it through the role of the elder son. People who see themselves as morally upright should be pierced by the final verses of this story. The older son's moral rigidity leaves him pouting outside the family home while his young sibling, who has acknowledged his guilt and received forgiveness, celebrates inside. It is reasonable to assume that many, perhaps most, people of modern Western society have more reason to identify with the older son than with the younger. Again, the meaning is fluid, not self-evident.

Others of Jesus' parables are even more cryptic. Was Jesus, for example, attacking the patriarchy of his time by making a woman the God-figure who searches for a lost coin (Luke 15:8-9)? Was he tearing to shreds other social conventions when he suggested that people from off the street—a group that would have included both rich and poor, ritually clean and unclean, male and female, lame and able—could enter the king's chambers and share in a feast to which a more exclusive group once had been invited (Luke 14:16-24)?

Richard Watts and Dominic Crossan said it well:

> A parable empowers rather than dominates an audience. It challenges them to think and judge for themselves. It is the most appropriate teaching technique for a Kingdom of God in which God empowers rather than dominates, challenges rather than controls.[9]

The teachings of Jesus are thus most accessible to those who are willing to search for elusive truths. Jesus did not give his followers a single vision of reality for all time—a one-size-fits-all approach to ethical living. Instead, his impressionistic canvas is offered so that people in each new setting can complete the painting in a style appropriate to their own circumstances.

◆

Where Knowledge Is Clearer

None of this is intended to imply that the New Testament is devoid of clear statements about human problems. Many people have found life-transforming answers in the teachings and actions of Jesus. Rare and happy moments occur when something Jesus said, or some activity of his, fits precisely with a person's modern concern.

Centered on This Present Life

On one issue there is increasing agreement among those who treasure and study the New Testament: Jesus' teachings focused on this world. He spoke time after time about the Kingdom of God. The phrase suggests the way human life would be organized if God, not Caesar, were in charge.[10]

The church has been especially dishonest on the subject of Jesus' focus on the present life. An uninformed visitor to most mainline worship services would be convinced that Jesus was concerned primarily about life after death. Such a visitor could easily conclude that the current life is only an obstacle course on the way to a blissful existence beyond the grave.

Jesus' actual teachings were very focused on the circumstances of the present moment. The prayer most closely associated with his teachings asked that God's will be done *on earth*. According to Luke, Jesus introduced himself to his hometown acquaintances by appropriating for himself Isaiah's concept of liberator and healer (Luke 4:16-19). His parables had the common theme of imagining a new, inclusive, just way of ordering our current lives.

Jesus, then, chose the most difficult of all possibilities for enlisting followers: a this-world-centered, this-moment-oriented, brick-by-brick construction of a new community. He seemed to know that his approach had a slim chance of success. People, then as now, were turned inward. He could quickly have won a large following by appealing to the narrow focus of their felt needs. He could have seized their attention by describing in detail a paradise that awaited them beyond the grave. Instead, he set out on the infinitely more difficult road of transforming the energy of their selfishness into concern for their neighbors. He was determined to challenge people to grow, rather than reinforce them in the tiny packages that result when individuals are wrapped up in themselves.

The modern church that makes the afterlife the near exclusive focus of religious attention is violating the most elementary of Jesus' commitments. Rather than expanding the horizons of people, it reinforces inwardness. Instead of challenging people to live as if God were in charge *right now,* the church offers its people an inexpensive ticket to the rule of God in an undefined afterlife. Instead of encouraging a broadened concern, the modern church allows people to remain in their consumer-oriented state: "What's in this for me?"

Other Clear Teachings

On particular issues, Jesus' ethical stance was clear but its application open to interpretation. His forgiving attitude toward a woman guilty of adultery (John 8:3-11),[11] for example, might be, in some circumstances, healing for a couple attempting to repair their marriage after acts of unfaithfulness. Even here, however, forcing this forgiveness on lives precariously held together by the frayed cords of yesterday's love is a risky procedure. The modern danger is that one member of a bruised relationship could use the story to try to extract a forgiveness that the other partner is not ready to offer.

The story of the woman taken in adultery is a good example of a New Testament narrative that seems clear on first glance, and then becomes more complex as it is reread. The real subject of this account is not sexual ethics but moral rigidity. Jesus thoroughly embarrassed those whose self-righteousness made them too quick to condemn others. Even moments of supposed New Testament clarity need to be approached with due care.

At certain points in the New Testament, the reader might wish Jesus' teachings were less clear. The challenge of some of the teaching attributed to Jesus is jarring. The 25th chapter of Matthew, for example, is quite specific about the overt requirements of discipleship. The follower of Jesus is to give attention to the needs of the prisoner, the homeless, the naked, the hungry.

Many students of the Bible, including the Fellows of the Jesus Seminar, dismiss the 25th chapter of Matthew as an addition to the Gospel record made by the young church. This is because of the passage's emphasis on an ultimate judgment and the introduction of the "son of Adam" or a king as the judge. Yet, even here, embedded as a truth-story within a larger story, a deeper insight can be found, one that brings us into intimate contact with the here-and-now message of Jesus.

In addition to the stern, overt calls to action found in the 25th chapter of Matthew, the shadow of a covert requirement can be detected. Disciples are to be concerned about their neighbors with *no thought for their own spiritual rewards.* In the passage, those who were welcomed into God's kingdom because of their unselfishness were surprised to be commended. Ruled out, then, is the calculating goodness (what might be labeled "selfish unselfishness") of those who compute that a certain number of hours of volunteer effort at the homeless shelter will bring them closer to eternal bliss. In Jesus' refreshing worldview (or Matthew's truth-story, whichever correctly describes these verses), time spent at the homeless shelter is commendable only when it is a loving response to the needs of one's neighbor. Fear of the fires of hell is not an acceptable motivation.

Thus, the clear ethical guidelines in the 25th chapter of Matthew are aimed at a query few Christians have the courage to pose: What *kind* of person does the New Testament call into discipleship? We fear to ask because the answer is overwhelming in its implications. Authentic followers of Jesus are persons whose center of concern is outside themselves, people who are willing to imitate Jesus' own style of living. Jesus was, we recall, the person whom Bishop John A. T. Robinson called "the Man for Others." Those of us who struggle constantly against the gravitational pull of self-centeredness find this call dizzying in its breadth. The attempt to respond to that challenge constantly prods us toward change and growth.

▲

People who find the most guidance in New Testament stories, chaos-tolerant people mostly, encounter in Jesus a person who wrestled with expressions of the world's primordial chaos— illness, death, enslavement, abject poverty. They know that the attempt to apply easy answers to such a difficult world will only expand the disorder. Thus these people have learned to look for helpful but not absolute answers. Whatever solutions they have found have not jumped off New Testament pages; they have been unearthed after much laborious mining. The answers they discover are not clear; they are not neat. They are not fixed for all time.

The honest church will present to its congregations the Jesus who invites followers on a search, not the Jesus who is the answer to unspecified questions. Why? Because this is the Jesus offered to readers of the Gospel stories.

◆

The Gospel of John: The Mystery Deepens

Chaos-intolerant individuals, those who want understandable and precise answers, might be forced to agree that the first three biblical accounts of Jesus' life, with their contradictory details and their open-ended parables, are not fertile grounds for their mindset. They might want to shift with more hope to the Gospel of John. John described Jesus as a lecturer more than a storyteller. By the time the Gospel of John was completed, the church had transformed the Resurrection from truth-story into dogma, from mystery into historical fact. John presents the pre-Easter Jesus as if he had already become the resurrected Christ, a divine being wrapped in an aura of spirituality so strong that it threatens to overwhelm any sense of Jesus' humanity.

The self-effacing Jesus of the Synoptics is gone. In John, Jesus makes elaborate claims for himself: "I am the truth." "He who has seen me has seen the Father." Those who are chaos-intolerant should, at first, be delighted. Isn't this an atmosphere in which absolutes can flourish?

The answer, in a word: no. The aura of spirituality in the Gospel of John is also an aura of mystery. The impressionistic painting of the earlier Gospels becomes, in John, almost abstract. The writer of the fourth Gospel is not concerned with history, as we today understand that term, but with those depths that can be probed only through symbolic language. Thus he spins out one truth-story after another. Even more input is required of those seeking understanding.

The Gospel of John begins with a poem that may have been adapted from an ode to a Greek philosophical concept. The poem, even in translation, is magnetic in its beauty and stunning in its depth. The poem centers on a Greek concept: *logos*. In English there is no precise translation for *logos*. *The Word* has become accepted as the best, though inadequate, translation.

Logos was, in the Greek culture, the divine means of communication. Logos radiated from the mind of God to the mind of humankind. In the Gnostic tradition (*gnosis* equals *mind* in Greek), only those with highly developed minds and spirits could receive messages sent via the logos. (Today, one could say much the same about the meaning of logos itself: Only a few persons adept in philosophy may understand the implications of this term. The rest of us stand on tiptoe to catch a glimpse of its profundity.)

Adapting this logos poem allowed the writer, John, to introduce his major themes, especially his love of opposites. "The light shines in darkness." Another juxtaposition of concepts creates an even sharper distinction. On the one hand is the logos, the pure emanation of the mind of God. On the other hand is the Greek word *sarkse*—human flesh with all its animal hungers and corruptibility. In a statement that should steal the breath from anyone who fully encounters it, John makes this audacious claim: The *logos* became *sarkse*. The pure thought of the divine became the flesh of humanity.

Can anyone fully grasp the majesty of these early sentences in John? The reader is alerted at the outset that what lies ahead is not clarity but an unfathomable mystery.

Later in the Gospel of John the reader encounters many other astounding claims. The true follower of Jesus must be born from above (John 3:3), a regeneration that has nothing to do with biology. The person who first heard this news did not understand, and Jesus said little to illuminate the idea.

Later yet, Jesus, as John described him, took another title upon himself: "I am the way" (John 14:6). The Jesus we meet in the fourth Gospel saw himself not as a fixed point but as a process. To be a follower of the Way is to join in a journey, to open one's spirit and mind to a search for truths too profound to ever be mastered.

Later still, John would describe Jesus' journey through death and Resurrection. Life and death are another of John's intertwined opposites. Jesus, even as he writhes in pain on the cross, is the carrier of more life than the soldiers who execute him. The mystery deepens.

Eternal Life in the Eternal Now

The Gospel of John shows that the emphasis on eternal life made by popularized Christianity is not entirely misplaced. Though the present life constitutes the center of gravity in Jesus' teachings, implications of an ultimate victory of life over death are scattered throughout the four Gospels. The implications are especially strong in the Gospel of John. In the fourth Gospel, people are introduced to a *condition* called eternal life, a state that is consistently described in the present tense. Eternal life, in the New Testament sense, can be entered at any current moment. When one has entered eternal life, one's basic interconnectedness with God and neighbor has become more important than any other reality. One continues to live in the present moment yet has transcended time. Eternal life is a condition that does not cease when the biological functions cease.

It is, above all, a quality of living that is worth preserving. To adapt a phrase from Paul Tillich, the Gospel of John attempts to teach us how to achieve eternal life in the eternal now.

Nonetheless, the pattern of these references to eternal life indicates that the topic may have been more important in the thought-world of John the writer than in the mind of Jesus. The earlier (and, therefore, probably more historically accurate) Gospels contain infrequent references to life beyond the grave. By the time the Gospel of John was completed, Jesus was being quoted frequently on this subject. The phrase "eternal life" occurs only twice in the Gospel of Mark, the book that is widely accepted as the earliest of the four Gospels. The same phrase is found three times each in Matthew and Luke. The Gospel of John, completed several decades later, refers to eternal life seventeen times. Eternal life was, then, a subject probably addressed by the historical Jesus. But the frequency with which it was addressed, especially in the later writings, seems to have been a function of the stage of church development.

The Resurrection story is the occasion for Christian theology to shift from this world to a future world. The Gospel of John makes this shift especially easy. Yet the Resurrection, even as presented by John, is open to interpretations that center on this present existence.

One quite ancient but still relevant interpretation of the Resurrection has been labeled the "Christus Victor" theory of atonement. In this understanding, the emphasis shifts from life after death to a victory over the forces that reject the values that Jesus incarnated. Walter Wink refers to these forces as "the domination system." The Resurrection, in this view, becomes a truth-story affirming that liberation, not domination, has the final answer to the perplexities of human existence.

In another interpretation, Jesus' victory over the tomb is an indication that a divine Spirit is available to assist us to rise above the many deaths that scatter themselves along the path of the living. Dreams die; precious relationships are severed; disease or accidents limit bodily functions; parents, siblings, even children and grandchildren disappear into graves. Death stalks us in countless guises. Many losses are so great that we are sure we cannot continue. Yet continue we do. A power wells up from an unknown source, and we find strength to repair our lives and move on. Shakespeare tells us that "Cowards die many times before their deaths"; the happy corollary of this is that people of faith experience resurrection many times before the angel of death touches them directly.

These alternative understandings of the cross and Resurrection allow the final acts of Jesus' life to fit seamlessly with his earlier concerns. To the end, he remained the Man for Others. These interpretations deny us permission to focus on our own rewards to the exclusion of the spiritual and physical needs of our neighbors. The church that allows that to happen, or that encourages that to happen, is guilty of turning a thoroughly unselfish religion into a completely self-centered faith. That is, emphatically, the action of a dishonest church.

The fourth Gospel gives the reader a different kind of savior figure from the man who was presented in the three Synoptic Gospels. Some people will be drawn to the earthy, emotion-driven, story-telling Jesus of the Synoptics; others will find themselves more challenged by the deeply spiritual teacher they find in John. On this all will agree: None of the four Gospel writers presents a Jesus who dispenses set answers to simple questions. The Jesus whom we meet throughout the New Testament is one who spins out puzzles. He invites his followers to join him on a journey of exploration, an encounter with Ultimate Mystery.

◆

Faith Like a Child's

Jesus refused to be the answer. Instead, he insisted on leading his followers on a search. The search will be most profitable for those who travel with the proper equipment. Key elements of this equipment are cognitive maturity and a childlike sense of wonder.

Adults whose cognitive development remains dependent on authorities will find the search difficult at best. Jesus, in one of the Gospels' most compelling truth-stories, was tempted in the wilderness to be an authority figure. He forcefully rejected this role.

What he did instead was to speak of, and to demonstrate by deeds, the potential rule of God in human life. The rule of God, as described by Jesus, is never authoritarian. No armed militia goes out to capture new recruits. No high gates keep citizens from escape. Being a part of the dominion of God is purely voluntary.

Instead of forcing people into compliance, Jesus opened doors that led to a new way of being. In his invitation he violated many of the established rules of those who seek to be popular. In place of security he offered the discomforts of a journey; in place of ease he offered difficult decisions and the pain of standing apart from the crowd. Maturity is required.

Ironically, Jesus is reported to have given a special invitation to mature people whose faith is like that of a child. A child! People whose cognitive maturity allows them to be comfortable amidst the moral clutter of life are also those who are able to recapture the spirit of the very young. A child readily embraces *phobeo*, the Greek word used frequently in the Gospels to describe the sense of wonder.

Jesus invited others to share the sense of awe he carried within himself: "Behold, the lilies of the field . . ." (Matthew 6:28). He found it amazing that nature could, with so little apparent effort, overwhelm the viewer with its beauty.

Instead of handing out packaged answers to petrified minds, Jesus seemed bent on eliciting a sense of wonder in those whose attitudes were childlike in their flexibility. In addition to the word *phobeo*, the term *traumatzo* is used thirty times by Gospel writers. "Astound" is one of the best English translations. In most of the cases where this word is used, people had been amazed at something Jesus had done or said. On a few occasions, *traumatzo* describes Jesus' reaction, either at the depth of faith he had encountered, or at the total lack of it. Pilate was *traumatzo*—astounded by Jesus' refusal to speak in his own defense.

Astonishment can be the result of cheap circus tricks; it can also be elicited by a demonstration of the difference between the world as it presently is and the world as it might, under divine rule, become. Jesus awed people through the second means. Jesus astonished people and opened them to further exploration. How can this be? What sort of man is this? Where will we go if we follow Jesus' style of life? How can I receive this life-giving power into myself?

Full engagement with the biblical Jesus, then, requires an interesting mixture of skills. Potential disciples must have moved far enough in cognitive development to deal with teaching stories that demand completion from the hearer. Followers must be willing to substitute encounters with mystery for set answers. Jesus invited his followers to a faith which, in its maturity, has come full circle, embracing once again the openness and sense of wonder of a young child.

◆

An Incarnation of Faith

A mature faith and a childlike sense of wonder sound as if they are mutually exclusive, a difficult if not impossible combination. I know, however, that the two are compatible. I have been fortunate to have encountered lives that brought these two together in a harmonious unity. John A. (Jack) Easley, a Professor Emeritus in Education at the University of Illinois in Champaign/Urbana, was one of those.

Jack's brilliant mind and open spirit made him equally at home in science and theology. As a scientist, he could look out over an ever broadening and constantly shifting body of knowledge. As a person of faith, he could be nourished by a deepening sense of the Mystery at the heart of the universe.

Jack found no conflict between his twin loves, religion and science. These were complementary means of encountering the unknown.

The conflict that did bother him was between rigidity and openness. All his life he fought fundamentalism. Fundamentalists in religion vexed him. Fundamentalists in science dismayed him. Fundamentalists in education infuriated him.

Anger was seldom evident in Jack. Yet he became visibly angry when he talked about what happened to children in the early years of schooling. Young minds full of curiosity, eager to explore, are filled, as he saw it, with the dry dust of unexamined facts. Soon their spirits die. Too often he had watched as a child's eagerness was buried under what he described as the "crushing weight of traditional schooling." What he witnessed in public schools he also saw in church school classes. He often expressed his distress over the church's tendency to substitute indoctrination for education.

Jack was confident that one of the primary channels through which the Creative Spirit moves into human life is the open mind of a young child. When inflexible educational methods shut off this channel, the result is more than personal tragedy. The loss is a matter of ultimate concern. The stifling of a child's spirit denies all humanity a closer contact with God.

A few months before his death, Jack accompanied a group of first-grade children to a playground for weather observations. They went out immediately following a rain. The children became more fascinated by the earthworms under foot than by any activity in the atmosphere. "Why do the worms come out of the wet soil?" one of the children asked. "Why do *you* think they do?" Jack asked in turn. Several responses by the children followed, answers that most adults would consider far off the mark. To each answer Jack responded, "That's an interesting thought." Later, the teacher, with detectable irritation in her voice, confronted him. "Why didn't you just tell them why earthworms come out of the soil after a rain?" To which Jack quietly responded, "Because I want them to enjoy the wonder!"

Likewise, Jesus refused to be the source of dry facts—to make his teachings like the crushing weight of traditional schooling. Instead, he told stories that were unfinished. He lived and acted in ways that stimulated a sense of awe.

Jesus gave no systematic description of the nature of God. He did not tell us the how of creation and refused to be drawn into a discussion of the way it will all end.

Many more people heard him than responded to Jesus' perplexing invitation to discipleship. A commercial success he was not. He was successful only at what he chose to do: challenge at least a few of his followers to grow toward the maturity that he embodied.

An honest church will stop teaching and preaching as if Jesus were a fixed answer, an identifiable point at which one may arrive. Instead, the honest church will celebrate the fact that Jesus invited us to be part of a search—to accompany him on the way. The honest church will help others grasp what Jack Easley understood about the venture of the Christian faith: Jesus wanted to help us all enjoy the wonder.

NOTES

1. John Howard Yoder, in his book *The Politics of Jesus* (Grand Rapids: William B. Eerdmans Publishing Company, 1972), offers an impressive, even overwhelming, list of biblical texts in which the follower of Jesus is called to imitate Jesus' style of living. Yoder's point: To be Christian is not just to benefit from Jesus' sacrifice; it is also to share in his sacrificial and nonviolent lifestyle.

2. Joseph Scriven, "What a Friend We Have in Jesus" (hymn).

3. Harry Emerson Fosdick, "God of Grace and God of Glory" (hymn).

4. N. T. Wright and Marcus J. Borg, *The Meaning of Jesus.*

5. Albert Schweitzer, *The Quest of the Historical Jesus: A Critical Study of Its Progress From Reimarus to Wrede* (translated by William Montgomery, 1910; reprint, New York: Macmillan, 1961).

6. Robert W. Funk, Roy W. Hoover, and the Jesus Seminar, *The Five Gospels: The Search for the Authentic Words of Jesus* (New York: Macmillan Company, Polebridge Press, 1993).

7. Walter Wink, *The Human Being: Jesus and the Enigma of the Son of the Man* (Minneapolis: Fortress Press, 2002).

8. Bernard Brandon Scott, *Re-Imagine the World* (Santa Rosa, California: Polebridge Press, 2001).

9. John Dominic Crossan and Richard Watts, *Who is Jesus?* (New York: HarperCollins, 1996).

10. The writer of the Gospel of Matthew used the phrase "Kingdom of Heaven." This was not an effort to move Jesus' concern to life beyond the grave. Rather, it was one of the ways in which the writer tried to make his material acceptable to the Jews—by avoiding use of the name of the divine. Nonetheless, "the Kingdom of Heaven" in Matthew's gospel means the same as "the Kingdom of God" in other New Testament books.

11. This story is considered by many scholars, including members of the Jesus Seminar, to be a creation of Gospel writer John—what I prefer to call a "truth-story" rather than a true story. Students of the Bible, however, are almost unanimous in the belief that this story captures the essence of Jesus.

8

Honesty Carries Us toward the Numen: God As Mystery

Here, in brief, is the root of the dishonesty that the church has practiced in regard to God: In its preaching and in its literature, the church has failed to challenge its members' childish concepts about the divine.

Through all the time of my ministry I have heard the word "God" used primarily as if it referred to an overwhelming exterior force that could be called on to bring safety and predictability into a person's private life. God is imagined to be a kind of genie from Aladdin's lamp. God is thought to be on my side even in regard to selfish goals. God is assumed to be unfailingly on the side of my nation in times of international conflict.

I hear these immature concepts embedded, sometimes covertly, in the conversations of lay persons and in discussions I have with religious professionals. I also see them on the pages of literature produced by respected church publishing houses. I hear them in sermons when I have an opportunity to visit other churches. If I listen carefully, I might hear the echoes of such thoughts in my own sermons. Habits of a lifetime do not change easily.

More encouraging, but much less frequent, are the times I have heard parishioners wrestle courageously with the idea of a God who is quite beyond human imagination and who may have an agenda in conflict with one's own. I referred earlier to one church member who, without any prompting from me, reminded the congregation in a lay sermon that "God is not my cosmic bellhop."

On the subject of the nature of God, the gap between professional and lay styles of faith is probably not so large as in other issues. As N. T. Wright observed, a common assumption is abroad that everyone shares the meaning of the word "God." When pressed, however, few among either clergy or laity would be able to provide a helpful definition. Both professionals and nonprofessionals tend to operate with vague, archaic, and intellectually insupportable ideas of God.

What the professional clergy do know, and fail to share with the laity, is that theology today is in ferment. Creative thinkers are pouring their best efforts into the search for an understanding of God that is mature, that has roots in the tradition, and that is not likely to be blown away by the next discovery of science. Yet information about this ferment is either withheld from congregations or is described as a threat to be avoided.

What a marvelous opportunity is being missed! Congregations could be invited into the most exciting search occurring in religious circles. They should be told of Paul Tillich's description of the divine as the "Ground of all Being" and his even more expansive idea of a "God above the God of theism."[1] Church members should be given an opportunity to wrestle with the meaning of "panentheism" and to compare their own beliefs with the insights of process theologians. ("Panentheism" and "process theology" will be defined and discussed in the final chapter.) Participants in these discussions would either modify their beliefs in light of new possibilities, or they could recommit themselves to their traditional beliefs, having examined and taken ownership of those beliefs.

Few such discussion groups take place. Again, professionals do not want to disturb the laity. So, bored church members miss another excellent chance to grow.

◆

A Problematic Word

In truth, no common understanding of the word "God" exists. With no clear definition, using the word with integrity becomes difficult for persons who value intellectual honesty.

The word "God" has had a shorter life span than is generally realized. According to the Oxford English Dictionary, it is of German ancestry and may originally have meant simply "what is invoked." Previously, in the Western world, the divine had been referred to as *deos* (from Latin), *theos* (from Greek), or *Jehovah* (from the consonants of the Hebrew name for God that was too holy to be used except in the most sacred settings). A word so recent to our tradition as "God" could be dismissed, if necessary, from that tradition, though its total abandonment in the foreseeable future is highly unlikely.

This much is clear about the word "God": It comes with unfortunate and often destructive associations. Since our language distinguishes between gods and goddesses, the word God is irredeemably masculine. Much of early Judaism envisioned the divine as the ultimate patriarch, the overwhelming force that would impose *his* will on humankind, even at the expense of enormous suffering, including, on occasion, genocide.

Several decades ago a group of theologians upset the religious community with their "God is dead" movement. They were not trying to rid the world of religion. They were trying to bury a concept of the divine that could, they believed, no longer be supported. It was in a similar, but less threatening vein, that Paul Tillich spoke of the "God above the God of theism"—the

God who appears when the gods we have designed disappear. His was an effort to accomplish the same goal.

Tillich captured the essence of the church's dishonesty in regard to the divine in a brief meditation on Psalm 130, *I wait for the Lord, my soul waits. . . .* Tillich commented: "Waiting means *not* having and having at the same time. . . . A religion in which that is forgotten, no matter how ecstatic or active or reasonable, replaces God by its own creation of an image of God. Our religious life is characterized more by that kind of creation than anything else."

Tillich then states why so much dishonesty exists in the church's statements concerning the divine:

> It is not easy to preach Sunday after Sunday without convincing ourselves and others that we *have* God and can dispose of Him. It is not easy to proclaim God to children and pagans, to skeptics and secularists, and at the same time to make clear to them that we ourselves do not possess God, that we too wait for Him. I am convinced that much of the rebellion against Christianity is due to the overt or veiled claim of the Christian to possess God, and therefore, also, to the loss of this element of waiting, so decisive for the prophets and the apostles.[2]

In other words, the church has pretended to know more about the Ultimate Mystery than it does. Once again it has confronted people with premature answers when questions are both more appropriate and more inviting.

Casualness

Because we pretend to know more than we do, persons of the Christian tradition use the word "God" with alarming intimacy. God is spoken of as if the divine were a long-term neighbor whose habits and history we know thoroughly. The overwhelming majority of Christian churches are guilty of not discouraging such cozy attitudes.

To avoid problems with the term, I chose not to use the word "God" in the title of this chapter. I have demonstrated, in many places in this volume, that I cannot avoid the term altogether. It is too deeply enmeshed in the language and the culture to be set aside easily. We need, instead, to expand our spiritual vocabulary. To this end, I will refer to the divine at times with two other terms: *Ultimate Mystery* and *the Numen*.

More precise meanings of these two terms will be offered later. For now, I want to acknowledge that I know each term is inadequate, as are all efforts to identify that which is beyond human understanding. The two are most helpful when seen together. "Ultimate Mystery" implies that we are confident a spiritual realm exists, while recognizing that our ignorance of this realm exceeds our knowledge. "The Numen" defines some of the important attributes we courageously and humbly believe can be attached to this spiritual realm.

Let me now try to unfold some of the meanings of these two terms. We must begin where we are.

◆

Child-Like vs. Childish

"Childish" is the word I used at the beginning of the chapter to describe the attitudes that linger in most Christian congregations. As I noted in an earlier chapter, *childish* must be distinguished from the *child-like* attitudes commended in the Gospels. "Child-like" means "full of wonder, ready to relish the search for that which is unknown." Mature Christians find it easy to incorporate child-like qualities into their stance toward life. Childish, in contrast, implies clinging to limited concepts that played a useful role in one's early years but which, in adulthood, have outlived their usefulness.

Childish attitudes toward God take at least three forms. A small child, just beginning to attempt to make sense of the surrounding world, usually wants concrete, definable ideas. While abstract thought is not impossible for children, they find abstract ideas difficult. Adults who do not move beyond this hunger for the concrete become literalists. Dogma, creeds, and scripture are seen in absolute and black-and-white terms. Narratives are either true or untrue. The concept that a narrative might be a truth-story, a container of truth, does not resonate with adults who continue to think in concrete, childish terms.

A second characteristic of the childish attitude is an obsession with power. Children are small. They compensate for their weakness by identifying with dependable centers of power. Young boys are especially enamored with power (a good argument for more female theologians!). They read Superman and Spiderman comics. They engage in competitive games ("My daddy can beat up your daddy" or "My baseball team hits more home runs than your baseball team"). An omnipotent deity fits neatly into the worldview of a child who is attempting to find strong allies in life.

A third characteristic of a child's worldview is the necessity to keep ideas at a manageable size.

A favorite finger-play that my wife likes to share with small children can help us understand this characteristic of very young minds. The finger-play demonstrates three sizes of ball. "Here's a ball" (the first finger is placed with the thumb); "and here's a ball" (the two hands make a circle); "a great big ball I see" (the arms form a circle, with fingers touching above the head). If a great big ball is the size of two human arms, then a ball the size of the earth is completely beyond the comprehension of a developing child. The size of God is limited, in the child's mind, to the approximate size of the largest adult they have met.

A childish attitude toward God is one that keeps the divine at a manageable size. Half a century ago an English cleric, J. B. Phillips, offered a helpful book entitled *Your God is Too Small*.[3] His section headings indicated the drift of his ideas: "Resident Policeman," "Parental Hangover," "Grand Old Man," "Heavenly Bosom." The honest church will help challenge its members to ask themselves if these same inadequate images are still held today.

If an honest church is to nudge its people beyond childish ideas of the divine, it must do so on these three levels. The concept of God must become less concrete; it must be less obsessed with power; it must be expanded in magnitude.

◆

Beyond Childish Concepts: God As Mystery

Over against the childish desire for concrete ideas, a mature and honest faith focuses as much on what we do not know as on what we know about God. Maturity leaves open spaces for future discovery.

Again it should be said: Questions draw people in; fixed answers are barriers holding most people out. In our search for new ways to describe the divine, we must look for terms that acknowledge both our knowledge and our lack of knowledge. "Ultimate Mystery" is helpful because it confesses ignorance. The term affirms that what we know about the divine is only an island of refuge in a vast sea of emptiness.

Mystery is present when we sense the presence of a reality, but the essence of that reality remains unknown. In the spirit of the Tillich quote given earlier, a mystery is something we can have and not have at the same moment. Mystery entices. It challenges. "Ultimate Mystery" suggests ultimate challenge, an exploration that requires the investment of a lifetime.

"Ultimate Mystery" points toward a search that cannot be completed in the few decades of life we are allowed on this earth. The extent of the unknown in the deity may be the best argument for an existence beyond the grave, a time beyond time when the Mystery shall slowly be revealed.

A few months ago my wife and I were visiting the St. Louis Art Museum. As we made our way through the section devoted to Asian art, I was taken by a disarmingly simple work done by the artist Aoki. With a broad brush stroke he had enclosed a circle, black on white. The inside of the circle, vacant space to a Western eye, was, as explained in the accompanying material, the critical center of the work. This space was given a name: *Ensô,* apparently from a Japanese word that means "performance." What the practical Western mind insists is open (and therefore wasted) space is, for this artist, the center of spiritual activity. That which the artist had left untouched carried profound significance. Aoki wanted us to consider the possibility that the focus of divine activity is not where we see something, but where we see nothing. The Western mind wants to rush into this space and fill it with attributes and dogma. We should pause before doing so. God is Mystery. Openness is necessary. Persons of the Buddhist tradition often speak of God as "Emptiness." Adapting at least a bit of that attitude could save the Western mind many idolatrous moments.

Over and over again, our tradition affirms that the divine is beyond human knowing. Question marks, not exclamation marks, characterize discussions of the holy. Biblical writers delighted in describing what God was *doing,* but they resisted efforts to understand what God *is.* These writers would deny that we can have intimate knowledge of the Mystery itself; they would posit that we can know only what Mystery is accomplishing. This distinction was so important that these writers assumed that anyone arrogant enough to want to look directly on the face of the divine would immediately die.

Not even Moses, the dominant figure of the Hebrew Scriptures, was allowed to look directly at God. In a truth-story concerning a burning bush (Exodus 3:1-15), Moses is said to have heard the divine voice. God asks Moses to lead the rebellion against Pharaoh and slavery. Moses wisely tries to wiggle out of this dangerous task. "I don't even know who you are," he replies to that challenging voice. Using a form of the Hebrew verb "to be," the voice responds: "I am the I Am." Other translations of this difficult passage include, "I am the essence of being," or, "I will be who I will be." (Walter Breuggemann, one of the most respected living biblical scholars, suggests, only half in jest, that the proper translation is: "I am not going to tell you my name!") However the words are translated, they clearly are intended to leave us with more questions than answers.

Names are more than convenient tags laid on objects. Names partake of the essence of what is named. Thus, Jews are reluctant to speak the divine name, fearing that in doing so they might limit the scope and depth of the reality to which the name refers. For the same reason, neither the observant Jew nor the follower of Islam will paint any picture or construct any form that represents God.

Additional reasons can be found for the refusal to assign a name to the divine. Names imply a separate reality, a being distinguished from other beings. Also, a word that represents God, or visual images that suggest the divine, imply that we know more than we do. A name for the divine would inevitably mislead. The second of the Ten Commandments codifies this prohibition on pseudo-knowledge: "You shall not take the name of the Lord your God in vain." Or, in a translation I find helpful, "You shall not use the name of the Lord your God for mischief." An assignment of any name to Ultimate Mystery opens the door to all manner of mischief.

The 33rd chapter of Exodus again affirms the mystery of God. This narrative has been put to music. Since childhood I have sung, "Rock of Ages, Cleft for Me." I assumed, until at least my middle adulthood, that I was singing about a rock that represented the strength and permanence of God. To be held in the cleft of that rock, I thought, was to be held in God's strong grip. A few years ago something caused me to remove my blinders and read again. The rock in this charming truth-story, I discovered, is not a reference to divine strength. The rock was a means of protecting Moses *from* God. To look on the divine face would have meant death. So God allowed Moses to hide in the cleft of a large rock while the divine presence moved by. Moses could glimpse the divine backside, but not the divine face. Moses was given mystery, not fact; questions, not answers.

Christians proclaim that much of the veil of mystery concerning God was lifted in the coming of Jesus. Indeed, many of the characteristics that we assume pertain to the divine are either revealed in or reinforced in the person of Jesus. Yet it is clear from reading the four Gospels that Jesus had a developed sense of the majesty and mystery of his Creator. Not even Jesus could manipulate the Holy. As the Gospel writers portrayed the story, he prayed to be released from crucifixion but was crucified anyway. On the cross he felt spiritually abandoned.

As was pointed out in the previous chapter, most of Jesus' teachings were cryptic. His parables were often enigmas. After Jesus, Christians who want to know God are left with clearer questions, not absolute answers. This is good news. God remains the Ultimate Mystery. The search goes on.

◆

Beyond Childish Concepts: God As the Numen

As it moves beyond the childish obsession with divine omnipotence, a mature faith will find ways to understand divine power that are less coercive. God is not Superman minus the cloak.

This shift will not mean the end of divine power. In this fresh understanding, God becomes less the focus of power and more the distributor of power.

Many modern Christians will find a shift away from a belief in a manipulative divine power extremely difficult. Too many people have never outgrown the childish need to be protected by a force bigger and stronger than themselves—bigger and stronger than any force that threatens them. Because this shift is so difficult, and yet so important, I will use a considerable number of words exploring the idea of a less powerful divine, and the way a non-omnipotent God fits into the Christian tradition.

Divine strength is a major theme of biblical writers. The Hebrew words *el-saddai,* usually translated *almighty God,* appear more than sixty times in the Hebrew Scripture. Clearly, our religious ancestors wanted to be under the protection of a strong divine hand.

Perhaps, however, the scriptural emphasis on divine power has been magnified in the process of translation. Precisely what *el-saddai* meant in early Hebrew history is unclear. *El* is clearly a reference to God, but the meaning of *saddai* is less obvious. The word was apparently taken from the Canaanites. Its roots are unknown. The contexts in which it is used indicate that it was concerned with power. It is likely that it referred to relative strength, a power greater than that of other deities. Whether it implies infinite power, in the sense of the English words "almighty" or "omnipotent," is one of many religious mysteries that will probably never be settled. "Omnipotent" comes from a Latin root that entered the tradition later. It implies total power and micromanagement. Using "omnipotent" as an equivalent for "saddai" quite possibly stretches the concept beyond what the Hebrew writers intended.

The reasons for the scriptural emphasis on divine strength are the same as the reasons children are obsessed with power. Israel was a small nation. Often the Hebrews' only hope for military victory lay in the possibility that their deity was more powerful than the deity of the opposing army. They assumed that Yahweh, their God, was one of many existing deities, each the sponsor of a particular ethnic group. Victory in war, they were confident, depended as much on the strength of a nation's deities as on the strength of its armies. Perhaps the Hebrews fought more fiercely because they were confident they fought in the name of Yahweh.

One of the marks of maturity is a more nuanced insight into the nature of power. As our understandings of life and relationships grow, we recognize that the kind of power that overwhelms, that forces compliance, is successful only in the short term. Over the long term, it carries the seeds of its own destruction. Coercive force is, at the end of the day, an expression of weakness. Hitler thought he had amassed such a formidable military that his Reich would last a thousand years. It imploded within less than two decades.

Christians are called to live out the implications of a radically different concept of strength. This alternate power comes from the courage to turn the other cheek, to love one's enemies, to submit to the cross.

The temptation stories, which three Gospel writers placed near the beginning of their narratives (Matthew 4:1-10; Mark 1:13; Luke 4:1-12), demonstrate Jesus' profound understanding of power. These truth-stories constitute a drama in three acts. The first temptation (in Matthew's account) offered Jesus the opportunity to bring people under his spell by meeting their physical necessities. Stones could be turned into bread. The second temptation was similar: People would follow him if he performed a spectacular act to prove his power over nature. The third act dealt with the rawest form of human power known: Jesus could become a ruler over political kingdoms, supposedly achieving this status by violent means.

Jesus emphatically rejected each of those temptations. Jesus knew that the methods suggested by the Tempter violated the nature of God. Jesus chose, instead, the slow, costly method of building human allegiance. He would love, teach, and serve people until they acknowledged his as the superior (and thus stronger) way to abundant life. His decision to die rather than do evil to those who would harm him was the ultimate demonstration of this alternate form of power.

Paul's writings reinforce the insights of the stories of temptation and the story of the cross. His words may be the most profound probing of the meaning of power in religious literature: *God's weakness is stronger than human strength* (1 Corinthians 1:25).

The Numen

Reconsidering the nature of God's power will mean rethinking our entire concept of the deity. The idea of the divine as a separate being, one that determines every human event, one that intervenes in life to force particular results, must be set aside.

Our long religious tradition has survived not because so many people have heard a divine voice or witnessed a miraculous act. The vast majority of people have done neither. Our tradition survives because so many people have, in a variety of ways, become aware of another dimension to life than that experienced through our five senses. This is the dimension that offers strength to move through and beyond life's reversals. This dimension gives meaning to existence; it gives meaning even to encounters with chaos.

To take a religious stance is not necessarily to look upward in search of a separate something called "God." A religious stance may cause one to look *down* to explore life's depth, and then to look *outward* to recognize the interrelatedness of all things. At times religion causes a person to look at a nearby object and to recognize that the object is the carrier of an essence that cannot be identified, a value that cannot be quantified. In whatever direction one looks, religion is seeing the universe through the widest possible lens.

If Christianity is to survive among intellectually alert people, fresh terms must be found to refer to the spiritual dimension that a religious stance attempts to explore.

The term *Numen* is an alternate way of referring to the divine that avoids some of the unfortunate associations of the word "God." *Numen* refers to a spiritual quality that permeates a space or a people. *Merriam-Webster's Collegiate Dictionary*[4] defines it as "a spiritual force or influence often identified with a natural object, phenomenon, or place." *The American Heritage Dictionary*[5] describes *numen* as "creative energy; genius." The word pertains to a role more than to an object. It is a noun with overtones of a verb. Like all terms that refer to the spiritual dimension, it is imperfect. Yet its use here may refocus the nature of the problem and breathe fresh air into the discussion.

Early in the 20th century, Rudolf Otto used the terms *numen* and *numinous* in his classic study, *The Idea of the Holy*.[6] Otto wanted an original way to refer to the awe-inspiring sacredness that points toward the divine, a way to describe the special aspect of all the persons and objects that become, in special ways, revealers of the Holy.

Those who are familiar with the term (I consider it fortunate that *numen* is not in common use; thus it carries less baggage into the religious arena) know that it also has roots in animistic religions. Animists consider that each person and object is inhabited by a force that gives it a special identify and helps it fulfill its purpose. This force is its numen. A rock is permeated by its numen, causing it to fulfill the role of a rock. The same is true of a spider and its numen. Each human being has his or her own numen, an empowering spirit instilled in a child as it is given a name.

These two sources of the term *numen* suggest meanings that are dramatized during the baptism of an infant. In that service, the child is given a name that distinguishes it from others. Its name is also its numen, carrying with it a sense of sacredness that binds it into a web of persons and sacred objects.

Just as each person and object has its own numen, so the entire universe is enlivened and held together by *the Numen*. The Numen is that which transforms our universe from a set of discrete, interacting units into an interrelated, interdependent organism, a totality in which the whole is much greater than the sum of its parts. This whole is the sacred web in which we and all reality are held.

Otto's description of the Numen was an effort to shift the concept of the Holy from an intellectual exercise to an experiential encounter. I identify with that effort. I have had too few spiritual breakthrough occasions to call myself a true mystic. But some such rare moments have occurred. Early in my adulthood I was living in Pakistan and had an opportunity to worship with a small Christian community near Lahore. The worship was conducted in Urdu, which meant I understood only a few words. I expected to be bored, homesick again in a strange setting. Instead I felt supported and permeated by a sense of holiness. Every person around me took on a *numinous* quality. For a few truly ominous moments the barriers between my fellow worshipers and me melted away. I retained my individuality, as did each of them. Indeed, our individuality was enhanced. Yet I experienced a remarkable wholeness, a unity within this highly diverse group. A sacredness invaded that service, binding me with others and empowering me to live out the remainder of a difficult assignment.

The implications of thinking of God in the role of the Numen are far-reaching. It is not my purpose to explore all these implications here. I hope simply to demonstrate that a fresh vocabulary can stimulate ideas that are able to move us beyond our childhood concepts of God.

A narrative (perhaps a truth-story) related by the Quaker mystic Rufus Jones may help unlock this different way of understanding the divine. The tale is set along Jones's beloved Maine coast.

> A church on the mainland discovered that children on a nearby island had no church home, and thus no religious education. One of its members volunteered to go to the island and hold a church school for a few weeks in the summer. Lacking a building, he gathered the island's children on a sandy beach. The instructor knew that good educational technique meant starting with something the children already knew. His first question was, "Will someone tell me about the ocean?" To his dismay, not a single hand went up. The faces before him contained blank stares. Then reality hit. The Atlantic Ocean, which in so many ways defined their existence—permeated their air, provided nourishment, livelihood and recreation for their families—had never, in the presence of these children, been called by its proper name. Its role in their lives had not been explained.[7]

What was true for the children of a Maine island in regard
to the ocean is also true for many modern people in regard to
the Numen. The central reality by which our lives are defined
and nourished has seldom been adequately identified. Because
people are looking for a separate being, they miss the spiritual
dimension in which they are constantly immersed.

This way of envisioning the divine suggests the act of
swimming in a deep, slow-moving river. The water supports
us, though that support requires our cooperation. We are free
to rebel, as it were, to resist the current by seeking a destination
of our own choosing. Rebellion requires extra effort, but it is
possible. Or we can cooperate with the current and be supported as we attempt to move in positive directions.

Otto's book was, in large part, an effort to focus religious
sensibilities on objects that carry a numinous quality. Those
objects are pointers toward the Numen. Otto knew that the
spiritual radiance that adheres to some realities is not a proof of
the existence of God. (The search for such proof is, at the end of
the day, a search for fool's gold; if such proof could be found, it
would turn the religious quest into scientific knowledge.)
Numinous qualities do not prove anything; they do, however,
powerfully suggest a depth and meaning to life.

As I read Otto's words, I find myself naming the settings
and moments in my life when I have been aware of a wonder
and an awe that can be called numinous. Here are a few:

- driving on a sunny October day along the Blue Ridge
  Parkway, when the sun makes astounding patterns
  through changing leaves;
- standing within the quiet dignity of the Meditation
  Chapel at St. Patrick's Roman Catholic Church in
  Urbana, Illinois;
- reading the Suffering Servant passages of the Book of Isaiah (Isaiah 40-55), especially the words relating to vicari-
  ous suffering (Isaiah 52:13-53:12);
- listening to the *Violin Concerto in D Major* by Beethoven;

- encountering a human face that emits compassion through wrinkles and scars;
- rereading the Beatitudes (Matthew 5:3-12);
- viewing any one of several paintings of water lilies by Monet.

While none of these moments proves to me that God exists, I find that when I encounter any of them, the burden of proof shifts. Logical reasons for believing in a realm of the spirit are no longer needed: instead, overwhelming arguments would be required to convince me that reality is restricted to what can be known by my five senses. The situations and moments described make it difficult to dissuade me from continuing to search for something deeper than the surface on which I appear to exist and for a source of value at the center of it all.

The Power of the Numen

The divine, when understood as the Numen, has power. But that power is expressed in a way quite different from the way the power of God is traditionally understood. If I am ill, for example, God does not have to be persuaded by the prayers of my friends to assist me to regain health. The Numen is already with me, encouraging me, enabling the forces of healing. The prayers of my friends may in some way focus this power, but those prayers are not required to summon the Numen from inactivity.

Without the healing strength that the divine provides, my chances of surviving illness are slim. With that power at work, my chances of survival increase significantly. In neither case is my recovery guaranteed. The Numen is strong, but not omnipotent. The divine enlivens my body's healing capacity. But the strength of illness can sometimes be so great that not even a spirit-empowered body can cope. The Numen coaxes toward health, yet it never *over*powers. Especially, the Numen does not overpower the physical laws that allow both life and death to do their work.

The Power of the Numen in Scripture

The concept of divine power that works quietly and gently is not at all foreign to our tradition. It will be found in surprising places. For example, the stories of creation, usually assumed to be God's mightiest acts, may be descriptions of a less manipulative form of activity than is usually assumed.

The usual reading of the opening verses of scripture seems to indicate that God, working from some distance, created the heavens and the earth *ex nihilo* (from nothing). It is easy to understand how this view has become popular. Churches have taught it for generations. The King James Version, essentially the only translation of the Bible used by Protestants for nearly three hundred years, implied as much. "In the beginning, God created the heavens and the earth" (Genesis 1:1).

Two factors push toward a reexamination of the earliest scriptural verses. The first comes from the secular world. As researchers probe the beginnings of our universe, they put question marks beside the idea of a starting point, of a time when time itself began. Steven Hawking discussed a remarkable possibility in *A Brief History of Time*.[8] He suggested that we might live in an undulating, cyclical universe without beginning or end. If his theory is true, then the Big Bang happened when matter became so compacted that an enormous explosion had to take place. That explosion pushed matter out into space, forming the expanding universe as we know it. After a time, the forces of gravity will reverse the movement, and the universe will gradually be drawn back into almost infinite mass. Another Big Bang. Another expansion, then contraction.

If this view prevails in the scientific community, Christians and Jews will be faced with a major problem. As Hawking himself puts it, the creator God then becomes unemployed. Attempting to cling to the idea of a God who wills a universe into existence will cause a conflict between religion and science as disruptive (and as embarrassing to religion, which always eventually loses such struggles) as the conflict between the concepts of evolution and creationism. Christianity cannot survive another such battle with science and pretend to keep its intellectual respectability.

The second reason for reexamining the early part of Genesis comes from the Bible itself. Over the past three centuries, scholars who specialize in biblical language have had an opportunity to look more deeply into these important verses. What has emerged is a growing confidence that the first lines of Genesis should be translated as a single sentence, with the opening verses as a dependent clause. This simple change of grammar creates a significantly altered meaning. *Ex nihilo* is no longer implied. The translators of the New Revised Standard Version, hesitant to offer such a radical change in the text itself, offer this possibility in a footnote:

> In the beginning, when God began to create the heavens and the earth . . .

Place these words with the verse that follows and we have this reading:

> In the beginning, when God began to create the heavens and the earth, the earth was a formless void and darkness covered the face of the deep, while a mighty wind from God swept over the surface of the deep.

Clearly, this different wording does not describe an entirely new reality being called into being. Instead, what is usually referred to as creation was a tidying up of the chaotic nature of something already present, the rearrangement of a mess not of God's own doing. In this reading, God (the Numen) is not the maker of the world but the force that works to overcome the chaos of the world.

As the story progresses, light—a major ingredient of order—was separated from darkness. The sea (a symbol of chaos in the ancient mind) was tamed and divided from the dry land. The stage was set for the creation of life, a continuation of the ongoing process. Life is the ordering of inanimate ingredients. Human life, as the second chapter of Genesis makes clear, transformed the dust of the earth into sentient beings. With remarkable depth of understanding, the narrator of the first creation story recounted how lower forms of life preceded the higher. Humankind, with its developed consciousness, with its ability to relate to one another and to a higher consciousness, came last. A remarkable amount of chaos had been tamed.

The writer of the second creation story (Genesis 2:4-25) adds a final touch. After the dust of the earth had been turned into human flesh, the resulting life required refinement. Into this "dirt-person" was breathed the very breath of the divine. The Numen had shared its numinous quality with humankind. Again, the creative act was not so much a new reality, but the reordering of ingredients already present.

One other fact is important. The Hebrew verbs used in the creation stories are not simple past tenses. These verbs imply activity that began in the past but continues in the present. *In the beginning, when God began to create . . .*

A Statement of Hope

As is true of almost every biblical narrative, the deeper meanings of the early stories of Genesis are seen only when they are placed in their human context. Many biblical scholars believe the final editing of these passages was done during the Jewish exile. The nation's situation had become desperate. Their nation, their tradition, and their faith had become a formless void. Hope was almost nonexistent. The stories of God's early activity were dramas thrown against the despair, visions that allowed people to believe that a meaningful future was possible.

Their reason for hope was this: The redemptive activity of the divine is ongoing. "God the creator" was continuing to do what God had always done: move across a broken and chaotic world bringing healing and order. Despite overwhelming problems, reasons for hope remained. Their situation offered the Numen another opportunity to move through their disorder and establish the conditions in which their community could be renewed.

The power of an honest faith to offer hope to despairing people is no less today than in the depth of the exile. The work of creation, rightfully understood, continues as the divine leans against the forces of chaos. The Numen never loses contact with those who are in despair and grief, holding them in a supportive, loving web of relationships. God's creative activity is made visible whenever the barriers of race, gender, nationality, age—all the walls we humans so ingenuously erect between ourselves—come tumbling down in acts of reconciliation. Here the story of the Resurrection and the stories of creation merge. Disorder will not have the final word.

The divine force of early Genesis is not a withdrawn CEO who luxuriates in an impressive skyscraper suite while controlling all the offices in the building below. The God of Genesis does not *control* at all. God has been called the anti-entropic force, the ever-present power that persistently encourages the forces of health and order. Entropy is the tendency of all created things to run down—to decay. The physicist J. Willard Gibbs has described entropy as the "mixed-upedness of a system." Yet the total system is not as mixed up as the laws of physics would expect. The world is not moving toward chaos as rapidly as the second law of thermodynamics predicts. Something is pushing in the opposite direction. The rich, Hebrew term *shalom*, usually translated "peace," is more accurately seen as an antonym of disorder. To be an anti-entropic force is to push toward *shalom*.

The divine's complex purposes and activities can be summarized in a simple phrase: The Numen works to bring order from chaos.

It becomes clear, then, how serious is the loss when a dishonest church, in an effort to pander to a small percentage of biblical fundamentalists, presents the Genesis creation stories as literal history. When this is allowed to happen, the defense of a pseudo-historic truth overwhelms profound truth. The basis for hope that revived and ultimately saved the Hebrew nation is buried in an effort to treat the opening chapters of the Bible as historic fact rather than truth-story.

God's role as the force toward order is reaffirmed in the magnificent poem we know as the Book of Job. Job's story is particularly pertinent here. This dramatic truth-story centers on a man who began with a square-cornered view of God and of God's world. He was confident that the divine held and exercised all ultimate power and was responsible for every detail of his own life. Serving God faithfully, he was confident, was the means of securing a long and prosperous life. Unexpected circumstances would prove him very wrong.

This poem was probably edited in its final form following the Jewish exile, a point in history when the theologians of Judah had a great deal of explaining to do. Previous religious leaders, much like the young Job, had insisted that God was in charge of everything. God would protect the nation, its Davidic kingdom, and its individual members forever.

Those promises were impossible to defend in the years following the exile. The nation had seen its royal family destroyed and had spent sixty years in exile. The writer of the 40th chapter of Isaiah said it well: Israel had been punished double for its sins.

How can a good God be in charge of such moral disorder? A poetic genius attacked the question. Using the framework of what may have been an existing poem, he told the story of an absolutely blameless man named Job who saw both his life and his views of God turned upside down.

Through chapter after chapter, Job demanded an explanation of the disasters that had nearly destroyed him. Why should he, a thoroughly righteous man, suffer the loss of his wealth, his children, and, finally, his own health? Three, later four, "friends" debated him, defending the justice of the universe and the honor of a God who must have found some flaw in Job's moral armor. Job, they insisted, was being punished for some noxious thing he had done.

The ending of the Book of Job seems strange, even to astute students of scripture. When, near the end of the drama of Job, God finally responds to Job's request to enter the debate, the divine voice seems to speak past Job's question. God's response to Job is, on the surface, literature's most monumental *non sequitur.* The words seem simply to defend God's right to do with the world whatever God desires. As an explanation of why divine power is not used to prevent suffering, this traditional interpretation is thoroughly silent.

Perhaps we have misread the Book of Job in our efforts to see it as an exploration of the meaning of suffering. It is partially that, but its basic purpose may lie elsewhere. Perhaps the writer's goal was to explain the role of the divine in the face of undeserved suffering.

From the whirlwind—the ominous setting from which emerged the divine voice—Job learned nothing about *why* God had failed to act as his protector. He was told *how* God had acted in pursuit of an entirely different goal. All during Job's suffering, the Numen had continued to do what the divine had always done: push back the threatening jungle of disorder to establish a clearing in which Job would be free to rebuild his devastated life. God, according to that voice, had been preserving the separation of sea from dry land. God had ensured that Leviathan, that mythic symbol of chaos, was kept safely distant in the ocean depths. God had not caused Job's suffering, nor had God prevented that suffering. God had been supporting Job throughout, holding back the chaos just enough so that Job could survive and rebuild (Job 38-42).

The radical nature of the book of Job lies in this: It represents the rejection of traditional, inadequate concepts of divine power. The Holy One who meets Job is not the divine monarch Israel had sometimes worshiped. Monarchs tried to control every event in their realms. The writer of the Book of Job compared that monarchial image with what he knew of human events and found the image wanting. That the book remains a difficult challenge to modern readers is an indication that the model of God as overbearing ruler still prevails.

In short, the Book of Job traces the transformation of its main character from one who was chaos-intolerant to one who had made his peace with the messiness that surrounded him. Job discovered that he could not fit evil into any comprehensible pattern. Suffering is entirely random. Even in this random universe, however, Job discovered that the Numen was on his side, but in a way he had not imagined. Job was surrounded by a supportive presence, a divine web that exercised no power to protect him. Instead, this spirit would lean with him against the destructive forces. The Numen would provide strength as Job began to pick up the pieces. The discovery that he had not been abandoned gave Job the strength to survive and the will to rebuild.

Honest and mature Christians will find the example of the ancient Job attractive. This dramatic poem allows us to set aside any idea of an omnipotent power that controls every event (and therefore is responsible for the world's enormous pool of suffering). We may embrace, instead, the concept of the Numen whose empowering presence is always at work supporting us in our efforts to tame the chaos that threatens existence.

Fred Rogers, of the long-running children's program *Mister Rogers' Neighborhood*, was asked during a television interview to account for the positive attitude he was able to convey to his young audience. In response, he offered advice given to him by his mother. Several times during his own childhood, Fred Rogers witnessed fires, auto accidents, and other disasters. His mother would comfort him by saying, "Look for the helpers."

He learned, then, to focus his attention on the firemen, the rescue squads, the concerned neighbors who arrived, often risking their own well-being to minimize the damage and to assist victims to survive and rebuild.

Our understanding of the role of God would be transformed if we, like Fred Rogers, could learn to look for the helpers. Instead of assuming an all-powerful deity who, for unknown reasons, allowed a particular disaster to happen, we might identify a different form of divine power expressed in a far more positive manner. We might recognize a constructive, numinous power in the confluence of forces that gather in moments of chaos, forces that will once again separate light from darkness and push Leviathan back into the depths of the sea.

This changed view of the power of God fits with the experience of people's everyday life. It also emerges from the wisdom of our spiritual ancestors.

An honest effort to describe the divine, then, will move us from the concrete to the mysterious. It will move us from envisioning a separate being exercising control to a concept of the Numen, always loving, never ceasing to gather us into webs of mutual support in which we find sustenance and hope.

◆

Beyond Childish Concepts:
A God of Adequate Size

A sure sign of an immature faith is its investment in a divine being small enough to be understood (and manipulated). Fortunately, belief in a small God becomes increasingly difficult as human knowledge expands.

Across many centuries, an expanding knowledge of the universe has prodded people of faith to move, though at a snail's pace, through several stages in their understanding of the divine. (Distinct vestiges of each stage remain in the worship and beliefs of modern people.) First there was the *egocentric* deity, one whose primary business was to protect the individual from the forces that threatened health and life. As the Hebrews encountered other ethnic groups, a wider religious vision led to a second stage; at this stage they worshiped an *ethnocentric* god, one who could be called on to protect a particular people and to lead that people's armies to victory. Later yet, some progressive thinkers tried to move religion on to a third level, an *Earth-centered*[9] faith. At this Earth-centered stage, divine concern was assumed to touch all people and all creatures of planet Earth. Each of these stages is worth examination.

Egocentric

Some of the most ancient fragments of scripture speak of God in purely personal terms. When Abraham first appeared in the biblical narrative, at a time when no nation had been formed, the God to whom he responded was known simply as "my God." In Genesis 15:1, Abraham (known then as Abram) described God in terms of a personal shield. Throughout the remainder of scripture, and through religious literature of a more recent vintage, the phrase "my God" occurs frequently.

The dangers of this individualized God should be obvious. If I build my self-esteem and my sense of safety on the idea that God belongs in some special way to me, I have set myself up for overwhelming disappointment. Events, as life unfolds, are sure to prove me wrong. Abraham's belief that the divine is a personal shield might be appealing at first. But massive loneliness will be the result, for my happiness must always then be posited against the best interest of the remainder of humanity. When our interests conflict, the divine will be for me, against you. A God who is primarily my personal bodyguard is either the result of or the cause of paranoia.

Yet the idea of a personal God is deeply embedded in our tradition. For good reason. The Numen is much more than personal. But the Numen is never less than personal. The divine *is* my God in a very real sense, just as the divine is my neighbor's

God, and my enemy's God, and the God of each of those billions of people with whom I will never have personal contact. The pathos and profound meaning of Jesus' cry from the cross, "My God, my God, why have you forsaken me?" (Matthew 27:46 and Mark 15:34) must not be lost.[10]

The egocentric concept of God is an important stage in religious growth. The spiritual journey, however, must move forward from there.

Ethnocentric

In the scriptural narrative, Abraham's offspring became numerous, fulfilling a divine promise. The Hebrew nation was formed. God called Moses, and through Moses provided freedom from slavery and guidance through the wilderness. The God of the Israelites also assisted the nation as it won its way into a land of its own. An ethnocentric concept of the deity was embedded in this entire saga.

Thus was the Hebrew commitment to nation intertwined with its commitment to God. By worshipping their unique God (whom they assumed to be one among many gods), they were confident they were strengthening and protecting themselves as a nation. A vital connection between religion and patriotism took deep roots and spread like a vine far beyond Israel's borders.

A large segment of the religious population has never progressed beyond this stage. National flags appear in sacred settings across the globe. The unspoken assumption of this patriotic symbol: The god who is worshiped here smiles especially upon this national or this ethnic group.

Redeeming features exist in the egocentric stage of religious development. It is difficult for me to find similar positives in the ethnocentric stage. Believing the divine to be a special protector of one's own ethnic group has caused more violence than can be computed. Wars are always made more brutal when religious concerns enter; battles for self-protection are turned to crusades and holy wars, the most vicious kinds of human struggle.

The damage done by the ethnocentric stage of religious development should be obvious to any person who examines human history. Sadly, the lesson has not been absorbed. Whenever the United States, for example, is threatened, or when its armies threaten others, a multitude of churches are quick to add patriotic songs to their hymns of praise.

The dishonesty of the modern church is nowhere so evident as here. Church leaders, whose individual faith has been broadened by years of meditation and study, seem to lack the courage to challenge their people to move beyond the ethnocentric stage of religious development. Thus the dangers associated with the marriage of God and country live on. As warfare becomes more destructive, the damage done by this unholy alliance grows.

Earth-Centered

One of the truly amazing aspects of scripture is that several of its writers, despite their ethnic fears, stood on tiptoe and gazed beyond their nation's borders. With their broader view, they recognized that there existed but one God, and that this God's concerns reached across national boundaries. These internationalists were few, yet they exercised an influence disproportionate to their number.

The short-story writer who penned the story of Ruth was one of the earliest to have a truly Earth-centered worldview. Underneath this writer's tender tale of human commitment and romance was a larger purpose: to celebrate the contribution of non-Jewish women to the Jewish nation. Another such writer designed the story of an oafish and narrow patriot named Jonah. Jonah was confident that God did not have any interest in the people of Nineveh, for Nineveh was a gathering place for the enemies of the Hebrews. Yet Jonah, resisting at every turn, was sent by God to convert the people of that foreign city.

The writer of the middle chapters of the Book of Isaiah was another internationalist. His vision was stunning in its breadth, and lives on in the Christian tradition by its influence on Jesus' self-understanding.

Earth-centered faith is the broadest view in scripture. A faith that embraced the entire planet was the most advanced view possible for these writers, since they assumed that the Earth was the center of the universe. Were these religious spokespersons, some of whom composed their works more than 2,500 years ago, too advanced for their age, and now too advanced for ours? Why have church leaders not done more to encourage their people to rise above the God-and-country, God-and-flag mindset to acknowledge that the Numen embraces and supports people on every side of every national boundary?

During a recent national crisis, the phrase "God Bless America" was encountered at every turn. One congregation in California placed on its signboard these words:

> God bless America . . .
> And everyone else.

Such public sentiments are rare. Few Christians have moved beyond the ethnocentric understanding of God. Few church leaders have encouraged them to do so.

The Next Stage

We are, then, at least two stages behind. Followers of Jesus should long ago have moved to the Earth-centered stage. The challenge of the 21st century is to move our minds into broader arenas.

A god of planet Earth is still entirely too small. The supportive spirit we call God must be large enough to participate in a universe that extends across fourteen billion light years and continues to expand. Our concepts of God must account for the strangeness of quantum mechanics, with its evidence that all this marvelous creation is interrelated and interconnected. Storms on the surface of the sun soon become storms in the atmosphere of Earth, and gravitational forces at the edge of the universe affect the swing of a pendulum in France. In the face of these facts, we can no longer be content with a God who is nothing more than planet Earth's private chaplain.

Astronomers who are privileged to look deep into the heavens see stars (and, presumably, their accompanying planets) being born, and other stars and planets in the process of dying. Chaotic forces continue to be tamed, perhaps bringing about new environments in which sentient beings can exist. The Numen is alive, well, and at work far beyond the planet we call home.

In an age when stunning information about the heavens appears with regularity, only a God whose presence fills that universe is worthy of worship. As people mature, the scope of their world enlarges. "A great big ball I see" may be, for a pre-school child, the size of two arms extended. "A great big ball" for that child's parents should be at least the size of the Milky Way. Some of those parents (and grandparents) are religiously mature enough to recognize themselves as citizens of a universe that includes a billion galaxies. As knowledge of that universe expands, giving oneself in worship to a deity that resides in a shadowy "heaven" next door to planet Earth will be seen as an investment of decreasing value.

The concept of a God whose influence reaches the edges of the universe puts our lives and our concerns in perspective. Seeing this larger picture does not lessen the value of my life or make my worries smaller. Instead, this larger view causes my life and my concerns to be placed beside a multitude of other issues. When distances are beyond the scope of human imagination, and time is measured in billions of years, I am forced to learn patience when the taming of chaotic forces by the Numen moves at a pace less rapid than I would like.

▲

The honest church, then, will acquaint its members with the excitement of the theological search currently taking place. In a few (entirely too few) congregations, people are being invited to set aside concepts of God that served them as children and embrace a more mature understanding. Among those people, the mystery of the divine is being celebrated. An omnipotent god is being exchanged for an empowering God. A small, manageable deity is giving way to something like what I have called the Numen—the redemptive spirit that is at work here and in astoundingly distant places—the divine force that holds this remarkable universe together in a supportive and healing web of love.

◆

An Honest Church in Action

As I was writing this chapter, struggling to find ways to describe what it means to know God as Ultimate Mystery, I attended a worship service led by a friend of another denomination. The service was both worshipful and informal, a difficult combination that this church manages with aplomb. The closing moments of the service included congregational sharing. Two families reported the agony of having to seek institutional care for elderly parents. One person who held an office of public trust asked for prayers as he faced a particularly thorny decision. Another acknowledged his gratitude to nurses in a local hospital, and requested prayers for them as they continued their efforts. Two persons requested prayers and support for projects for peace and justice.

Not a single person asked the congregation to persuade God to change any of the difficult circumstances in his or her life. No one asked for intervention by any outside, overwhelming force. Each asked, instead, that persons of faith be aware. They wanted to know that other members of their faith community held them in prayerful concern as they sought, to the best of their abilities, to be faithful in the tasks and choices before them. I recalled Paul's description of the church: It is the body of Christ. The church, the closest thing we have to a physical manifestation of divine care, was the channel through which spiritual support was being expressed. "This," I found myself thinking, "is what it means to serve a God whose agenda is love rather than power." These people, revealing a wisdom I have come to respect in ordinary church people, knew themselves to be part of a web of divine concern. They asked only for prayers that would affirm that supportive web.

The honest church will do many of the things the congregation just described is doing. It will believe profoundly that an ever-present, persuasive Spirit can make, and is making, a difference. Through worship, the honest church will stress those foundational beliefs that motivate us: that the power/powerlessness of the Numen has been lived out through Jesus of Nazareth, and that the search for ways to encounter and serve the Ultimate Mystery gives breadth, depth, and meaning to life. The honest church will help its members live out the implications of their relationship to this creative, supportive spiritual web in which we exist. In so doing the honest church will remain securely rooted in its tradition, while reaching forward in hope.

NOTES

1. Paul Tillich, *The Courage to Be* (New Haven, Yale University Press, 1952).

2. Paul Tillich, "Waiting," in *The Shaking of the Foundations* (New York: Charles Scribner's Sons, 1948). Note that Tillich, a product of his time, assumed the masculine nature of the divine.

3. J. B. Phillips, *Your God is Too Small* (New York: Macmillan Publishing House, 1961).

4. *Merriam-Webster's Collegiate Dictionary, Deluxe Edition* (Springfield, Massachusetts: Merriam-Webster, Inc., 1998).

5. *The American Heritage Dictionary* (Boston: Houghton Mifflin Company, 1994).

6. Rudolf Otto, *The Idea of the Holy* (Oxford: Oxford University Press, 1923).

7. This is taken from one of the most precious books in my library, *Rufus Jones Speaks to Our Time,* edited by Harry Emerson Fosdick (New York: The Macmillan Company, 1951).

8. Steven Hawking, *A Brief History of Time* (New York: Bantam Books, 1998).

9. I would love to have used the term "Earthnocentric," but my exacting editor—and, more importantly, my wife—advised against it.

10. As the story is related by the Gospel writers, Jesus, at the moment of death, turned to his religious heritage: the words of Psalm 22.

9

Signs of Hope

The landscape remains bleak. In too many places and in too many ways, church professionals are engaged in a rear-guard defense of the "Faith of Our Fathers, living still . . ." The words of that hymn are ambiguous: Which is being kept alive—fathers or faith? *Rigor mortis* is a danger in either case. I am reminded of Pelikan's comment: *"Tradition* is the living faith of the dead, *traditionalism* is the dead faith of the living." The modern church must make a clearer choice between the two.

Nonetheless, several oases of hope are appearing at scattered places across the religious landscape.

In Chapter 6, I noted several reasons for optimism—reasons that had to do with changes taking place at the core of the current life of the church. Here, in this final chapter, I want to point to new realities occurring on, or just beyond, the cutting edge of church life. Some of these new realities, such as changes in the field of science, have no religious roots at all. They represent, nonetheless, external pulls toward religious renewal.

In a few cases, individual thinkers and writers, and even whole congregations, are joining to produce organized groups whose mission is to share fresh insights across the professional/

laity divide. Most of these groups remain modest in size and scope. (The Jesus Seminar is the exception. It is large enough to draw both attention and abundant critical reaction.) Small but dynamic, the other movements are sure signs that congregations cannot remain insulated from the thought-worlds that surround them. Mainline Protestantism must, to borrow a phrase from the Roman Catholics, open its windows and let fresh breezes blow, else its gradual decline in numbers and influence will continue until it is no longer worth preserving.

◆

Expansion of Interest

A major sign of hope is the explosion of interest in the renewal of Christianity. Books and magazine articles that call for new thinking abound. Those who want to defend dogma developed centuries ago, who measure truth by its antiquity, are everywhere under attack.

In a visit to the web page of a major bookseller, I searched for titles using the keywords "Religion, renewal." More than four hundred books were described. A quick and unscientific survey indicated that approximately half of these books were asking for sweeping changes in church life. The other half were requests for alterations of a modest sort, alterations in the way evangelism, worship, or some other single aspect of religious life is carried on. The calls for limited change were usually the products of denominational publishing houses and were efforts to control, rather than stimulate, the forces of change. Yet, even these were acknowledgments that the problems of modern church life cannot be ignored.

Religion and Science

Especially significant is the expanded interest in the relationship between science and religion.

Ian Barbour, in *When Science Meets Religion,* described several ways in which science and religion have related to one another. *Conflict, independence, dialogue,* and *interdependence* are the four major ways these two fields have met—or chosen not to meet. *Conflict* takes place when, for example, religious literalists argue that the Book of Genesis represents a more accurate account of history than the concepts of evolution. *Independence* means the two operate in different realms: religion in the realm of the spirit, science in measurable phenomena. *Dialogue* means they overlap at points, and thus must enter into conversation. *Interdependence* means they are partners in the encounter with mystery.

I want to suggest a fifth possibility, one that can grow out of Barbour's third or fourth options. Science and religion can and should be *mutually corrective.*

Several modern writers are well equipped to help scientists and people of faith interact. The first is Ian Barbour himself. He is the emeritus Bean Professor of Science, Technology, and Society at Carleton College in Minnesota. He has written and lectured on issues in science and religion for several decades. His early work, *Issues in Science and Religion,*[1] has long been considered a basic text for those interested in the interaction of these two fields. His more recent works include *Religion in an Age of Science*[2] and *When Science Meets Religion.*[3] A second major writer is John C. Polkinghorne, who has taught religion and science at Queens College, Cambridge, and is Canon Theologian of Liverpool, England. His book *Belief in God in an Age of Science*[4] consists of the Terry Lectures given at Yale University and is a summary of a lifetime of living at the intersection of science and faith. A third writer of note is Arthur Peacocke, who is a priest and Canon in the Church of England and has worked in the field of physical biochemistry for most of his adult life. Peacocke, too, has published a summary of his work and thought. His book is entitled *Paths from Science Towards God.*[5]

Barbour, Polkinghorne, and Peacocke demonstrate the profound and balanced thinking that is needed as science and religion encounter one another. These three do not always agree.

Polkinghorne approaches the Christian faith from a traditional stance. Barbour is influenced by process theology (a concept that will be discussed shortly). Peacocke is situated somewhat between the two, but closer to Barbour; he, too, is influenced by process theology. Each, nonetheless, is a helpful guide for all those who want science to be guided by the insights of religion, and faith to be influenced by the findings of science. These three are representative of many writers in this expanding and exciting field.

■ Impact of the Encounter of Religion and Science

As Christians attempt to develop mature understandings of the Numen, help can be found in surprising quarters. Science, which is sometimes considered an antagonist of faith, has proven that it can provide helpful insights and useful metaphors.

As Barbour has pointed out, science and religion can be interdependent, allies in their encounters with mystery. Some differences in approach will always exist between these two fields. Science sees each unknown issue as a challenge and wants to move immediately to its solution. Religion, in contrast, is nourished by mystery and is threatened by insights that unfold too rapidly—insights that expose us to truths for which we are unprepared.

Rather than putting the two at odds, however, these differences in approach show how much science and religion need one another. The two are, as Barbour points out, *interdependent.* Beyond that, they need one another in a *mutually corrective* sense. Without religion, science has demonstrated in tragic ways how it can lose sight of its central goal of serving humankind. Experiments using human subjects, especially the disabled, done in both Germany and the United States, are well-known examples of what happens to unbridled science. The development of weapons of mass destruction is another area in which science has moved without due caution and with inadequate dialogue with students of human ethics.

Humankind is deeply threatened when science proceeds with no concern for a larger vision of human welfare and sells its findings to the highest bidder. Unbridled science, that is, science that has attempted to take over the role of religion, should be called by its proper name: "scientism."

On the other hand, religion needs to open itself to the corrective influence of science. Without science to urge it forward, religion is in danger of stagnating and becoming lazy in its embrace of outdated dogma.

Science may seem a strange place to start in expanding one's vision of life's spiritual dimension. Yet what better place to begin than in the study of the world in which the sacred is encountered? Scientific thinkers such as Galileo, Sigmund Freud, Charles Darwin, and Stephen Hawking are sometimes perceived as critics of religion. It is possible to accept them, instead, as friends. They have encouraged people of faith to do what they should have done without outside help: reach for a larger and more sustainable concept of God. They have forced religious people to expand their understanding of the inner workings of the human psyche, to see the interconnections of all things, and to confront the almost unimaginable scope of the universe.

Science, quite inadvertently, has taken the lead in narrowing the gap between its own insights and the insights of religion. Recent developments at both the quantum (tiny) and astronomical (huge) levels have forced many leading scholars of physics to talk and write like philosophers, or even at times like theologians. The questions that scientists ask today are quite open-ended. How can one explain a world in which the old laws of cause and effect are no longer entirely dependable? How can one deal scientifically with light when light fits at least two mutually exclusive descriptions? How can one rely on measurements of our environment when the very act of observing changes the nature of what is observed, so that one can no longer make a clear distinction between object and subject? What is the nature of consciousness, that strange ability of the mind to stand apart and observe itself? Is consciousness simply the result of a certain degree of complexity in the mental processes? Can it occur in a computer once the computer has achieved this critical mass of complexity? These issues require the scientist to move outside the comfortable world of mathematical measurements and cope with ultimate issues. At times scientists find themselves calling on colleagues from disciplines such as ethics and theology.[6]

As science moves closer to religion, religion finds itself strengthened by new insights. Scientific progress has forced the church to reopen an issue discussed in the previous chapter: Are the concepts of God we carry with us adequate for the age in which we live?

Some years ago an interesting story circulated among members of the clergy. Supposedly, a religious educator had polled a group of early teenagers on this question: Does God understand radar? The vote, or so it was reported, was lopsidedly negative. The story sounded apocryphal. I decided to test it. I asked the same question to a confirmation class made up of unusually bright early teens. The first response was a moment of perplexed silence. Then laughter. The group admitted, almost unanimously, that their first reaction was to vote "no." They immediately saw the importance of the insight this simple inquiry engendered. Their ideas of the divine needed revision.

Many new insights of science help challenge our views of God. While most church members do not understand the intricacies of quantum physics (nor, indeed, is the local pastor likely to be comfortable in this realm), both pastor and parishioners have been exposed to news reports about this fascinating, developing field. They know that quantum physics refers to a strangeness at the foundation of being. At the quantum level, the level of the smallest building blocks of matter, nature seems to become capricious, to free itself of the usual laws of cause and effect. At this level the predictability of normal physics vanishes. Waves are transformed, when observed, into particles, and vice versa. The distinction between the observer and the observed, which Western minds once considered obvious, is eliminated. We influence the quantum world simply by trying to measure it. We cannot remove ourselves and study with accuracy what remains, for in stepping aside we have altered what is to be studied. We are part of the world, and the world is part of us, in ways that we are only dimly beginning to imagine.

The world of objects is interconnected in strange ways. For example, two quarks (tiny particles) that have been together, then separated, remain related through some unknown force, though they may be miles apart. When one quark alters direction, its former partner will *at the same instant* also change direction, even though no known way of communication connects the two.

Barbara Brown Taylor, in a brilliant and helpful article, described the change in religious thinking that must accompany this new worldview of physics.

> It is no longer possible to see [our world] as a collection of autonomous parts, as Newton did, existing separately while interacting. The deeper revelation is the degree to which the world is interconnected. The observer is not separable from what is observed. Or, in [Werner] Heisenberg's words, "The common division of the world into subject and object, inner world and outer world, body and soul, is no longer adequate."

Later in the article, Taylor speculates on the theological meaning of these scientific insights:

> Where is God in this picture? All over the place. Up there. Down here. Inside my skin and out. God is the web, the energy, the space, the light—not captured in them, as if any of those concepts were more real than what unites them, but revealed in that singular, vast new web of relationship that animates everything that is.
>
> It is not enough for me to proclaim that God is responsible for all this unity. Instead, I want to proclaim that God *is*

the unity—the very energy, the very intelligence, the very
elegance and passion that make it all go.[7]

What Taylor, reacting to quantum physics, has written
sounds surprisingly similar to a speech attributed to Paul and
given to a group who were trying to cope with divine mystery
(a truth-story that has had a profound impact on Christian concepts of the divine): "The God who made the world and everything in it, he who is Lord of heaven and earth, does not live in
shrines made by human hands, nor is he served by human
hands, as though he needed anything, since he himself gives to
all mortals life and breath and all things. From one ancestor he
made all nations to inhabit the whole earth, and he allotted the
times of their existence and the boundaries of the places where
they would live, so that they would search for God and perhaps grope for him and find him, though indeed he is not far
from each one of us. For in him we live and move and have our
being" (Acts 17:24-28).

Quantum mechanics has forced science to move closer to
theology as both try to deal with what cannot be explained. As
science moves closer, it creates a gravitational pull that draws
religion away from its tired and inadequate concepts of the
divine. Traditional theology is based on a now-discarded para-
digm: separate beings interacting with one another, with each
action causing a predictable reaction. God was once considered
one of those distinct, separate beings. But the world of cause
and effect, the world of separate entities, is gone now. We must
learn to speak of God in new ways—ways such as the Numen,
or Ultimate Mystery.

In the late 16th century, Galileo shared his observations that
proved the Earth was not the center of the universe. The
Roman Catholic Church responded by putting the astronomer
under house arrest. In the later part of the 20th century, the
church publicly, and for the first time, admitted its error.

The scientific advances of the present time are at least as
far-reaching as those of Galileo's time. And they have the

potential of making equally unsettling changes in the theological world. This time, I predict, the church will not have the luxury of four hundred years to adjust.

By adjusting its views, the church is not surrendering to science. It is allowing science to be the prod that brings theology back into harmony with its own most profound insights.

■ Illustrations and Metaphors

Science assists religion in another way. In addition to expanding our minds, science offers rich illustrations and metaphors that help us begin to penetrate the divine mysteries.

A helpful illustration of the mystery that science and religion share comes from what astronomers call "dark matter." When measurements of the total mass of the universe are made, what can be seen explains the gravitational force of only about 10 percent of what exists in the heavens. As much as 85 to 90 percent of what makes up our universe is inaccessible to humans through our five senses.

Timothy Ferris gives this more precise definition of the issue:

> A ghostly clue that there may be such undetected material in the universe today is proffered by what astronomers call the dark matter problem. The masses of galaxies and their clusters can be deduced by measuring the velocity at which stars orbit the centers of the galaxies to which they belong, and at which galaxies orbit the centers of clusters of galaxies. In case after case, this turns out to add up to something like five or ten times the mass of all the visible stars and nebulae. The startling implication is that everything we see and photograph in the sky amounts to only a fraction of the gravitationally interacting matter in our quarter of the universe.[8]

What Ferris has described is one of the most astounding discoveries of the modern age. The majority of everything that exists in our universe is unseen and as yet unknown! It was not even imagined to be present until recently.

I am not attempting to build a case that equates God with dark matter. Instead, I find it remarkable that we live within and are dependent on something real, something that participates in the systems that make up the universe, yet cannot be seen, heard, touched, tasted, or smelled. Add to this information the fact that we are also surrounded by unseen electronic impulses, some of which are also necessary for life, and some of which can be translated by a variety of modern receiving devices. *It is also quite conceivable that we are, at every moment and in every place, immersed in, surrounded by, saturated with, a spirit-world that is not subject to detection by our usual means of knowing.* Is this not what the words attributed to Paul implied? "In [God] we live and move and have our being."

Science helps, also, by reinforcing and enriching metaphors that the church has used for centuries. Religious persons have always searched for ways to symbolize what cannot be intellectually grasped. Worship usually takes place in the presence of such symbols. As culture changes, some of these symbols lose their power. Fortunately, the opposite can also occur: New insights can expand the symbolic power of ancient symbols.

"God is light": This is one example of a religious symbol that has been enriched by scientific discoveries. The phrase does not mean that God is equated with light. "God is light" is poetry, metaphor, simile. People of almost every religious faith light candles to celebrate the presence of the divine. Architects design places of worship to maximize the impact and beauty of light.

Humanity has always known basic facts that helped light become a central religious symbol. Light guides; it is essential to growth; it even purifies. Now, with the aid of science, we know even more about the appropriateness of light as a religious symbol. Light has power, especially when it becomes focused in the form of laser beams. This power can both heal and destroy. More fascinating yet, light surrounds itself in mystery. For example, the speed of light appears fixed at precisely

186,272 miles per second. Yet, if a space traveler is moving from Earth to Mars at half the speed of light, that person will experience the light traveling from Mars toward Earth as being precisely the same as if the spacecraft were standing still. Why? No one knows.

Other scientists have tried to determine whether light is a wave, or whether light is made up of particles. In some experiments light acts as a particle; in other experiments it is a wave. Logic says it cannot be both. Yet it is both. Its nature remains an enigma.

Paul Tillich remarked that a symbol must participate in the essence of what is symbolized. To symbolize the Ultimate Mystery, we could hardly do better than the mystery that is light. Science has enriched this symbol.

Music is used as frequently as light to evoke a sense of the deity. Singing and dancing, organs and a variety of other musical instruments, have been used in praise of God. Rhythms and melodies are stimulants to lively worship. The beauty of music is a conduit into the depths of worship, evoking the divine in ways that words cannot.

Now science is strengthening the connection between music and faith. Many physicists believe that the most basic building block of matter is a substance so tiny that its size must be expressed mathematically. It is called a "superstring." Superstrings vibrate. The frequency of their vibration determines their mass. The more energetic the vibration, the greater the mass. Scientific instruments can detect superstrings only when they vibrate together in groups of three. Then they make up protons, neutrons, and electrons. The astrophysicist Trinh Xuan Thuan describes with eloquence the implications of this insight.

> The music of an atom, which is made up of protons, neutrons, and electrons, is played by even more musicians [superstrings] in an even larger orchestra. In this way, strings sing and vibrate all around us, and the universe is in fact a vast symphony.[9]

Music has been described as shorthand notes brought back by visitors to another world. A Bach prelude, or indeed any suitable musical composition, has long been known to be an effective means of preparing a congregation for worship. This, we now suspect, is no accident. Music not only mimics the creative work of God by organizing sounds into harmonies; it also participates in the essence of reality.

Yet a third symbolic way of speaking of God is enriched by insights of science: "God is love." This statement, so central to a Christian's understanding of the divine, has been, unfortunately, used as if it referred to a sweet feeling, an insipid emotion lacking power to impact the real business of living.

Quantum physics has put muscle into the concept that God is love. This branch of science reports that our world is, through and through, relational. Nothing exists apart from its role in a larger system. Superstrings have an independent existence, but that existence is meaningless apart from their participation in quarks. Quarks exist to be part of the building blocks of atoms, which exist to be the basis of all larger objects. In a similar way, we could say, each human being has an independent existence, but that existence is authenticated by relationships to other human beings, to the world of nature, and to the divine. The Earth can be defined in itself, but it would sail off into frigid space if it were not related to the other objects in the solar system.

What power holds all these particular beings together in the web of relationships that makes genuine existence possible? The Numen is the web that binds us all in a remarkable interrelatedness. God is, indeed, love.

Love, then, is more than sentiment. Love is, as the songwriter wrote more accurately than he knew, "what makes the world go 'round." The power that holds families together also holds atoms in molecules, and binds us all into a web of mutual responsibility that reaches out into the heavens. As Barbara Brown Taylor said in the article quoted earlier, "I want to proclaim that God *is* the unity—the very energy, the very intelligence, the very elegance and passion that make it all go." *God is love* takes on deeper meaning as science enriches the religious vocabulary.

▲

Thus a basic point becomes clear: A gigantic tragedy is perpetrated when, in the name of a literal view of the Bible, religion is pitted against science. When cutting-edge secular knowledge is banished from the sanctuary, parishioners are left with their childhood pictures of God unchallenged. In those childhood images, God remains a separate Being, a Super-Santa who dwells somewhere out there, whose concern is limited to planet Earth, and whose primary business is keeping current his list of who's naughty and nice. When the wealth of scientific knowledge is welcomed in the sanctuary, the concept of God is infinitely expanded and the symbols of God become more effective in evoking a sense of Ultimate Mystery.

As I have insisted at several earlier points, the fresh approach to religion needed for today does not take us away from our tradition. A more open and honest view of scripture reveals that our spiritual ancestors were not anti-science. They consistently used their best understanding of their physical surroundings to help understand the relationship between the divine and their world.

> When I look at your heavens, the work of your fingers,
>> the moon and the stars that you have established,
> what are human beings that you are mindful of them,
>> mortals that you care for them?
>
> (Psalm 8:3-4)

We live in an age of phenomenal, mind-bending new insights. Yet much of the information that appears to be new actually reinforces ancient insights. For centuries, in almost every culture, light and music have helped carry people to the depth of life. Now science is telling us that light and music are, indeed, at the core of reality. How sad it is when religion and science spend energy pushing each other away. Instead, progressive religion and modern science have a unique opportunity to enrich and correct one another as they encounter, each in its unique way, the Ultimate Mystery.

◆

Organizations Dedicated to Honesty

Another reason for hope is the appearance of organized groups dedicated to bridging the gap between the faith of the religious professional and that of the religious laity. Individuals who press for change can be significant, but they are never enough. Ideas must be housed within ongoing institutions if they are to survive long enough to make a difference. Several institutions committed to spreading the excitement of the religious search to those who occupy church pews have emerged in the past few decades.

Here are some organized movements that offer hope.

The Westar Institute

The best known, and by far the most controversial, of the groups pressing for an honest faith is the Westar Institute. The Institute sponsors a group of New Testament scholars known as "The Jesus Seminar," a group already described in Chapter 6. In their material, the Institute defines its purpose in these words: "To renew the quest of the historical Jesus and *to report the results of its research to more than a handful of gospel specialists*" [italics added]. Clearly, this organization has seen itself as a means of bridging the gap between an informed religious elite and a less informed religious laity.

The Jesus Seminar began in 1985 with thirty scholars and has grown to include more than two hundred. Their initial task was to achieve a clearer view of Jesus of Nazareth. Their method has been to look at each of the sayings attributed to Jesus in the Gospel stories and to assign to each a level of *probability of authenticity.* Voting was done by placing colored beads in boxes. Red equaled a high degree of probability that Jesus actually said the words attributed to him; black equaled a very low probability. Pink and gray represented intermediate positions. Using this method, only 18 percent of the words attributed to Jesus in the Gospels were judged likely to have been said by him.

These findings are unfathomable to a biblical literalist, and shocking even to those who approach the scripture with a degree of sophistication. Members of the Jesus Seminar explained and defended their choices in a work already referred to in Chapter 7, *The Five Gospels.* (The number five is due to the inclusion of the Gospel of Thomas, a collection of Jesus' sayings discovered relatively recently, along with the four biblical Gospels.)

Using the sayings that they assume to be authentic, members of the Jesus Seminar have developed a profile of the historical Jesus. (The profile was helpful to me as I wrote Chapter 7 of this volume.)

The historical Jesus, according to the Jesus Seminar, did not see himself as the founder of a new religion. Nor did he perceive his role to be that of sacrificial lamb in a cosmic conflict between God and Satan. He was never one to present quick answers to simple questions. Instead, he lived out the meaning of faithfulness to a realm in which God's will is paramount. He was a stimulant for new ideas, a framer of questions. Rather than seeing himself as divine and therefore separate from others, he saw himself as the essence of humanity.

The Jesus Seminar meets twice each year to discuss research papers that have been prepared and read in advance. Between meetings, they publish their findings, and send their scholars to any local church that invites them for weekend lectures and discussions. These weekend sessions are called "Jesus Seminars on the Road."

The often blatantly hostile opposition engendered by the Jesus Seminar indicates that their activity has struck a nerve. The controversial nature of their work is not the issue. Scholars are accustomed to disagreeing among themselves. As long as the disagreement is kept quietly within the walls of academia, the arguments are restrained. When, however, a group takes concepts once confined to the academic community out into the larger marketplace of ideas, the reaction can be nasty. Critics have claimed, for example, that none of the members of the Jesus Seminar are outstanding scholars, nor do they teach at major universities.

Such critics no doubt have their own definition of "outstanding scholars" and "major universities." In point of fact, though, members of the Jesus Seminar teach at colleges and universities all across the United States (including an institution as distinguished as Stanford) and hold doctorates from Oxford, Harvard, Yale, and other respected schools.

The method of voting, by colored beads, seems to bother the critics, too. But is there, one might wonder, a better way of indicating the nuanced nature of decisions in the complex matter of determining the genuine sayings of Jesus?

The Jesus Seminar has covered so much material that criticism of some of its decisions is inevitable. Members of the Seminar no doubt welcome a certain amount of notoriety. Discussion of serious issues, not agreement, is their goal. They disagree among themselves. That is why they vote, and why they vote with degrees of probability.

A more serious criticism is that, despite their desire to communicate with persons in local pews, they can sometimes radiate a self-defeating air of self-importance. Their book on the sayings of Jesus includes their own translation of the Gospels. This translation delightfully captures the vernacular of the koine (earthy) Greek in which the New Testament was written. Unfortunately, they choose to call this *The Scholars' Translation*, a title that can be off-putting to those who are not part of an academic community. The name also carries the implication that other translations have been done by persons who are less prepared academically.

This, however, is a minor criticism compared with the heavy attacks leveled against the Jesus Seminar by some defenders of the status quo. The fury of the attacks is a sure sign that a deeper issue is at stake. The issue is the same as that pursued in this volume: an honest faith. Or, seen from an opposite standpoint, the issue is the preservation of a dishonest faith. The Jesus Seminar has sinned by telling tales out of school. They have violated the unwritten rule that says that religious professionals should have one style and quality of faith while offering another style and quality of faith to the laity. For shame!

Fortunately for those who want an honest bridging of the pulpit/pew gap, the Jesus Seminar presses on with its work. As this is written, they are looking at the writings attributed to Paul with the same critical eye used in analyzing the Gospel accounts. No doubt more controversy is ahead.

The Center for Progressive Christianity

The Center for Progressive Christianity (TCPC) is a network of congregations that are committed to bringing Christianity into the 21st century. As explained in a previous chapter, they encourage congregations to make the search for truth a higher priority than the preservation of dogma. The number of churches that have affiliated with TCPC is growing. It now includes congregations across the entire United States as well as in Canada, Europe, New Zealand, and Australia. TCPC invites into its fellowship churches that are stimulated more by enticing questions than by set answers. It offers encouragement and literature to churches that are engaged in the otherwise lonely task of questioning the rigid truisms of yesterday.

Process and Faith

Process and Faith, which was founded in 1984 and has its headquarters in Claremont, California, is another network of individuals and churches seeking to explore effective ways to be followers of Jesus in the modern world. It seeks to disseminate concepts based on the insights of the philosopher/theologian Alfred North Whitehead. *Process theology* is the name given to Whitehead's views.

As stated in the brochure of Process and Faith, process theology offers a relational vision of reality where:

- Science and religion need not contradict each other;
- Concepts of the divine and human natures make sense;
- Other faiths are respected and valued;
- Creative transformation of self and world is a possibility alive in every moment.

Process and Faith publishes literature, provides speakers, and produces a quarterly magazine—all efforts to move the insights of theologians out to the general public. After confining their early activity mostly to southern California, the group is now seeking to reach a larger audience. They have developed the Road Scholar Program as a means of providing speakers, sharing literature, and leading workshops in process theology. A goal of the Road Scholar Program is to form study and action groups in cities across the United States and Canada.

More will be said later in this chapter about process theology. For now, it is important to note that those views are being disseminated by an active, organized group.

◆

Actions at the Local Level

Perhaps most hopeful of all is the fact that many local churches are involved in activities that ensure that fresh breezes will blow through outworn concepts. Congregations that are committed to new ways of thinking and being are inviting lecturers from the Jesus Seminar or from Process and Faith. They are banding together to support one another in structures such as TCPC. They are discovering creative ways to utilize their unique resources in a search for new truths.

A United Methodist Church in Oak Ridge, Tennessee, sponsors an annual Science Fair in which workshops, demonstrations, and lectures highlight advances in science and explore the religious implications of those advances. Here, in the city where some of the awesome advances in science have begun, a mainline Protestant congregation is exploring ways to relate itself to the new realities that many of its own members helped birth.

Creative congregations find other ways to turn faith into an exciting venture. A Catholic parish in Champaign, Illinois, applied for and received a grant from the Illinois Council on the Arts for a lecture series called "Ushering in the New Millennium." The series invited secular and religious speakers to explore ways in which religious faith and the secular world can interface. A Presbyterian congregation in Roanoke, Virginia, uses the income from an endowment fund to bring outstanding scholars to the city for a series of lectures. This lecture series, like many other similar ones across the nation, brings the academic world in contact with the pew. Walter Breuggemann, one of the outstanding biblical scholars of the present day, was a recent participant in the series. He used one of his evenings to take the congregation through the story of the Hebrew escape from Egypt (Exodus 1-14). At the end of the talk he remarked, calmly, "There is not a shred of evidence that any of this ever happened. Yet the story remains a pivotal part of our religious foundation." No murmur of displeasure came from this mainline congregation. As I tried to read their faces, I was confident that I saw people who recognized that they had been respected. They seemed to know that Breuggemann had offered them information that was both spiritually profound and historically correct.

Breaking Out of Religious Isolation

Here is another reason for hope: In many ways, members of local churches are attempting to break out of the isolation created by Christianity's claims to exclusive access to God. When other faiths are considered to be basically bogus, little motivation can be found to learn about those faiths. So, across many generations, Christians have developed negative attitudes toward world religions of which they knew practically nothing. With instant communication and rapid travel shrinking the global village, Christian ignorance of the remainder of the world becomes increasingly intolerable.

When the Gulf War broke out in the early 1990s, the congregation in central Illinois where I was pastor determined that they could no longer live in isolation from the other major world religions. We made contact with the local mosque. The leaders of the mosque were delighted to send lecturers for a series of encounters. They invited our church to a Friday evening service. The contacts were pleasant (though occasionally bruising to old assumptions) and broadening for both sides. After the events of September 11, 2001, these contacts were renewed.

Many other congregations have made similar efforts to expose themselves to other faiths. Christians are no longer content to read what other Christians write about Islam, or Buddhism, or Hinduism. They want to hear honest evaluations of those faiths by persons who speak from within those faiths.

One thing is beyond question: People of different religions will encounter one another with increasing frequency. Churches, therefore, do a service to the entire community when they arrange organized and productive settings for interfaith contacts. This communication lessens the chance that such contacts will take place in unstructured settings where misunderstandings might be multiplied.

The United States is no longer the Christian culture (or even the Judeo-Christian culture) it was once assumed to be (and probably never was). Immigration policies of the United States over the last hundred years have ensured that, as Diana Eck has indicated, the United States is now the most religiously diverse nation on Earth. In her book, *A New Religious America*,[10] she has catalogued the amazing growth of non-Western religious practice in this nation. In this volume she describes the Parliament of World Religions held in Chicago in 1993. That gathering brought from across the globe leaders of all the major world faiths. Yet, Eck insists, the sessions could have been held using only people from the Chicago area. Communities of every significant world religion can be found in that single metropolitan area. And that is only one major city! She points out that Hindu temples and Islamic mosques are rising in both urban and rural areas all across the land.

Eck's book is the result of years of study done in cooperation with her students, who are part of the Pluralism Project of Harvard University. Her findings not only give a clear picture of the ethnic and religious makeup of the United States at a particular point in time, but also hold profound implications for those who practice the Christian faith. No longer can Christians make assumptions about the "heathen" who live in distant places. Those assumptions will be tested by human contacts in places of business and leisure. Stunningly beautiful places of worship, constructed lovingly by faithful Buddhists or Muslims and placed in quiet neighborhoods, belie the sentiments of Christian hymns that dismiss those faiths as centers of darkness and despair.

Occasionally, a vignette offers insight into the otherwise subtle changes that are taking place around us. I was shopping in a relatively small midwestern city when a fascinating scene emerged in front of me. The salesperson I saw was a young woman dressed in the distinctive garb of Islam. She was assisting a large black man whose silver cross necklace dangled between them as they leaned together to examine the piece of jewelry he was considering. Here, I found myself thinking, is the new American—perhaps the new world—culture.

This emerging social milieu may be one of our most important reasons for hope. Our new neighbors will force us to rethink many of our previously comfortable but destructive assumptions. If Truth is large enough to distribute itself among the major religions, then Christians have much to learn as well as much to share. We will be forced to change our self-image. Instead of always being the teacher, we must sometimes be the student. Dogmatic statements will often give way to questions.

Or, to put all of this in a slightly different way, if honest reform does not come from the professional leadership of the church, it will be forced upon that leadership by relentless social forces. The laity are immersed in those forces. They are the ones who, in their workplaces or in their evening reading, come across the findings of science that create dissonance with traditional faith. They are the ones who, in social events or in the marketplace, have contacts with Buddhists, Hindus, Sikhs, atheists, Jews, and others—contacts that batter their prior assumptions concerning non-Christians. The laity will increasingly demand to hear intelligent discussions of the points of intersection between these varied forces and varied faiths. If these issues are not honestly addressed, the laity will (and should) continue to do what millions have already done: They will vote with their feet. They will quietly disappear.

Two Helpful Movements

Here is yet another reason for hope. New ways of discussing the Ultimate Mystery called God are emerging out of the religious ferment of the present day. Two that I want to describe have remained faithful to the living tradition of Christianity while challenging the dead traditionalism that has poisoned the modern church.

■ Process Theology

The first of these movements, *process theology*, has already been introduced. As the term implies, process theology shifts the emphasis from things to events, from nouns to verbs. God is to be found in the interaction of what we once thought of as separate realities.

Process theology insists that God is not a static, overwhelming presence from beyond, but a participant in the interrelated web of the universe. God is, as indicated earlier, the anti-entropic force that is always present and always carrying out the work of replacing chaos with order. Process theology has no quarrel with science. Instead, process theology celebrates the insights of quantum physics, especially those that recognize the indivisibility of all things. Process theology and quantum physics agree that the universe works together, not as a great machine of separate parts but as a magnificent, interrelated system in which no single item can exist without the remainder. Systems interact with and affect other systems; they join in making ever larger systems. The largest system of all embraces the entire universe *and includes the divine.* By interacting with the created world, God continues to change just as the universe continues to change. God, too, is in process, just as the universe is in process.

Advocates of process theology will recognize many themes that have been explored in this volume—themes that process theologians have developed in a compelling way. In particular, they would agree that God works to transform chaos into order. Whitehead wrote in a similar vein of the amazing capacity of the universe to create patterns of beauty. Process theology stresses that the Numen's method of working with the world is loving persuasion; the divine does not have the dominating "power over" other events that is an important part of traditional theology. God's power is the power to empower. The deity is forever at work luring us toward our highest and best. Yet we can choose to disregard this influence. We are free to act in ways that decrease the harmony of the world. Acting in this negative way, however, will bring pain to ourselves and to God, who feels the suffering of all sentient beings. For all of these ideas, I am indebted to process theologians.

The Jewish theologian/philosopher Abraham Heschel has suggested that biblical references to the wrath of God are metaphors for the pain of God. Process theology embraces this concept. The Numen, as part of the ultimate unity of all things, is impacted by human rebellion. On the other hand, human rebellion is restrained by the gentle urgings of the Spirit. In process theology, cause and effect move back and forth, from divine to human, from human to divine.

■ *Panentheism*

A second relatively new way of speaking of the divine is called "panentheism." This is a concept that was put forth at the University of Chicago by Charles Hartshorne, a philosopher of religion who did his major work in the middle of the 20th century. His ideas have been incorporated into other modern thought patterns, including, often, process theology. Most process theologians embrace panentheism, although not all panentheists are process theologians.

Panentheism sounds at first like a slight twist on an old idea: pantheism. Pantheism insists that God is everything, and everything is God. The problems of pantheism, however, are enormous. It assumes that God is entirely immanent. All sense of transcendence is lost. How can we equate the divine with all reality, the destructive no less than the constructive? How can reality be assigned different degrees of value if everything is ultimately divine?

The inclusion of the syllable "en" responds to the problems of pantheism. The Numen, according to the panentheists, is *in* all things and upholds the being of all that is, but is not to be equated with all things. All things are also in the Numen. This also allows us to acknowledge that the divine is both in and beyond us.

Panentheism, unlike pantheism, stresses that each person, and each object we encounter, has a separate existence, yet is held together by participation in the Numen. John B. Cobb, Jr. explains this:

Hartshorne suggests that we think of the relation of God and the world as like that of the psyche or soul to the body, or most particularly to the brain. Hartshorne thinks of each cell in the brain in each moment as an individual subject that receives from others and in turn acts on others. Each cellular event or experience is also taken up into the unified experience of the human person. This experience is not just made up of all the cellular experiences added one to another. Instead it integrates them into a single coherent experience with its own memories and anticipations. Similarly, all of these human (and other creaturely) experiences are taken up into the unified cosmic experience that is God. Hartshorne calls this doctrine *panentheism*.[11]

▲

Both panentheism and process theology carry us a good distance from the monarchial divine, the overpowering, dogmatic deity that characterizes the theology of most current Christians.

These two approaches to God combine fresh insights with a deep respect for the wisdom of the past. Both are firmly rooted in our religious tradition, though they differ significantly from the ways that tradition has commonly been taught. The biblical Abraham left for a new home, having sensed an invitation from a spiritual Mystery. This Mystery beckoned Abraham toward an unknown land. Process theology and panentheism both ask that modern day believers continue Abraham's journey in search of an infinite and ultimate truth that shall never be entirely uncovered.

For at least three thousand years, Jews (and later, Christians) have embraced Abraham as a model. They have explored new terrain of the spirit world while being embraced and nourished by Ultimate Mystery itself. Our membership in this great cloud of witnesses motivates us to press on in this search. Discovering new ways to envision and speak of the loving force that holds the universe together is another way to bring Abraham's adventurous spirit into the modern age.

◆

Implications

Let us imagine that what has been said so far is true, or at least points us in the direction in which truth can be found. Let us assume that both a broad religious tradition and modern scientific knowledge discourage the concept of an overpowering, controlling deity to which humankind is called to submit. Let us assume that we are, instead, immersed in the Numen, a spiritual reality whose agenda is not innate power, but empowerment. God's role, therefore, is not to micromanage but to transform dissonance into harmony. Symbols such as light and music, both enriching and empowering realities, replace patriarchal, power-saturated symbols for comprehending the divine. The implications of all this for our style of life are broad.

One of the most helpful things the church taught me in my teen years was a simple poem that began, "God has no hands but our hands to do His work today." Those who taught me those words no doubt wanted to reinforce the idealism of youth and to make me feel needed in the Christian enterprise. They succeeded, perhaps beyond what they had intended. Not only did I hear the surface sentiments of this simplistic poem; I also heard intimations of a God for whom the word "omnipotent" is inappropriate. The deity who is the subject of this poem is not self-sufficient; this God is part of the interrelated system of the universe, a reality that is incomplete without the cooperation of faithful servants. I have spent much of my adult life attempting to work out the implications of a God who "has no hands but our hands."

Here are some topics that come to mind when we ask how we might be the hands and feet of a God who is concerned with increasing the order of the universe. I mean to do no more than suggest a few of the appropriate topics.

- ◆ *Eco-justice:* The God who celebrates life calls all Christians to be concerned for the magnificent, interrelated world of nature. Life, in all its forms, is the orderly arrangement of otherwise inanimate materials.

♦ *Medical research:* Support of the medical profession as it searches for cures for debilitating diseases is more than self-interest; it is part of the religious vocation. A subtopic of this larger theme is the study of the relationship between spiritual health and physical health.

♦ *Christians and state-sponsored violence:* If the Numen's primary work is to overcome chaos, Christians must ask themselves whether they can continue to rationalize their participation in and support of the ultimate chaos that is war.

♦ *Capital punishment:* If human life and human consciousness is the most complex result of divinely willed order, what does it mean for the government to be our agent in executions?

♦ *Economic and social justice:* In the biblical tradition, justice refers to a fair distribution of goods and services, a distribution that allows all persons to have the resources for a life of dignity. Just societies tend to be stable societies. Injustice, in the form of oppression, ensures an eventual rebellion and an attendant increase in chaos. Oppression may bring a form of orderliness for a brief time. In the final analysis, however, people refuse to be used as cogs in machines of repression. Political dictatorships are a formula for short-term order and long-term disorder.

♦ *Understanding the role of love:* Love is the power that pushes toward reconciliation. Once we recognize that God is love, we then seek to allow the healing power of love to flow through us. Jesus, and his followers who wrote the Christian portions of scripture, treated love as an action that can be the result of conscious thought. The religious understanding of love is the opposite of the secular, romantic notion wherein loving actions take place only after a person has been overwhelmed by the emotions of love. Those who wrote about Jesus were confident he had wanted concrete, compassionate actions, with or without emotion. Paul was also confident that love was action, not emotion. He used a different set of descriptive verbs and nouns: Love is patient, kind, slow to take offense, quick to shed the gunny sacks of past grievances, hopeful (First Corinthians 13).

♦ Shalom: The Hebrew concept of peace, *shalom*, is a final summary of all that can be said about serving as the hands of the Numen. Shalom begins as the absence of violence. It is more than that. Shalom occurs when an individual or a community is in a state of well-being. Shalom represents the triumph of a loving, sacred power that constantly plants seeds of order within the ever-threatening forces of chaos. Everyone who wants to be a servant of the divine will pray with St. Francis: "Make me an instrument of your peace (shalom)."

In summary, those who wish to align themselves with the will of the Numen, the loving, supportive web at the core of the universe, will do specific things. They will strive to enrich life and expand justice. They will give themselves in sacrificial love in the effort to establish communities of peace and reconciliation. These things constitute the religious vocation, applicable to both lay and professional followers of Jesus.

♦

A Final Word

The ideas and movements discussed in this chapter are the ingredients of hope for those of us who are convinced that change is necessary. If the major Protestant branches of Christianity are to survive, the dynamic aspects of their traditions must be exposed and explored. Creative individuals in growing numbers, often banding together to multiply their effectiveness, are doing just that. Living, changing traditions are being rescued from the deadly bonds of traditionalism.

Those who take an opposite position, who want to preserve some ancient form of Christianity in an unaltered form, will see these same ideas and movements as reasons for despair. They know the difficulty of keeping any church member in a state of religious innocence while voices calling for change become numerous and compelling.

Religious professionals may hope that their constituents will ignore the theological ferment around them. This hope is vain. Very few people who occupy the pews of Protestant churches are waiting for the experts to tell them what they should or should not ignore. The cognitive development of most church members has moved to higher levels. An increasing number of Christians want to participate in the ferment; they have come to value well-formed questions above prepackaged answers. Church professionals cannot keep their secrets hidden any longer.

Local pastors find themselves in an almost intolerable bind—a bind partly of their own making. They are fearful of disturbing a single chaos-intolerant member of their shrinking congregations. So they tend to become walking repositories of a dysfunctional faith, believing one way in the secret places of their hearts while openly reinforcing their congregations in a quite different way of believing. They do not seem to recognize that they are addressing congregations sophisticated enough to sense that something is horribly amiss. This is how churches become seedbeds for disharmony, the settings for conflicts waiting to happen.

The result of all this is tragic beyond description. People who are committed enough to remain in such churches are encouraged to move backward in their mental development and prodded into cognitive dissonance. They are denied affirmation as people capable of growth. They are cheated, cheated by being handed a lifeless *traditionalism* when they are eager to participate in a living *tradition*. They learn to distrust their spiritual guides.

Fortunately, a growing number of exceptions to this dreary situation are appearing. Across the Christian map courageous people, both lay and professional, are insisting that the church stop playing safe and begin to take whatever risks are involved in playing honest.

Paul Tillich is credited with the phrase *belief-ful realism.* Belief-ful realism implies that one can be fully in touch with the visible world and fully accepting of the truths discovered by researchers in secular fields—all the while placing that realism in the context of an ever present, ever supportive numinous Mystery. The church of the 21st century must aspire to a belief-ful realism.

NOTES

1. Ian Barbour, *Issues in Science and Religion* (Englewood Cliffs, New Jersey: Prentice-Hall, 1966).

2. Ian Barbour, *Religion in an Age of Science* (San Francisco: Harper and Row, 1990).

3. Ian Barbour, *When Science Meets Religion* (San Francisco: HarperSanFrancisco, 2000).

4. John C. Polkinghorne, *Belief in God in an Age of Science* (New Haven: Yale University Press, 1998).

5. Arthur Peacocke, *Paths from Science Towards God* (Oxford: Oneworld Publications, 2001).

6. See, for example, the stimulating book by Matthieu Ricard and Trinh Xuan Thuan, *The Quantum and the Lotus* (New York: Crown Publishers, 2001). The book consists of conversations between Ricard, a scientist turned Buddhist monk, and Thuan, an astrophysicist on the faculty of the University of Virginia.

7. Barbara Brown Taylor, "Physics and Faith: The Luminous Web," *The Christian Century,* June 2-9, 1999.

8. Timothy Ferris, *Coming of Age in the Milky Way* (New York: Anchor Books, Doubleday, 1988).

9. Ricard and Thuan, *The Quantum and the Lotus.*

10. Eck's book suffers somewhat from use of inflated membership figures for some faiths. Even so, it forces all Americans to acknowledge the new religious reality in which we live.

11. John B. Cobb and C. Robert Mesle, *Process Theology: A Basic Introduction* (St. Louis: Chalice Press, 1993).

Bibliography

Barbour, Ian. *Issues in Science and Religion*. Englewood Cliffs, New Jersey: Prentice-Hall, 1966.

———. *Religion in an Age of Science*. San Francisco: Harper and Row, 1990.

———. *When Science Meets Religion*. San Francisco: HarperSan Francisco, 2000.

Belenky, Mary Field, Blythe McVicker Clinchy, Nancy Rule Goldberger, and Jill Mattuck Tarule. *Women's Ways of Knowing*. New York: Basic Books, 1986.

Cherry, Conrad, Betty DeBerg, and Amanda Porterfield. *Religion on Campus*. Chapel Hill: The University of North Carolina Press, 2001.

Cobb, John B. *Reclaiming the Church*. Louisville: Westminster/John Knox Press, 1997.

Cobb, John B., and C. Robert Mesle. *Process Theology: A Basic Introduction*. St. Louis: Chalice Press, 1993.

Crossan, John Dominic, and Richard Watts. *Who is Jesus?* New York: HarperCollins, 1996.

Dostoyevsky, Fyodor. *The Brothers Karamazov*. New York: Random House, 1950.

Eck, Diana L. *A New Religious America: How a "Christian Country" Has Become the World's Most Religiously Diverse Nation*. New York: HarperSanFrancisco, 2001.

Ferris, Timothy. *Coming of Age in the Milky Way*. New York: Anchor Books, Doubleday, 1988.

243

Fosdick, Harry Emerson, editor. *Rufus Jones Speaks to Our Time.* New York: The Macmillan Company, 1951.

Fowler, James W. *Faithful Change: The Personal and Public Challenges of Postmodern Life.* Nashville: Abingdon Press, 1996.

Funk, Robert W. *Honest to Jesus.* San Francisco: HarperSanFrancisco, 1996.

Funk, Robert W., Roy W. Hoover, and the Jesus Seminar. *The Five Gospels: The Search for the Authentic Words of Jesus.* New York: Macmillan Company, Polebridge Press, 1993.

Goggin, Helen. "Children and the Church in the 21st Century." *Creative Transformation,* Volume 7, Number 4 (Summer 1998).

Good, Jack. *The Bible: Faith's Family Album.* St. Louis: Chalice Press, 1998.

Hawking, Steven. *A Brief History of Time.* New York: Bantam Books, 1998.

Hoge, Dean, Donald A. Luidens, and Benton Johnson. *Vanishing Boundaries: The Religion of Mainline Protestant Baby Boomers.* Louisville: Westminster/John Knox Press, 1994.

Kushner, Harold. *When Bad Things Happen to Good People.* New York: Schocken Books, 1981

Mesle, Robert, and John B. Cobb. *Process Theology: A Basic Introduction.* St. Louis: Chalice Press, 1993.

Oswald, Roy. *Crossing the Boundary between Seminary and Parish.* New York: Alban Institute, 1980.

Otto, Rudolf. *The Idea of the Holy.* Oxford: Oxford University Press, 1923.

Peacocke, Arthur. *Paths from Science Towards God.* Oxford: Oneworld Publications, 2001.

Perry, William, Jr. *Forms of Intellectual and Ethical Development in the College Years: A Scheme.* New York: Holt, Rinehart and Winston, 1968.

Phillips, J. B. *Your God is Too Small.* New York: Macmillan Publishing House, 1961.

Placher, William C. "Helping Theology Matter: A Challenge for the Mainline." *The Christian Century,* October 28, 1998.

Polkinghorne, John C. *Belief in God in an Age of Science.* New Haven: Yale University Press, 1998.

Ricard, Matthieu, and Trinh Xuan Thuan. *The Quantum and the Lotus.* New York: Crown Publishers, 2001.

Robinson, John A. T. *Honest to God.* Philadelphia: Westminster Press, 1963.

Roof, Wade Clark. *A Generation of Seekers.* San Francisco: HarperSan-Francisco, 1993.

Rosenblatt, Naomi H., and Joshua Horwitz. *Wrestling with Angels.* New York: Doubleday, 1995.

Rubenstein, Richard. *When Jesus Became God.* New York: Harcourt Brace and Company, 1999.

Schweitzer, Albert. *The Quest of the Historical Jesus: A Critical Study of Its Progress from Reimarus to Wrede.* Translated by William Montgomery, 1910; reprint, New York: Macmillan, 1961.

Scott, Bernard Brandon. *Re-Imagine the World.* Santa Rosa, California: Polebridge Press, 2001.

Shinn, Roger. *Education in the Christian Community.* New York: The Pilgrim Press, 1960.

Smith, Huston. *The Religions of Man,* revised edition. San Francisco: Harper and Row, Perennial Library, 1986.

Taylor, Barbara Brown. "Physics and Faith: The Luminous Web." *The Christian Century,* June 2-9, 1999.

Tillich, Paul. *The Courage to Be.* New Haven: Yale University Press, 1952.

———. "Waiting." In *The Shaking of the Foundations.* New York: Charles Scribner's Sons, 1948.

———. *Systematic Theology,* Volume Three, Part V, Section II. Chicago: The University of Chicago Press, 1963.

Wink, Walter. *The Human Being: Jesus and the Enigma of the Son of the Man.* Minneapolis: Fortress Press, 2002.

Wolfe, Alan. "The Opening of the Evangelical Mind." *The Atlantic Monthly,* October 2000.

Woodruff, Paul. *Reverence.* New York: Oxford University Press, 2001.

Wright, N. T., and Marcus J. Borg. *The Meaning of Jesus: Two Visions.* New York: HarperSanFrancisco, 1999.

Yoder, John Howard. *The Politics of Jesus.* Grand Rapids: William B. Eerdmans Publishing Company, 1972.

Zaleski, Carol. "Faith and Doubt at Ground Zero." *The Christian Century,* December 19, 2001.